POETIC DRIVE

CULTURAL FRAMES, FRAMING CULTURE

Robert Newman, Editor
Justin Neuman, Associate Editor

POETIC DRIVE

American Poetry in the Age of Automobility

JOEL DUNCAN

UNIVERSITY OF VIRGINIA PRESS
Charlottesville and London

The University of Virginia Press is situated on the traditional lands of the Monacan Nation, and the Commonwealth of Virginia was and is home to many other Indigenous people. We pay our respect to all of them, past and present. We also honor the enslaved African and African American people who built the University of Virginia, and we recognize their descendants. We commit to fostering voices from these communities through our publications and to deepening our collective understanding of their histories and contributions.

University of Virginia Press
© 2025 by the Rector and Visitors of the University of Virginia
All rights reserved
Printed in the United States of America on acid-free paper

First published 2025

9 8 7 6 5 4 3 2 1

LIBRARY OF CONGRESS CATALOGING-IN-PUBLICATION DATA

Names: Duncan, Joel author
Title: Poetic drive : American poetry in the age of automobility / Joel Duncan.
Description: Charlottesville : University of Virginia Press, 2025. | Series: Cultural frames, framing culture | Includes bibliographical references and index.
Identifiers: LCCN 2025035829 (print) | LCCN 2025035830 (ebook) | ISBN 9780813954028 (hardcover) | ISBN 9780813954035 (paperback) | ISBN 9780813954042 (ebook)
Subjects: LCSH: American poetry—History and criticism | Automobiles in literature | BISAC: LITERARY CRITICISM / Poetry | LITERARY CRITICISM / Modern / 21st Century | LCGFT: Literary criticism
Classification: LCC PS310.A87 D86 2025 (print) | LCC PS310.A87 (ebook)
LC record available at https://lccn.loc.gov/2025035829
LC ebook record available at https://lccn.loc.gov/2025035830

This book was supported by funding from the European Union (ERC, OffRoad, 101044725) and from the Centre for Cultural Inquiry (ZKF) at the University of Konstanz.

Cover art: Midtown skyline of New York City seen from Queens, Danny Lyon, 1974, from *DOCUMERICA: The Environmental Protection Agency's Program to Photographically Document Subjects of Environmental Concern, 1972–1977.* (National Archives, NAID 555938)
Cover design: Joel W. Coggins

CONTENTS

List of Illustrations | vii
Acknowledgments | ix

Introduction   1

1 William Carlos Williams Drives a "Hot Little Baby"   27

2 Frank O'Hara Crashes Charles Olson's Car   57

3 Driving Through Catastrophe with Eileen Myles   97

4 Not Driving While Black with Claudia Rankine   133

Coda   165

Notes | 171
Works Cited | 189
Index | 207

ILLUSTRATIONS

Flossie Williams with baby Bill	32
Frank O'Hara in *Presenting Jane*	84
Promotional image for *The Last Clean Shirt*	91
Eileen Myles in *The Trip*	129
Casper in *The Trip*	130
Jim Crow Rd., Michael David Murphy	145

ACKNOWLEDGMENTS

One of the pleasures of writing this book has been talking with so many different people about car cultures, from a Zen nun in Uppsala to Volvo workers in Gothenburg. During these conversations I have often been introduced to new poetry, stories, music, movies, and scholarship, some of which has made it into this book. I have likewise encountered many exciting examples of how to read literature and make art in relation to petromodernity, while sharing this project at conferences, in seminars, in Swedish media, and at Göteborgs Konsthall. All these encounters have made writing this book a collective affair, to which these acknowledgments cannot fully do justice.

The germ for this book was sown in my doctoral dissertation at the University of Notre Dame, which was supervised by Stephen Fredman and Laura Dassow Walls. I am thankful to Steve for reading and commenting on the whole of my book manuscript and for letting me know early on that I was the right person to write it. Laura has also offered lively encouragement and thoughtful reflections, especially as regards my uncertain entry into the field of ecocriticism. My intellectual community at Notre Dame included many others to whom I am grateful, not least the dynamic poetry and poetics workshop. It bears mentioning that while living in the Midwest

I owned my one and only car, a used Buick Century with a bench seat in the front, which shuttled me between Notre Dame, Chicago, Ypsilanti, Detroit, Buffalo, and Maine. Last I heard, another poet and scholar is still driving it around the Midwest.

This book would never have gotten off the ground without funding from the Swedish Research Council, which allowed me to work as a researcher at the University of Gothenburg for several years. Thank you to Håkan Möller for supporting my application. I am also grateful to all my colleagues at Gothenburg who responded to parts of this research, including the members of the research seminars in VitKrit (critical whiteness studies), Poesi som kunskapsform (Poetry as a Form of Knowledge), and the participants in the work-in-progress seminars at both the Department of Languages and Literatures and the Department of Literature, History of Ideas, and Religion. A special thanks to Marius Hentea for feedback on my writing and for general career advice, as well as to Anders Westerström for all our informal writing retreats.

While teaching for a year in the English Department at Uppsala University, I likewise had many supportive colleagues who asked compelling questions that informed my writing. I am grateful for lively conversations hosted by the Swedish Institute for North American Studies, the Poetry Reading Group, the Uppsala Travel Writing Seminar, and the Talking American Literature at Uppsala series run by Daniel Kane. Daniel, who taught me some of the poetry in this book when I was an MA student at the University of Sussex, has also given me invaluable feedback on my writing. My intellectual community has furthermore included the Critical Petroaesthetics research group led by Sissel Furuseth at the University of Oslo, as well as everyone involved in the Modernist Studies Association's Special Interest Group in Modernism and Environment, especially our brilliant reading group initiative.

I finished writing this book at the University of Konstanz, where I had the privilege of participating in the European Research Council–funded project "Off the Road: The Environmental Aesthetics of Early Automobility," led by Timo Müller. I am grateful to Timo and the rest of the Off the Road team—Jannis Buschky, Melanie Frey, Gilberto Mazzoli, and Otilia Teodorescu-Stadler—as well as the American Studies Research Colloquium, for providing me with an incredibly well-informed audience for drafts of this book. The Off the Road team organized a conference titled "Cultures of Automobility" in October 2024, and the many wonderful presentations and discussions that took place in Konstanz during the conference expanded my sense of our field. I also had the opportunity to teach an advanced seminar called "Poetic Drive" at Konstanz, and was inspired by my students' engagement with much of the material in this book. I am especially indebted to one of those students, Sophie Hyllus, who assisted me in preparing this manuscript for publication.

Fellow scholars have been generous enough to respond to drafts of my chapters and share their own publishing experiences, including Red Chidgey, Bryan Santin, Myka Tucker-Abramson, Brian Glavey, Jack Parlett, Prudence Bussey-Chamberlain, Fredrik Portin, and Christine Fouirnaies. I also want to thank Andrew Epstein for his supportive and helpful correspondence. I am especially grateful to Justin Parks for reading the whole manuscript and for encouraging me to take this book's title seriously. An early conversation with Peter Riley about publishing first books provided me with a mantra that perhaps other new authors can also write by: "There are two kinds of books: perfect books and published books."

I am thankful to Angie Hogan and her colleagues at Virginia for making this a published book, as well as to my two anonymous readers, whose detailed feedback led to a reframing of my argument. Thank you as well to Sophia Editing for the expert copyediting, and to Nancy du Plessis for creating the index. Parts of this book appeared in different versions as articles in *Arizona Quarterly*, *Modernism/modernity*, and *Women's Studies*, and the anonymous reviews I received from these journals also proved formative for the direction of *Poetic Drive*.

My family and friends have been consistent enthusiasts for this project, especially my parents, Susanne and John Duncan, who read most everything I publish and provide useful reflections. This book is dedicated to them; to my feline companion, Daniella; and to all of my friends and neighbours in Biskopsgården who took care of DD and cheered me on while I was traveling around writing about poetry and cars.

POETIC DRIVE

INTRODUCTION

IN THE MID-1950S, during the height of the postwar boom that has come to define our image of American automobility, Robert Creeley penned an anxiously manic poem from the perspective of the driver's seat. Entitled "I Know a Man," its opening lines throw the reader into the middle of a seemingly never-ending conversation between two men that sounds much like the mad talk at the center of Jack Kerouac's iconic road novel, *On the Road* (1957). In contrast to Kerouac's sprawling homage to the thrills of the open road, though, Creeley's short poem seems to be careening toward disaster:

>   As I sd to my
>   friend, because I am
>   always talking,—John, I
>
>   sd, which was not his
>   name, the darkness sur-
>   rounds us, what

> can we do against
> it, or else, shall we &
> why not, buy a goddamn big car,
>
> drive, he sd, for
> christ's sake, look
> out where yr going.[1]

"Drive, he sd" could serve as an alternative title for this book.[2] The phrase is one of the most poignant poetic illustrations of the twentieth century's imperative to drive, an imperative that became synonymous with a certain form of American life, which included crashing and death. The masculine pronoun in the phrase "Drive, he sd" also speaks to the persistent gendering of this imperative. Creeley's poem is well known, and yet critics have seldom discussed it in terms of automobility but have rather seen it as a confrontation with "existential despair" and "the horror of the void."[3] The poem may well confront existential dread, but what are we to make of the fact that this drama takes place in an automobile? Indeed, with its propulsive short lines and abrupt ending, it is as though this poem were about to crash into us while we are reading it.

I recommend listening to the recording of Creeley reading this poem on the Poetry Foundation's website, where he emphasizes its line breaks, making the poem's overextended syntax sound broken and desperate. We must drive on, his voice seems to be imploring us, and yet driving in this way won't end well. Michael Davidson has pointed out that the very word *drive* faces, syntactically, at least two ways: "'drive' could equally be a continuation of the previous lines (Why not buy a car and drive somewhere?), or it could be the beginning of an imperative spoken by 'he' ('drive... look out where you're going')."[4] "I Know a Man" thereby offers a double view of driving that ostensibly looks forward, toward the road ahead, but in seeing catastrophe there, abruptly ends the poem, exiting both it and the car. That this poem was written during the height of the postwar boom begs the question of why two presumably white men are so recklessly driving while fantasizing about buying "a goddamn big car," rather than basking in the social and economic benefits that the era is supposed to have conferred upon them.

Questions like this one, which link historical conditions to poetic form, are central to *Poetic Drive*. While there exists a small library of work on the role of cars in American culture, mainly in relation to films and novels, this is the first book about automobility in American poetry.[5] Previous scholars such as Cotten Seiler and Ann Brigham have laid the groundwork for my own approach by showing how "mobility is foundational to an understanding of American identity. It means freedom, rebellion, or reinvention; there exists the promise of escape."[6] In novels such as Sinclair Lewis's *Free Air* (1919) and Kerouac's *On the Road* and movies such as *Thelma and Louise* (1991) and *Queen and Slim* (2019), the road trip narrative has foregrounded the travails of self-realization across the expanse of the American landscape. In considering stories of the open road, Brigham and, more recently, Andrew Vogel and Myka Tucker-Abramson show how the road trip narrative emerged and developed as a genre.[7] In contrast to the road novel, the trips in many of the poems I analyze are short or nonexistent, sometimes never leaving the parking lot or even getting into the car. Moreover, in writing about poems, I am compelled to attend to how social conflicts around automobility have been formally inscribed *as* poetry. My readings elucidate the distinctive ways in which automobility is versified, which means considering history, subject matter, and form together. Whether looking at imagist and documentary poetry or poets' experimental movies, *Poetic Drive* reveals not only how American poetry is a crucial and underappreciated site in the contested cultures of automobility but also how American poetry has itself changed through its vexed articulation of these cultures.

The contradiction that emerges in "I Know a Man" between the will to drive, seemingly for its own sake, and the alarm sounded by not knowing "where yr going" encapsulates many of the ways US poets have reckoned with automobility and its elusive promise of both social and technological progress. The "poetic drive" of my book's title refers to this will or compulsion to drive, as well as the creative impulse to craft poetry that both evokes and critiques American automobility. We can see Creeley's poetic drive, for example, in the way that his poem emerges on the open road while seeming at once to veer toward a violent exit from automobility. This double vision is inherent in automobility itself, and is not unique to the United States, even if it has become synonymous with American identity. As the novelist

J. G. Ballard put it in the British motoring magazine *Drive* more than half a century ago, "I think that the 20th century reaches almost its purest expression on the highway. Here we see, all too clearly, the speed and violence of our age, its strange love affair with the machine and, conceivably, with its own death and destruction."[8] Automobility drives us manically forward while portending its and even our own destruction. There is much more to say, though, about the texture of this contradiction, both in terms of the variety of social experiences of automobility in the United States and the ways in which poets have harnessed and critiqued it. Creeley's and Ballard's double view of automobility reappears in different guises throughout this book, for while driving on the open road can provide some poets with free mobility, that mobility is always premised on the alienation of assembly-line production and includes myriad social and ecological hazards. The freedom to drive is also unevenly available to poets depending on their social position, revealing how this freedom is largely a fiction; indeed, the mythology of the open road is most prominent in narrative-driven genres such as novels and films. Rather than affirming what Marshall Berman calls "the easy confidence of our official culture, the civic faith that America could overcome its inner contradictions simply by driving away from them," American poets versify the contradictions of automobility, whether by attending to the alienating social relations that undergird mass automobility or by showing how the open road is as much a place of discrimination and violence as one of self-realization and freedom.[9] As Brigham points out, despite the promise of the open road, "mobility is not a method of freeing oneself from space, society, or identity but instead the opposite—a mode of engagement."[10] The various poetic drives in this book are precisely modes of engagement with the contradictions of automobility, even as many poets seek to drive past these contradictions and sometimes past the very limits of poetry on the page.

This book makes clear how the contradictions of Creeley's poetic drive in "I Know a Man" are part of a longer trajectory in American poetry, which began with the modernism of William Carlos Williams in the 1910s and leads up to Vickie Vértiz's *Auto/Body* in 2023 and beyond. In chapter 1, we see how Williams developed his imagistic poetics in the 1910s and '20s, but when mass automobility came to dominate the American landscape, he distanced himself from his earlier machine aesthetics.

The second chapter explores how Creeley's poetry partner Charles Olson's "Projective Verse" (1950) confronts the rigors of Fordist production after the Second World War, while his poetry uses cars and motorcycles to reckon with the status and skills of white men in mid-century America. I contrast Olson's work with that of Frank O'Hara, who couples driving with both the Civil Rights Movement and the production of poetry, providing in effect a riposte to the poetics of white, male authenticity in Williams and Olson. Chapter 3 examines how this critique of masculinist poetics becomes much more explicit in the work of Eileen Myles, whose transfeminist petropoetry, some of which is dictated while driving, explores the imbrication of climate catastrophe with poetic self-possession. The final chapter looks at how Claudia Rankine's work inhabits experiences of driving while Black, revealing the ways that African American drivers have been excluded from what Cotten Seiler has termed the "republic of drivers." For Rankine, the stopped car becomes a site for mourning white violence against Black drivers and a mode of critiquing the exclusions of white mobility. In the coda, I turn to Jericho Brown's and Vickie Vértiz's recent queer reckonings with their fathers' versions of patriarchal automobility.

Across the book's chapters, I show how American poets have both versified automobility's pleasures and thrills and confronted its sometimes deadly social exclusions as well as its environmental consequences. In the United States, automobility has historically been the privilege of white men, though, as we will see, women and Black drivers have also been on the roads since before mass automobility took off in the 1920s. In his cultural history of American automobility, Seiler has argued that "automobility emerged as a 'technology of the self,' organizing a compelling mode of self-government anchored in liberal notions of freedom."[11] Scholars such as Seiler have foregrounded the biopolitical role of automobility in crafting a liberal American subjectivity coded as white and male, and we can indeed see poets such as Williams versifying the "right of way" (the title of one of his poems) he enjoys while driving. Although the ideal of privatized mobility looms large in interpretations of American automobility, the story of how American poets have harnessed and critiqued cars and oil is significantly more complex than this ideal would suggest.[12] Indeed, American poets consistently reveal how the same technology used to express American personhood can at once undermine free mobility, social equality, and the very existence of the planet as we know it.

In order to attend to the breadth of American poets' reckonings with driving, I employ a wide-ranging conception of the term *automobility* that attends to both its social and infrastructural aspects. Here I take inspiration from sociologists such as John Urry, for whom "automobility can be conceptualized as a self-organizing autopoietic, non-linear system that spreads worldwide, and includes cars, car-drivers, roads, petroleum supplies and many novel objects, technologies and signs."[13] The poets in this book write not only of the car on the open road but also of the parked car, the crashed car, the view of motorcyclists on the beach, violent meetings in parking lots, roadkill, gas stations, and assembly lines. Urry understands the system of automobility as "autopoietic," but the way that automobility has been reimagined by poets has so far only been hinted at by critics.[14] For example, Laurence Goldstein writes that "much more than fiction, poetry responded to the cultural conditions impressed on verbal art by the technology of motion."[15] He goes on to argue, "unlike the Whitmanian ideal of either being a *flâneur* enjoying the random sensations of a vibrant city, or of hiking the open road like a pioneer or pilgrim, the freeway poem tends to focus on whatever stops or stalls the driver, as trivial and tedious as finding a parking spot or horrific as a car crash or shooting."[16] Goldstein rightly points out how driving poems upend our conception of the open road. As we shall see, though, it is possible for driving to be conceived of as Whitmanian, and car poems can very well include the random sensations of the road. As the chapters of this book show, poets' engagements with cars, trucks, motorcycles, oil, roadway construction, parking lots, gas stations, traffic, and police stops are more complex and compelling than previous studies have recognized. They expand our conception of what the culture of automobility looks, feels, and sounds like, while confronting the political and ecological consequences of automobility, which much of American society has yet to fully digest.

The poets in this book have developed a wide variety of poetic forms for reckoning with the system of automobility, including Williams's imagism, Olson's and O'Hara's time signals, Myles's petropoems, and Rankine's post-lyric prose poems and film scripts. These forms are never merely formal but demand to be read in relation to the social contexts they engage, whether Fordism, fossil fuels, petromasculinity, or the travails of driving while Black. Poets' poetic drives do not, then, stop at the edge of the page or the screen but, to quote Margaret Ronda and Lindsay Turner, "might be understood as an enactment of struggle and contradiction rather than an embodiment of achieved order or closure."[17] The poets in this book craft poetic forms through engaging with the contradictions of automobility, and the result, whether on the page or the screen, speaks to their work's fraught history of creation. Such history is multivalent not only across time but also in any given moment, depending on the social position and aesthetic commitments of the poet. It is the ambition of this book to provide an initial road map of the variety of poetic drives in the United States since the early twentieth century, in the hope that others will subsequently deepen its contours, not least as poets continue to drive their work in new directions.

The rest of this introduction is organized into three sections, through which I frame the themes of this book: "Fordism and Modernism," "Automobility's Others," and "Petropoetics." "Fordism and Modernism" considers how both car production and driving inspired modernist writing about automobility, as well as a particular conception of poetic experimentation that is still being debated today. Despite varying politics and aesthetic commitments, Ezra Pound, Gertrude Stein, and Williams all coupled modernist experimentation to automobility in ways that could be socially exclusionary. "Automobility's Others" introduces some of the social struggles, such as the Civil Rights Movement, which have fought against automobility's exclusions based on race and gender. These struggles appear, for instance, in the work of Wanda Coleman, a Black mother living in the Watts neighborhood of Los Angeles in the last decades of the twentieth century, and for whom the dream of liberal progress coupled to technological development becomes instead the nightmare of petromodernity. The poetic drives of Coleman and the other poets in this book can be understood as forms of "petropoetics," a term I use to merge the somewhat disparate insights of contemporary petrocultures research with those of the broad field of ecopoetics. Petropoetics is an especially useful term for reading the poetry of Gary Snyder later in this introduction and Eileen Myles in chapter 3, since, for these poets, driving also means confronting the ecological death brought about by mass automobility. While this ecological death shows no signs of abating, the decline of the internal combustion engine is nevertheless upon us, providing an opportunity to appreciate how American poetry both embodies and confronts Creeley's imperative to drive into the darkness, an imperative that continues to define our relationship to an ever more perilous road ahead.

FORDISM AND MODERNISM

Any study of American automobility during the twentieth century must reckon with Fordism, a term that spread after the publication of Henry Ford's *My Life and Work* in 1923.[18] *Fordism* was an economic system inaugurated with Ford's relatively affordable Model T in 1908, the implementation of a moving assembly line at his Highland Park plant in 1913, and the introduction of the five-dollar-a-day wage in 1914, which gave workers the possibility to buy the cars they were producing. This coupling of "mass production"—a term that Ford coined to describe the dominance of the assembly line—with mass consumption relied on a social contract that privileged white men, who became Fordism's main breadwinners and the people for whom driving was most accessible.[19] Fordism was, though, not only an economic system. As David Harvey explains, Fordism was "a total way of life. Mass production meant standardization of product as well as mass consumption; and this meant a whole new aesthetic and commodification of culture."[20] This way of life depended, especially after the Second World War, on the social infrastructure of the nuclear family and the welfare state, the physical infrastructure of interstates and suburbs, as well as the mass culture that came to define the American Century. As we shall see in chapters 1 and 2, Williams's, Olson's, and O'Hara's poetry is driven by the excitement and anxiety of Fordism's emergence and boom. The Fordist way of life began to change in the 1970s, though, when post-Fordist restructuring and neoliberal globalization led to a more precarious existence for many, especially those groups who were already marginalized by the Fordist social compact. Later in this introduction with Coleman, and in chapters 3 and 4 with Myles and Rankine, we shall see how poets reckon with the diminishing returns of driving during Fordism's long eclipse.

The two pillars of Fordist automobility—mass production and mass consumption of cars—depend upon and diverge from each other in important ways. Although assembly-line production suggests repetition and uniformity of product, the myth of the open road implies self-discovery and adventure. Without the production of cars there would, of course, be no road trips. The fact that so many modern American poets drive, while few work on assembly lines, helps explain why much of the poetry in this book concerns the driving, rather than the production, of automobiles. Nevertheless, to fully understand poets' relationship to driving, we should attend to mass production as well. Throughout this book's chapters, I therefore seek to offer a perspective that takes in both sides of mass automobility—production and consumption—to show how the supposed freedom of the open road can be a response to the inherent alienation as well as social exclusions of productive relations. As the Language poet Barrett Watten reflects about his adopted hometown, "it is difficult to find the connection between avant-garde writing and the social space of Detroit, which is one reason I am fascinated by what it means to live here. What is literature at the point of production?"[21] Watten answers this question by attending to the work of Gertrude Stein, who herself compared assembly-line production with modernist writing. Indeed, "modernism itself might be understood as the culture of Fordism," as Michael Denning puts it.[22]

The first modernist poetics of automobility emerged not in the US, though, but in Europe, and explicitly celebrated both masculinity and the destructive powers of cars. In his "Futurist Manifesto" (1909), the Italian soon-to-be-fascist Filippo Tommaso Marinetti offers a manic homage to fossil-fueled speed. Marinetti describes crashing his group's car into a ditch, from which he nevertheless declares that "we intend to hymn man at the steering wheel."[23] Indeed, in his car poems, he praised the automobile in mythic terms as a "Centaur" and a "Pegasus."[24] Andreas Malm and the Zetkin Collective have argued that Marinetti was the progenitor of a fossil fascism that "dreamed of a mechanical existence free from the botheration of nature and women," which has been inherited by later fascist and far-right movements.[25] American factory workers worried about this connection between automobility and fascism as well, with the United Auto Workers declaring in 1937, "Fordism is Fascism! Unionism is Americanism."[26] For Marinetti, mechanization demanded not only a new politics but also a new literature. In the "Technical Manifesto of Futurist Literature" (1912), he expressed, while sitting on an airplane's fuel tank, "a raging need to liberate words" and "destroy syntax."[27] This conception of modernism's violent break with realism was shared to varying degrees by Pound, Williams, and Stein, even though none of these Americans had quite the single-minded hubris of Marinetti in "preparing [for] the creation of the **mechanical man with interchangeable parts**."[28]

But modernist literature didn't need to be explicitly fascist in order to be racist. Natalia Cecire has persuasively argued that experimental modernist writing "constructs its own modernity by way of contrast with what is nonmodern," with the latter, as Timothy Yu puts it, providing "passive inspiration for the active creative energies of European and American modernists."[29] In this version of experimentalism, "some places, practices, and people are scientific and temporally forward, and others are not."[30] Modernists could themselves be attuned to this technophilic racism. D. H. Lawrence, for instance, parodies the marriage of free verse and machines in his *Studies in Classic American Literature* (1923) when he anachronistically places Walt Whitman behind the steering wheel:

> He was everything and everything was in him. He drove an automobile with a very fierce headlight, along the track of a fixed idea, through the darkness of this world. And he saw Everything that way. Just as a motorist does in the night.
>
> I, who happen to be asleep under the bushes in the dark, hoping a snake won't crawl into my neck; I, seeing Walt go by in his great fierce poetic machine, think to myself: What a funny world that fellow sees!
>
> ONE DIRECTION! toots Walt in the car, whizzing along it.
>
> Whereas there are myriads of ways in the dark, not to mention trackless wilderness. As anyone will know who cares to come off the road—even the Open Road.
>
> ONE DIRECTION! whoops America, and sets off also in an automobile.
>
> ALLNESS! shrieks Walt at a cross-road, going whizz over an unwary Red Indian.
>
> ONE IDENTITY! chants democratic En Masse, pelting behind in motor-cars, oblivious of the corpses under the wheels.[31]

For Lawrence, Whitman's all-encompassing poetics necessarily means sidelining the words and experiences of others by driving them off the road. Free verse, in short, isn't free for everyone, even if it is meant to have mass appeal. Indeed, Lawrence lambasts Whitman's poetics in obliquely racialized terms: "Just a horror. A sort of white flux."[32] Lawrence's conception of the automobile speaks to his own historical moment at least as much as it does to Whitman's. As we shall see in chapter 1, Whitman's shouting car sounds a lot like the "hot little baby" in Williams's *The Great American Novel* (1923), which was published the same year as Lawrence's study.

Aside from Lawrence's Whitman, it is Ezra Pound who explicitly envisions aesthetics in relation to Fordism. Pound began his modernist career defending the craft of literature against an increasingly Taylorist mass culture defined by timed efficiency. As James Knapp writes, "Pound the aesthete, who carried poetic experiment to unprecedented lengths, was also Pound the man who felt that eyes and limbs were threatened by the likes of Henry Ford and Thomas Edison."[33] It is therefore fitting that rather than craft a poetics of driving, Pound seeks to harness car production itself for aesthetic appreciation.[34] In his underappreciated essay "Machine Art" (1927–30, unpublished in his lifetime), Pound seeks to turn Ford's factory into music to the benefit of the workers. Drawing inspiration from George Antheil's *Ballet Mécanique,* which was first performed in 1925, Pound imagines orchestrating the sounds of assembly-line production so that they become sonorous, rather than being irritable noise.[35] He writes, "the idea that a factory, or at least the more highly organized and organizable parts of a factory can not be 'harmonized' is no sillier in 1927, than the idea that a horseless carriage could move, was in, let us say, 1880. The only reason the engineers have not done it already is because no one had thought of it."[36] Making factory noises pleasing is as plausible for Pound as the very movement of cars. He continues, "when I consider the disagreeable noises I have heard in factories it seems to me that they are mainly disagreeable for one sole reason, namely they are not organized. Some screech continues too long; some repeat is irregular in an unpleasant manner.... No one has thought of utilizing them for the ease and refreshment of the workers."[37] By turning factory noises into music, Pound hopes to make car production more efficient while entertaining workers who might otherwise engage in labor struggles. Indeed, Pound praises Ford's managerialism as "probably feudal" and he came to share both Ford's antisemitism and Marinetti's fascist politics.[38] Nevertheless, he contrasts his own vision of poeticized factory noises with the futurist veneration of machine noises for their own sake.[39]

Gertrude Stein also marries her poetics to techno-scientific imperatives, "mingling automobiles with Emerson," as she put it in *The Autobiography of Alice B. Toklas* (1933).[40] Like Pound, she was interested in assembly-line production as an analog for modernist literature; in her lecture "Portraits and Repetition" (1935), she writes, "I cannot repeat this too often any one is of one's period and this our period was undoubtedly the period of the cinema and series production."[41] Indeed, the repetitive and constructivist syntax of much of her work makes it sound like she's producing it on an assembly line. As Watten writes, "Ford and the automobile are the sites of a periodic meditation on mass production, social mobility, and repetition for Stein, a synecdoche for social modernity as interpreted in the process of her work."[42] Both thematically and formally, her work reflects on its own production through its engagement with automobility. For example, while Stein was an avid driver, in the *Autobiography* it becomes apparent that she didn't know how to reverse, which as Zena Meadowsong has pointed out, serves as "a powerful figure of her embattled position in the literary vanguard."[43] Toklas-as-narrator recounts, "wrong or right, said Gertrude Stein, we are going on."[44] It is as though the Ford is propelling Stein, much like an assembly line sets its workers into motion, rather than the other way around. Yet she also underscores the affective side of automobility, naming her cars "Auntie" and "Godiva," which then become characters in the *Autobiography*.

In a sense, Stein produced the machine art that Pound hoped to see coming out of Ford's factory, but in contrast to Pound, her poetry does not claim any practical application. Take, for example, this driving poem from her ironically titled *Useful Knowledge* (1928):

THE FORD
It is earnest.
Aunt Pauline is earnest.
We are earnest.
We are united.
Then we see.[45]

"Aunt Pauline" is another name for "Auntie," Stein and Toklas's Model T, which they drove around France for the American Fund for French

Wounded (AFFW) during World War I. The poem's short, repetitive sentences link together "Aunt Pauline" and "we" as earnestly plodding ahead to "then." This opaque but insistently forward motion is the poem's poetic drive, which humorously mimics an assembly-line logic of repetition and progression, which in the final line of the poem allows for a new kind of sight. Stein's earlier driving poem "The Work" (1917), which she published in the *AFFW Bulletin,* includes the matter-of-fact rhyme "We call our machine Aunt Pauline," evincing another kind of playfulness. She entitled yet another driving poem, "Work Again" (1922), suggesting how even in writing about driving she was thinking about production.[46] In all these poems, Stein assembles what Watten calls a "motor of desire" that puts in motion an analogy between car production, driving, and the composition of poetry itself.[47]

Yet the relationship between American poets and automobility is consistently more vexed than Pound's and Stein's enthusiastic embrace would suggest, with other poets critiquing and turning away from cars and oil in their work as much as they seek to inhabit the energies of driving or car production. As we shall see, Williams's poetics went ultimately in the opposite direction from Pound's and Stein's when he came to distance himself from mass automobility as the '20s and '30s wore on. In *The Embodiment of Knowledge* (written in 1928–30, unpublished in his lifetime), he writes—as though in criticism of Pound's contemporaneous "Machine Art"—that "to stop before any machine is to make of it a fetish attended by its metaphysical priest the engineer."[48] Williams hopes that Americans will come to love their poets as much as they worship their engineers, while betraying his own fascination with machines.

In her own fanciful way, Marianne Moore inadvertently confirmed the impossibility of a harmonious marriage between automobility and American poetry when, in 1955, she was enlisted by the Ford Motor Company to dream up a name for their new car. In the entertaining correspondence between herself and Ford's Marketing Research Department, Moore proposed names such as "THE RESILIENT BULLET," "THE INTELLIGENT WHALE," "ANTICIPATOR," "PASTELOGRAM," and, most wonderfully, "UTOPIAN TURTLETOP."[49] The following year, she was informed that the company had settled on the name "Edsel"—the name of Henry Ford's deceased son, who had also been president of the company.

The Edsel was a flop, though. Moore, for her part, refused financial renumeration for her efforts and received a bouquet of twenty-four roses instead.

AUTOMOBILITY'S OTHERS

The relationship between automobility and identity has a varied history. At the turn of the twentieth century, automobile owners were few and wealthy, and cars incited antagonism from workers, who saw horseless carriages as unattainable playthings for the rich. The fashionability of automobiles was often presented by critics as effete, and early electric cars were perceived as "ladylike," not least since they were easier to start and covered shorter distances than gasoline-driven motors.[50] Many of the earliest accounts of automobile touring were penned by rich women, even if they most often had male servants doing the actual driving. Sinclair Lewis's *Free Air* plays on this state of affairs when its protagonist-driver Claire Boltwood, in crossing the country, also definitively crosses class boundaries by starting a romance with a mechanic. Indeed, Cotten Seiler has explained that while "automobility has been a vital compensatory practice and exclusionary discourse of American men in the twentieth century, white women have been among its participants at least since Geneva Delphine Mudge of New York became the 'first recorded woman driver' in 1898. The next three decades saw the image of the woman driver undergo repeated renegotiation as the automobile itself made, in [Virginia] Scharff's words, 'the transition from toy to tool.'"[51] Seiler intimates how the authors of early American touring narratives were, regardless of gender, united by their whiteness. He writes that these authors, "male and female alike, invoked a wilder America, put themselves and their machines in it, and, so positioned, claimed fellowship with the generation of white conquerors that had preceded them."[52] Indeed, this is the lineage in which D. H. Lawrence places Whitman as he drives "over an unwary Red Indian."

While foregrounding the link between automobility and masculinity risks eliding women and trans drivers, this linkage also reveals something crucial about the social formation of mass automobility, and Fordism in particular. As Mimi Sheller points out, "women are often defined as lacking a 'mobile subjectivity,' being rooted in place and home, while narratives of masculine becoming often hinge on travel, hitting the road, and escape from home."[53] During Fordism, white men were the main breadwinners, while white middle-class women reproduced the conditions for male labor, a dynamic we shall see at play in Williams's early poem "The Young Housewife" (1916). Williams both gazed at women through the car window and compared them with automobilities, as other male writers also have. For example, in E. E. Cummings's 1926 car poem "XIX: she being Brand," his idiosyncratic typography dramatizes how to "give // her the juice,good," where "her" is both a new car and a virgin woman.[54] Similarly, Brigham has shown how being "on the road" in Kerouac's novel is synonymous with the sexual consumption of women who don't have the same freedom of mobility. As Guillermo Giucci puts it, "the woman and the car went together. Both belonged to the same world of objects. There was no incompatibility between the eroticism of industrial and corporeal products."[55]

Yet in the United States, automobility's coding as white has arguably been more intransigent than its masculinity. For white Americans the automobile has been coupled to fantasies of the open road, to the freedoms afforded by autonomous mobility, and to American empire. Free mobility has often been denied African American drivers, though, whose relationship with automobility remains fraught.[56] As Seiler puts it, "the 'open road' has always been an oxymoron. Not only has taking to the road voluntarily been a prerogative only of those ascribed full personhood; the road itself is a device by which territories and subjects can be measured and surveilled."[57] On the one hand, cars have provided all Americans who can afford one with unprecedented opportunities for mobility. During the era of Jim Crow, for example, driving gave African Americans living in the South a means of avoiding the discrimination inherent in other forms of transport such as buses and trains, and even "facilitated the Civil Rights Movement by providing transportation for bus boycotts, rental cars to get to and from airports, and general transportation for people and supplies," as Gretchen Sorin explains.[58] Yet, on the other hand, Black drivers often had trouble finding lodging, restaurants, gas stations, and rest stops that would serve them, especially in the South, and they were excluded from the American Automobile Association (AAA). Guidebooks such as *The Negro Motorist Green Book,* published between 1936 and 1966, tried to fill the gap, providing Black and brown motorists with listings of establishments where they could stop on long trips.

There are many literary examples of Black drivers causing white resentment, such as the character Coalhouse Walker Jr. in E. L. Doctorow's historical novel *Ragtime* (1975), whose very name suggests the coupling of the politics of race with those of energy and mobility. Coalhouse is a musician who proudly drives his Model T soon after its release. In New Rochelle, New York (across the Hudson River from where Williams freely drove his Model T), a group of volunteer firemen block his way, demanding he pay a twenty-five-dollar fee for passing on the road, which Coalhouse refuses to do. They prevent him from driving away, and he walks off to seek support from the police, who are uncooperative. When Coalhouse returns, his car has been moved and desecrated, and he is subsequently arrested for refusing to drive his damaged car, precipitating the major plotline of the novel, where he unsuccessfully seeks recompense for these injustices, eventually resorting to terrorism. Coalhouse's Model T is trashed again and again as the novel progresses, finally ending up in a swamp, as it comes to symbolize his dashed hopes of social mobility, and the overwhelming forces of white supremacy standing in his way. Ralph Ellison's 1973 short story "Cadillac Flambé" likewise highlights the frustrated hopes of a Black musician driver, this time in the 1950s. Baited by a racist senator's radio broadcast complaining that the Cadillac has been ruined for white drivers because of its popularity among African Americans, the musician sets his own Cadillac on fire on the senator's lawn. Over the flames of his Cadillac, the musician gives an impassioned speech describing his awakening to the fact that his automobile is really a "Coon Cage," and informing the senator that "you have unconverted me from the convertible."[59]

Of course, we do not need to limit ourselves to literary examples of racism on the road. The real-life Jack Johnson, who was the first Black heavyweight boxing champion, lived at the same time as the fictional Coalhouse. When Johnson won the heavyweight title in 1908—again, the year of the first Model T—he caused disbelief among white Americans, who attempted to assert the illegitimacy of his having the title at all. The ensuing contest over the legitimacy of his title became displaced onto a car race in 1910 that pitched Johnson against the white auto-racing champion Barney Oldfield. Oldfield won over the amateur racer Johnson, leading to headlines like that in the *New York Sun,* "OLDFIELD SAVES WHITE RACE."⁶⁰ Such blatant racism did not deter Johnson, though, who was also pulled over by the police for speeding. He is rumored to have offered one Southern police officer $100 instead of the $50 fine, and when the officer said he didn't have change, Johnson told the officer to keep the money as he'd be driving back the same way.⁶¹ Despite Johnson's flaunting of speed limits, it is nevertheless fair to say, as Paul Gilroy does, that he "was among the first African-Americans to fall foul of the law for the informal crime of 'driving while black.'"⁶² Over a hundred years after Johnson's race with Oldfield, Black drivers still struggle for acceptance in professional car racing, with only one full-time Black driver, Darrell Wallace Jr., in NASCAR's top racing series. In 2020 Wallace successfully persuaded NASCAR to finally ban the confederate flag from its events, causing an uproar among some white fans.

The dangers of driving while Black still include being pulled over by police about 20 percent more often than white Americans, incurring more fines and arrests, and also a greater risk of being killed by police.⁶³ As Claudia Rankine puts it, "space itself is one of the understood privileges of whiteness."⁶⁴ Jeremy Packer notes that "the origination and continuation of the term *driving while Black* in African American culture and communities points out the fact that race does matter when traversing public space by automobile."⁶⁵ The persistent anxiety of Black drivers on American roads flies in the face of the automobile's iconic status as a symbol of both technological and social progress. Black Americans have not shared that progress equally with whites, something that Black poets and writers have been attuned to in their reckoning with automobility.

Reading the poetics and politics of automobility in relation to identity makes apparent, in Brigham's words, how "mobility does not function as an exit from society/home/the familiar, but instead emerges as a dynamic process for engaging with social conflicts."⁶⁶ Who gets to drive, where, and when, are, then, questions that get taken up from various social positions and in different historical moments throughout this book. In seeking redress for those excluded from the right of way, Mimi Sheller has coined the phrase "mobility justice." As she writes, mobility justice "is concerned with sexual harassment as much as transport access, and with racist violence as much as resource extraction. It allows us to think more clearly about the intertwined relations between bodies, streets, transport systems, urbanization (including not just cities but also suburbs and the rural hinterlands), regional and transnational infrastructures, national borders, and wider planetary mobilities. It reveals the relation between the urban crisis, the migration crisis, and the climate crisis."[67] Taking its cue from Sheller, *Poetic Drive* attends to the ways that poets have inhabited the many sites of automobility in order to engage its social and ecological exclusions, whether that means anxiously benefiting from them, or seeking automobility justice. While poets such as Williams and Olson figure automobility as the privilege of white men, other poets in this book more or less explicitly confront the injustices of privatized automobility, whether it is Myles's auto-fictive character in *Chelsea Girls* surviving the sexual violence of "good-looking suburban guys, 18 or 19, same as me, who all owned cars" in 1960s Boston, or the ways that Rankine illustrates the continued risks of driving while Black in the supposedly postracial Obama era.[68]

An underappreciated poet who has written about the social struggles of automobility is the Los Angeles writer Wanda Coleman. In "I Live for My Car" from her book *Imagoes* (1983), Coleman dramatizes the difficulty of attaining and maintaining automotive citizenship, by contrasting the imperative to "live for my car" with the shame that her actual "struggle buggy" causes her. The poem begins, "can't let go of it. to live is to drive," and goes on to detail the time and money that the poet must spend to keep their car on the road.[69] The page-long poem ends where it began, while elaborating where the imperative to live for their car comes from:

> my car's an absolute necessity in this city of cars where
> you come to know people best by how they maneuver on the freeway
> make lane changes or handle off-ramps. i've promised myself
> i will one day own a luxury model. it'll be something
> i can leave my children. till then i'm on spark plugs and lug nuts
> keeping the one i have mobile. i live for it. can't let go of it
> to drive is to live[70]

In a lo-fi black-and-white video of Coleman reading this poem, available on YouTube, she utters the last lines as if in a trance, humorously underscoring the pathos of driving to live. She dreams that her "car is transformed into a stylish / convertible," but such "dreams become nightmares" when struggling to keep her actual car legally running in a city where driving is a primary form of social encounter.[71] Coleman gestures toward the disjuncture between the American promise of social and spatial mobility and her own lived situation, which in LA maps onto the social distance between Hollywood and Watts. As Krista Comer writes, "by the mid-1970s, Coleman sees the writing on the wall; she anticipates the decline in decent jobs for the nation's underclass that comes with globalization, and she worries that the consequences of these declines will be catastrophic for the residents of her hometown, Watts, and for black America generally."[72] Indeed, the automotive imperative of "keeping the one i have mobile" and the inability to "let go of it" underscore the profound burden of keeping up with Hollywood—Coleman worked in the '70s as a writer on the soap opera *Days of Our Lives,* for which she won an Emmy—while living in poverty.[73] As we shall see in chapter 4, such struggles against the delimiting of Black social and physical mobility have continued into the twenty-first century.

Coleman associates a lack of access to affordable mobility with being on the margins of the white literary establishment. In "Things No One Knows," from her book *Bathwater Wine* (1998), she writes that "my car / was stripped and stolen months ago and i have no / money with which to repair or replace it. my mentors have / exiled me to the outskirts of nappy literacy" (136). The "stripped" and "stolen" car is here akin to the "nappy literacy" leading to her erasure, figured perhaps by the lower-case *I*s populating her poems. Yet there is an energy to these poems, at once angry and humorous, that seems to outpace the fates of her automobiles. As John Yau writes, "Coleman pulls the reader in with long, sinuous lines that keep driving forward, pulling you along."[74] The lure of these lines contrasts with the burden of keeping her struggle buggy on the road as well as the effort of not giving in to her "frequent fantasies about running over people i don't like."[75] While Creeley's "I Know a Man" ends with a warning to "look / out where yr going," "I Live for My Car" runs on a poetic drive where the kids "scream / 'mama!'" from the back seat to get her to stop.[76] For Coleman the impulse to drive into things is born of frustration rather than freedom, and it is as though she were wryly answering Creeley's bombastic question, "why not, buy a goddamn big car," by simply describing the conditions that prevent her from driving in luxury.

PETROPOETICS

The most compelling recent scholarship on automobility and culture has considered automobility as a form of petroculture, a term which seeks to encompass all of our uses of fossil fuels, from gasoline and plastic bags to road movies and makeup. In *Living Oil: Petroleum Culture in the American Century* (2014), Stephanie LeMenager has made clear how ubiquitous oil is to cultural production writ large, including the production and distribution of academic books such as this one. LeMenager writes that "oil itself is a medium that fundamentally supports all modern media forms concerned with what counts as culture—from film to recorded music, novels, magazines, photographs, sports, and the wikis, blogs, and videography of the Internet."[77] She shows how novels such as Vladimir Nabokov's *Lolita* (1955) and Kerouac's *On the Road* perform the contradiction of the road trip as an escape from the very ills of social conformity associated with mass automobility. As we have seen, the same can be said of Creeley's "I Know a Man," but LeMenager does not consider car poetry at any length.

LeMenager is one of many scholars of petrocultures who have instructively foregrounded the centrality of oil to modern culture while asking difficult questions of literature as to its lack of a direct engagement with fossil fuels. Such questions were first posed in a much-cited 1992 article from *The New Republic,* where the novelist Amitav Ghosh wonders about the absence of oil in novels. He asks his readers to "try and imagine a major American writer taking on the Oil Encounter. The idea is literally inconceivable."[78] As others have pointed out, presumably Ghosh wasn't aware of Upton Sinclair's novel *Oil!* (1926–27), the basis for the 2007 film *There Will Be Blood.* In focusing on the absence of oil, subsequent petrocultures scholars have come to talk of an "oil unconscious." For example, Patricia Yaeger proposes periodizing literary epochs by their fuel sources, whether whale oil or gasoline, which would define the "energy unconscious" at work in each epoch.[79] Imre Szeman worries, though, that "such a periodization fails to capture . . . the almost complete absence of oil as subject matter (direct or allegorical) in the literature written during the era when it is dominant."[80] LeMenager is likewise concerned with the oil unconscious, asking, "*Why is oil so bad?* Because of the mystified ecological unconscious of modern car culture, which allows for a persistent association of driving with being alive."⁸¹ LeMenager's coupling of liveness and driving has been formative for my readings of the poets—such as Coleman—discussed in this book. Yet poets are often conscious about this coupling, rather than mystifying it. Eileen Myles, for instance, explicitly grapples with the way that their own aliveness while driving is burning the planet. It seems, then, that the framework of reading for an ecological or oil unconscious accords better for novels and films than poetry, which often wears its unconscious on its sleeve.⁸²

The dogged focus of petrocultures researchers on the absence of oil as subject matter provides a quintessentially *paranoid* reading of aesthetic production, a form of attention which, as Eve Kosofsky Sedgwick puts it, "knows some things well and others poorly."⁸³ Petrocultures scholars know, for instance, that oil is everywhere, yet their assertion that it is nowhere in modern literature is unsatisfactory. Some of the poets I consider are also paranoid about oil, worrying over the death that is central to driving to live. Yet their poems can also be *reparative*—the other side of Sedgwick's dichotomy. Rather than seeking, through exposure, to forever stave off the same trauma of catastrophe, many of the poets in this book live with and find ways to relate to catastrophe while creating space for mourning and even joy. To varying degrees, their poems "emphasize forms of complicity in environmental destruction and convey collective feelings of vulnerability, hopelessness, and dread," to quote Margaret Ronda.⁸⁴ By reading such poetry reparatively, we can foster, in Nicole Seymour's formulation, "a criticism that is nonnormative, self-reflexive, and noninstrumentalist—or, at the very least, open to the multiple possibilities of cultural works."⁸⁵ Environmentalists might be frustrated that the poetry in this book "makes nothing happen" and is instead "a way of happening," as W. H. Auden famously put it.⁸⁶ Yet learning from the difficulties and pleasures of such ways of happening is crucial even, or especially, amid catastrophes.

One of the aims of this book is to bring petrocultures scholarship into conversation with the burgeoning and shifting study of ecopoetics. Early scholarly understandings of ecological poetry focused on the theme of pristine nature, not least in writing by the British Romantics and the American Transcendentalists. In the new millennium, though, critics in the environmental humanities have questioned the very category of nature, a shift epitomized by Timothy Morton's influential book *Ecology Without Nature:*

Rethinking Environmental Aesthetics (2007). In contrast to affirming the values of pristine nature, postnatural ecopoetics scholarship has come to focus on diverse forms of poetry that explore the relationships between human and non- or more-than-human life, from cars and the internet, to ants, glaciers, and roadkill.[87] For example, Joshua Schuster has argued that the ecological poem might also be understood as a commodity poem that "sees itself in connection with as well as in distinction from the world of goods that circulate around the planet."[88] Rather than separating nature from culture and society, then, the ecological poem can interrogate the commodified relationships that define petromodernity, in part by mimicking them, as we saw with Stein's assembly-line-like poetry. As Kristin Ross points out, the automobile was arguably "the commodity form as such" during the American century, a reality which has paradoxically led to the car being "consign[ed] . . . to the edges of historical discourse."[89] Reading poetry in relation to automobility is therefore inherently ecological, regardless of the environmental content of any given poem.

While petrocultures scholarship has focused nearly exclusively on narrative-driven genres such as novels and films, ecopoetics scholarship hasn't had a lot to say about oil. Indeed, the term *ecopoetics* risks, in its capaciousness, saying very little in and of itself about what makes a particular poem or poet worthy of study. At the marriage point—to use a car production metaphor—of petrocultures scholarship and ecopoetics is the nascent study of petropoetics. Melanie Dennis Unrau offers this definition of the term: "*petropoetics* is world-making through collaboration and co-constitution between humans and fossil fuels. It is also art-making that participates in, describes, contemplates, or critiques this poetics."[90] Petropoetics, then, makes ecological poems focused on how humans interact with fossil fuels. Petropoetics is also a kind of "energy ecopoetics," a phrase Margaret Ronda and Kristin George Bagdanov use to "highlight the flow, stock, and interchange of energy as it powers and unmakes entities and environments."[91] While Unrau and others using the term *petropoetics* have been focused on poetry written in relation to oil production in Canada, I am interested in how American poets are writing about some of that very same oil as it fills their gas tanks south of the border.[92] Throughout this book poetry is energized by fossil fuels, though the degree to which poets explicitly reflect on the imbrication between poetry, cars, and oil varies greatly.

Indeed, poets in the new millennium are generally more environmentally conscious than their modernist forebears were. Lynn Keller has shown how twenty-first-century poets such as Evelyn Reilly, Juliana Spahr, and Ed Roberson "seek to better understand the nature and scope of the changes humans have wrought in the Anthropocene, and the impact of those changes on human and nonhuman bodies and lives."[93] Keller adds that "none of these writers imagines that poetry will save the world," but it is clear from her account that they are on the right side of ecological history, which admittedly hasn't always been the case.[94] As Christoph Irmscher warns, though, we risk smugness in foregrounding our own ecological consciousness: "As comforting as it might seem to think of ourselves today as equipped with an environmental awareness that previous generations lacked, it is also true that our planet is now close to, or has already reached, a point of no return.... Current disasters have a long genesis, and American poets long before the present moment already felt a sense of urgency about the changes they witnessed."[95] While the critique of automobility is as old as the first horseless carriages, it also seems clear by now that increased awareness of the ills of petromodernity is insufficient for addressing the climate crisis. While *Poetic Drive* affirms that poets have been more environmentalist in the twenty-first century than early in the twentieth century, it also seeks to unsettle critical narratives that find an unconscious affirmation of petromodernity in literature before the advent of modern environmentalism. Williams, for instance, came to turn away from the car as a driver of his poetry as soon as mass automobility took root in the 1920s and '30s. Similarly, Frank O'Hara confronted the deadly consequences of driving, during the height on the 1950s boom in car production and highway construction.

Michael Rubenstein and Justin Neuman provide another postwar example of petropoetics when they consider Elizabeth Bishop's 1965 poem "The Filling Station" as "a petrofiction—both in Ghosh's sense of the term as a fiction about oil and in Szeman's sense of the term as a fiction composed in the time of petromodernity."[96] In Bishop's droll exclamation about the filling station that begins the poem—"Oh, but it is dirty!"—Rubenstein and Neuman hear "something much bigger as the allegorical subject of the poem: petromodernity itself."[97] The same thing might be said about "For the Union Dead" (1960), one of the most famous poems by Bishop's poetry partner Robert Lowell, which ends with the lines: "Everywhere, / giant finned cars nose forward like fish; a savage servility / slides by on grease."[98] (The other candidate for most famous Lowell poem, "Skunk Hour," is even more explicitly about automobility.) "For the Union Dead" is written during both the civil rights and the nuclear eras and is framed by the contrast between the derelict South Boston Aquarium that Lowell visited as a child and the building of a new car park below Boston Common. While eyeing this construction project, the poet laments the contemporary absence of the heroism celebrated in the Civil War memorial at the edge of the Common, *Memorial to Robert Gould Shaw and the Massachusetts Fifty-Fourth Regiment,* honoring a regiment that was made up of Black soldiers. In contrast to this heroism, the poet seems always on the outside of events, including crouching in front of his television set, where "the drained faces of Negro school-children rise like balloons."[99] Lowell's petromodernity is at once the society of the spectacle, where white men seem to be stuck watching history as though looking into an aquarium and where a "goddamn big car" like Creeley's is unambiguously "savage" rather than liberatory.[100]

For a more explicitly environmentalist petropoetics, we must look ahead a decade or so to the work of Gary Snyder. Snyder published his Pulitzer Prize–winning book of poems, *Turtle Island,* in 1974, and it includes a section called "Plain Talk," where he inveighs against both nuclear power and fossil fuels. As Brian Ladd points out, "the years before the oil crisis, the late 1960s and early 1970s, may have been the golden age of car-bashing in the U.S. and Europe."[101] In one of the subsections of "Plain Talk," entitled "Four Changes," Snyder considers the problem of pollution, and advises "the community" to "use less cars": "Cars pollute the air, and one or two people riding lonely in a huge car is an insult to intelligence and the Earth. Share rides, legalize hitch-hiking, and build hitch-hiker waiting stations along the highways. Also—a step toward the new world—walk more; look for the best routes through beautiful countryside for long-distance walking trips: San Francisco to Los Angeles down the Coast Range, for example."[102] When "Plain Talk" was written in 1969, Snyder did not know about global warming but, rather, sought to encourage his readers to drive less for the sake of preserving air quality. He was also worried about peak oil, and the prospect of increased use of nuclear power when the oil runs out.[103] Sharing rides, hitchhiking, and walking will help save us from nuclear disaster, according to Snyder, and in the case of walking, has its own aesthetic pleasures.

Considering the scholarly reception of *Turtle Island* sheds light on why many twentieth-century poets might have shied away from incorporating explicitly environmental concerns into their poetry. (We find another potential reason for this avoidance, when Williams is fined the equivalence of a year's salary for slandering the owner of a local gas station.) Critics such as Michael Davidson, who appreciate the "haiku-like sparseness" of Snyder's earlier poetry, see his discursiveness in *Turtle Island* as undermining his "Buddhist naturalism."[104] The poem that Davidson chooses to illustrate this discursiveness—entitled "Tomorrow's Song"—ends with the lines "we need no fossil fuel / get power within / grow strong on less," a form of sloganeering that Davidson laments as "authorial intervention."[105] Such readings risk unmooring Snyder from the radical aspirations of his moment, which we would do well to recover. For example, Margaret Ronda has read Snyder's book alongside Diane DiPrima's extraordinary *Revolutionary Letters* (1968) as forms of "revolutionary pastoral" that offer "a sustained thought experiment in imagining an ecologically oriented commons not determined by present values and political frameworks."[106] The work of imagining another world in *Turtle Island* leads to a poetry of plain statement that turns a haiku-like simplicity toward political ends.

Forty years after *Turtle Island,* Snyder published the poem "Mimulus on the Road to Town" in his collection *Danger on Peaks* (2004), which offers a more subdued, but no less poignant, form of urban pastoral:

> Out of cracks in the roadcut rockwalls,
> clumps of peach-colored mimulus
> spread and bloom,
>   stiffly quiver in the hot
> log-truck breeze-blast
> always going by—
> they never die.[107]

These mimulus flowers live in the cracks caused by roadway construction, a relationship brought home in the rhyme of the final two lines, which links the never-ending rush of trucks with the undying flowers. Snyder had himself worked as a logger, and this poem echoes an earlier one, "Why Log Truck Drivers Rise Earlier than Students of Zen" from *Turtle Island*, which ends with the koan-like statement, "There is no other life."[108] Petromodernity is, among other things, this double bind, where this life means navigating the planetary cracks caused by automobility, not least while driving. Much of the poetry that follows takes place inside cars, but it can also feel like the tenacious mimulus flowers, blooming in the fissures of the open road. Taken together, this poetry provides us with a profound sense of what it means to "spread and bloom" alongside American automobility, often while yearning for a life and art beyond it.

I

WILLIAM CARLOS WILLIAMS DRIVES A "HOT LITTLE BABY"

> For many years, for all the years I had a car, I would always carry around the complete poems of Wm. Carlos Williams in my trunk because I always thought it was somehow necessary to have them there.
> —BERNADETTE MAYER, letter to Alice Notley, January 27, 1980

WILLIAM CARLOS WILLIAMS (1883–1963) bought his first car in October 1913, a Ford Model T that freed him from his mare and buggy (the mare was named Astrid), which he had been using to make his house calls as general practitioner in Rutherford, New Jersey, and the surrounding area.[1] It was nearly a year after he had married Florence and the same year as the famous Armory Show of modernist art in New York City, which Williams may or may not have attended.[2] In the course of his career driving around Rutherford, he delivered thousands of babies, and in between house calls he would sit in his car jotting down poems about women in labor, driving, and of course wheelbarrows and other industrial products. Williams has therefore rightly been coupled with automobiles both in the popular imagination and in his scholarly reception. In the wonderful *Voices and Visions* documentary that aired on PBS in 1988, a driver on the open road stops to write poetry on his "William C. Williams, M.D." prescription pad. Decades later, in Jim Jarmusch's 2016 film *Paterson,* Adam Driver's character drives around Paterson, New Jersey, writing and reading poetry, not least that by Williams. Yet Jarmusch's coupling of driving with the long poem *Paterson* (1946–58) is anachronistic, as little driving occurs in that poem, where we can read in book 5 (1958) that "you can't see anything / from a car window."[3] Rather than in *Paterson,* it is in Williams's earlier work, and especially that from the 1920s, where he comprehensively develops a technique of perspectival collage, which harnesses the view from the driver's seat. After the financial crash of 1929—which was in part brought on by the expansion of personal credit as the market for cars became saturated[4]—Williams associates cars and Henry Ford with monotony and stagnation, leading to his retreat from automobility as a source of poetic inspiration.[5] As he writes in *Pictures from Brueghel and Other Poems* (1962), "how / shall we / escape this modern // age / and learn / to breathe again."[6]

It was middle-class professionals, including physicians like Williams, who were responsible for the initial spread of automobiles beyond the luxury market.[7] Cotten Seiler has noted, "especially for the working-class and middle-class white men who would acquire automobility with the advent of the low-cost Ford Model T in 1908, driving's compensatory value depended on cars being what the early critics (and more recent ones) maintained they were: instruments for the display of blithe, arrogant, potentially destructive power—'insolent chariots,' as one later author would put it."[8] As his elder son Eric attests, Williams could himself be a reckless, aggressive, and overexcited driver.[9] Seiler outlines the centrality of speedy driving to a masculine version of consumer self-possession, where "one's competence behind the wheel indicated the capacity to thrive in capitalist modernity."[10] We can see Williams putting his own automotive competence on display in this humorous anecdote from the *Autobiography* (1967):

> To drive the streets at all seasons is also my delight, alone in my car, though it is only to return home at the end of an hour. It is not unexciting,

either. It is a formal game. It is also moderately dangerous. The duels with the other guy—or woman—who takes a wide swing into the right of way are a test of skill. Any moment's heedlessness is a potential accident. I pride myself on my escapes. No cowboy on the range could be happier in the chances he takes. Once a car and a coal truck were coming down Union Avenue abreast, over the crest of the hill. I was coming up at a good speed. There was no chance, apparently, to avoid a crash. I was lucky, of course, but it gave me a big kick to drive in over the gutter to my left, dodge between two trees, ride twenty feet up the sidewalk, duck out again between trees and skim past a police car following the coal truck.

"Hi, Doc!" is all they said.[11]

Driving could be dangerous, but this danger provided an opportunity for showing mastery and skill. The "formal game" of driving has, furthermore, parallels with the imagist and collage aesthetics Williams developed after he began driving, which relied on the hard edges of short lines as well as the associative leaps that such enjambment could facilitate. Williams's recklessness had its victims, though, including his wife; when he sped over a railroad crossing, Floss's head hit the tin roof of their Ford, crushing a vertebra and causing her neck problems for the rest of her life.[12]

Williams's experience as a driver before mass automobility took root has parallels with his work as a doctor making home visits, a sort of craft vocation that was in the process of becoming obsolete. As the above quotation from the autobiography attests, he styled himself as a kind of cowboy gentleman, all the while protected from police interference by his professional standing and his whiteness. In contrast to this pastoral New Jersey landscape through which he first navigated his Model T as a doctor, the brave new world of mass automobility was something else altogether, full of traffic and roadside debris. The sheer increase in the number of cars and gas stations during this period is astounding. In 1900 around eight thousand automobiles were registered in the United States.[13] By 1910, just before Williams acquired his first car, that number had increased by 450,000, and by 1929 the number of registered cars was just over 23.1 million.[14] To meet the demand for fuel, roughly 265,000 curbside and drive-in filling stations covered the country by 1927, while Americans consumed 382 million barrels of gasoline in 1929, four times more than a decade before.[15]

While Williams stood out as an early driver of the Model T, he joined the mass during the 1920s when, as James Flink writes, "automobility became the backbone of a new consumer-goods-oriented society and economy that has persisted into the present. By the mid-1920s automobile manufacturing ranked first in value of product and third in value of exports among American industries."[16] No longer just another commodity, cars became an industry at the heart of the American economy, inaugurating what Stephanie LeMenager has termed "the natureculture of petromodernity" in the United States.[17]

In considering the ecological stakes of poetry from this period, Joshua Schuster has asked, "where is the oil in modernism?"[18] As this chapter will show, we can find it in the cars in Williams's poetry and especially in the oil trucks in his experimental prose. Indeed, Williams's modernist experimentation with words was driven by the energy provided by fossil fuels. In claiming that there are "no ideas but in things"[19] (1927) and that a poem is a "machine made of words" (*CP II,* 54) (1944), he sought to harness the powers of US industry toward a petropoetics that at once critiqued the proliferation of oil and cars during this period. Enda Duffy is therefore mistaken when he claims that high-modernist writing "lack[ed] the means necessary to represent" car rhythms, and that its pacing was closer to that of the flaneur.[20] In valorizing pop culture's embrace of speed, Duffy underplays the central, if ambiguous, role of automobility for modernist poets such as Williams.[21] After the Great Depression, though, Williams did denounce the vantage point of the automobile and turned towards a pacing closer to that of the flaneur. As LeMenager has pointed out, by the mid-twentieth century, walking could be part of a refusal of automobility, a periodization that accords well with the arc of Williams's career.[22] This chapter will consider twenty-four years of that arc—from "The Young Housewife" (1916) to "Sketch for a Portrait of Henry Ford" (1940)—when Williams developed his poetic drive of experimental writing fueled by oil and driving, only later to leave the automobile behind as stalled junk during his "definite retreat" from his avant-garde commitments, as Marjorie Perloff put it.[23] This retreat was, in part, a bid to keep intact the craft of his poetic vocation, which relied on his experience as a cultural outsider in suburban America.

Williams's ambivalence toward automobility helps explain the contest he sets up in his work, between the productive powers of US industry and those of mothers, powers he sought to harness in his poetry. As we shall see in the experimental prose of *The Great American Novel* (1923), the generative powers of mothers, petrol, and electricity vie with each other to birth a new literature. The poet-doctor-narrator resolves this contest by himself becoming the ultimate mother of modernism, attending to the "hot little baby" of avant-garde literature. At the same time, Williams has no problem objectifying women as so many parts, a logic that is at work in "The Young Housewife" and *Spring and All* (1923). He nevertheless worries over the effects that automobility has on young women when "the pure products of America / go crazy" (*CP I*, 217), as he put it in the latter book. Like an anxious parent, he repeatedly thematizes driving's threat to women, while his own driving poems mechanize his male gaze. These two seemingly contradictory positions have a fascinating rendezvous in his all-but-neglected story, "The Five Dollar Guy" (1926), where the narrator-doctor jokes with an actual mother about the licentious joys and pitfalls of automobility.

The contest that Williams sets up between automobility and maternity is hinted at in a 1914 photograph that he took of his wife holding their first child, William Eric, with his new Model T Ford in the background. Flossie stands in the foreground with her face turned toward the infant; both their eyes are closed and they are smiling. This part of the photo is overexposed and somewhat out of focus, a sort of whiteout against the sharper background of the Ford parked by a hedge. The sturdy body of Williams's Ford seems of a piece with his wife's firm hold on baby Bill, her wedding ring visibly shining in the light. *Williams seems to be gathering his primary attachments in this photo with a kind of motherly care that is hard to distinguish from patriarchal possession.* Indeed, it is as though his Ford were vying with mother and child for his attention, as it will do in *The Great American Novel*.

Sixty-six years after this photo was taken, the poet Alice Notley published a pamphlet where she conceived of herself and fellow poet Bernadette Mayer as Williams's literary heiresses, an inheritance that I will return to at the end of this chapter. Strikingly, Notley couples Williams's sexual mobility with her own immobility while pregnant, thereby restaging the logic of his engagement with maternity from a poet-mother's perspective. While Notley is immobile, Mayer is driving around with William's collected works in the trunk of her car (see the epigraph for this chapter),

Flossie Williams with baby Bill and Ford, taken by Williams in 1914. (William Carlos Williams, MD, Estate, in care of the Jean V. Naggar Literary Agency, Inc.; image courtesy of the Beinecke Library at Yale University)

suggesting an ambivalent form of care for his poetry. Although these feminist poets probably never saw Williams's photo, I want to suggest that they are in imaginative solidarity with Flossie, who had to live with the physical consequences of Williams's reckless driving, his marital infidelity, as well as his round-the-clock work delivering babies and—thankfully—writing poetry.

EARLY POEMS

Williams's first modernist poems are a departure from his Keatsean juvenilia, and driving is central to this transition. The automobile provides Williams with a distinct vision and experience that is crucial for his imagist innovations, which reach their apex in *Spring and All*. Yet, from the beginning, Williams also figures automobiles as dangerous, especially for young women. In "The Young Housewife" (1916), his first poem to take place completely inside the automobile, his own position as solitary driver is compared to that of the solitary housewife. There is a stark imbalance of power between these two modern figures, encapsulated in the subtle violence perpetuated by the automobile. While troubling, this poem is elegant and understated in comparison to the later poem "Romance Moderne" (1919), where the poet's transgressive sexuality causes a car crash and leaves him in the ditch, recalling Marinetti's origin story for Italian futurism. Unlike the futurists, though, neither of Williams's poems celebrates the destructive powers of technology for their own sake. Rather, in these poems Williams stages the tension between poetry and machines in ways that would come to define his work.

Here is "The Young Housewife" in its entirety:

> At ten A.M. the young housewife
> moves about in negligee behind
> the wooden walls of her husband's house.
> I pass solitary in my car.
>
> Then again she comes to the curb
> to call the ice-man, fish-man, and stands
> shy, uncorseted, tucking in
> stray ends of hair, and I compare her
> to a fallen leaf.
>
> The noiseless wheels of my car
> rush with a crackling sound over
> dried leaves as I bow and pass smiling. (*CP I*, 57)

The self-possession provided by the poet's car is inseparable from what Rachel Blau DuPlessis has read as the poem's "mechanism of 'the [male] gaze.'"[24] One can't help but wonder how many times the poet has driven past the same house "again" in order to be able to account for so much activity. There is a clear imbalance between the poet and housewife, for while she is kept within "the wooden walls of her *husband's* house," the poet drives by "solitary" but free in *his* machine (emphasis added). Unlike "the ice-man" and "fish-man," the poet has no discrete function to perform. Nevertheless, his final act is to "bow and pass smiling." Why is he bowing, and how does one bow while driving? Bowing was indeed still possible in the Model T due to its high cab, allowing its inhabitants to wear hats. This minute formality nevertheless highlights a difference between the violence of "the noiseless wheels of my car," which "rush with a crackling sound over / dried leaves," and the poet's middle-class propriety. This propriety helps explain the policeman's greeting to the reckless driver in the *Autobiography:* "Hi, Doc!" Perhaps only a gentleman who bows while driving could be accorded such freedom, and yet this bowing while driving remains odd, as it seems to collapse the distance between the performance of social niceties before and after the emergence of automobiles.

Indeed, central to "The Young Housewife" is the mechanical distance between people that the automobile inaugurates. Nevertheless, the doctor's cruising enacts a fantasy of contact across the gendered division of labor so central to Fordism. Linda Kinnahan has argued that "Williams enacts a critique of a poetics, and ultimately of a cultural ethos, that chooses mastery over contact."[25] "The Young Housewife" is full of contact, though, but mostly between things: wooden walls and negligee, stray ends of hair, leaves, and car. These things are the erotic constraints that the housewife and the poet have in common. She is "tucking in / stray ends of hair" at the same moment that Williams's syntax is itself tucked in, or broken, to continue at the beginning of the next line. The poet is also tucked into his automobile, while his gaze and fantasy sprawl outward, which he then forms into a restrained little poem. Rather than describing the housewife's beauty as triumphant, the poet will "compare her / to a fallen leaf" and perhaps his bow mirrors her falling. Since Walt Whitman, "leaves" must also call to mind the pages of a book—*Leaves of Grass*—and the poems therein. But the leaves in Williams's poem are also the young housewife, and driving over them suggests femicide. In contrast to Whitman's poetics of immediate contact, in "The Young Housewife" the destructive "rush" of the doctor's car makes for the only explicit contact between poet and world, where the "crackling" of leaves signals the constraints on intimacy that "sound" the depths of this unnerving poem.

A few years after composing "The Young Housewife," Williams imagines the relationship between machinery and poetic contact somewhat differently. In "Belly Music," his closing statement for the final issue of the little magazine *Others* (July 1919), he updates Whitman's imagery by linking leaves to engines: "Poets have written of the big leaves and the little leaves, leaves that are red, green, yellow and the one thing they have never seen about a leaf is that it is a little engine. It is one of the things that make a plant GO."[26] Williams's leaves of poems can also be little engines, but he is at pains to assert the primacy of poetry over machinery. The artist, he declares, "writes in order to escape the mechanical perfection of sheer existence. He writes to assert himself above every machine and every mechanical conception that seeks to bind him. He writes to free himself, to annihilate every machine, every science, to escape defiant through consciousness and accuracy of emotional expression."[27] Williams's anxiety over the predominance of machines in American culture is in full bloom here, evincing the conflict between machines and artworks that Theodor Adorno would articulate half a century later when he writes that "modern works ... must show themselves to be the equal of high industrialism, not simply make it a topic."[28] Indeed, rather than simply writing about machines, Williams sought to craft a poem that is itself a "machine made of words."

Williams's poetic drive to exceed the powers of industry gave his destructive impulses free reign, which we can also see in his 1919 poem "Romance Moderne," where he maneuvers between a Romantic conception of nature and the machine aesthetics of futurism. The poem begins by describing the view of a "flickering mountain" in the "rain and light" and "a lake,—/ or brown stream rising and falling / at the roadside" (*CP I*, 147). One might be reminded of Mont Blanc, which was so central to Romantic conceptions of the sublime. This vision, though, is contrasted with "the other world—/ the windshield a blunt barrier." The barrier between what is inside the car and the view outside is compounded by a sexual drama within the car. As A. Walton Litz and Christopher MacGowan bluntly paraphrase "Romance Moderne," "the poet is flirting with a young woman in the back seat of an automobile, while her husband and the poet's wife are seated in front" (*CP I*, 496–97). Not content to flirt with the driver's wife, though, the poet has a go at the driver himself, and thereby manages to break through the barrier between the car and the outside world:

> Lean forward. Punch the steersman
> behind the ear. Twirl the wheel!
> Over the edge! Screams! Crash!

> The end. I sit above my head—
> a little removed—or
> a thin wash of rain on the roadway
> —I am never afraid when he is driving,—
> interposes new direction,
> rides us sidewise, unforeseen
> into the ditch! All threads cut!
> Death! Black. The end. The very end—(*CP I*, 148)

The poet's bravado and attempt to make contact at all costs appears to be self-defeating. Breaking through the social barrier of marriage, the practical barrier between passenger and driver, and the phenomenological barrier between the car and the outside world, leads to death. But the poet's attempt to take control of the car, and the deathly consequences of his actions, are as farcical as they are serious. He survives despite himself.

Sitting by the roadside after the crash, the blustering poet attempts to balance the pathetic and the grandiose:

> I would sit separate weighing a
> small red handful: the dirt of these parts,
> sliding mists sheeting the alders
> against the touch of fingers creeping
> to mine. All stuff of the blind emotions.
> But—stirred, the eye seizes
> for the first time—The eye awake!—
> anything, a dirt bank with green stars
> of scrawny weed flattened upon it under
> a weight of air—For the first time!—
> or a yawning depth: Big!
> Swim around in it, through it—
> all directions and find
> vitreous seawater stuff—
> God how I love you!—or, as I say,
> a plunge into the ditch. The end. I sit
> examining my red handful. Balancing
> —this—in and out—agh. (*CP I*, 148–49)

The poet painfully and ecstatically attempts to balance the "in and out" of his perspective, which resides somewhere between the romantic vision of a mountain in the rain and the actuality of a pile of dirt by the roadside. It is first by sitting in a ditch, though, that he sees the stars; the poet's "eye" is "awake!" Finally, the poet has made contact—"the touch of fingers creeping / to mine" even though this contact seems creepily like death.

In writing this poem, Williams may well have been influenced by Filippo Tommaso Marinetti's futurist manifesto, which had been published in Italian, French, and English ten years previously. In the manifesto, Marinetti and his friends race cars into the night until the narrator, confronted by two bicyclists in the road, rolls over into a ditch: "Oh! Maternal ditch, nearly full of muddy water! Fair factory drain! I gulped down your bracing slime, which reminded me of the sacred black breast of my Sudanese nurse. . . . When I climbed out, a filthy and stinking rag, from underneath the capsized car, I felt my heart—deliciously—being slashed with the red-hot iron of joy!"[29] Arising from this ditch, Marinetti and his comrades declaim their manifesto "to all the *living* men of the earth."[30] Being stuck in the muddy water reminds the futurist of his Black nurse, so that his own mobility is premised on Black servitude. As with "Romance Moderne," a car crash becomes the birthing ground of a modernism premised on violence. The tract ends: "Lift up your heads! // Standing erect on the summit of the world, yet once more we fling our challenge to the stars!"[31] While the futurists arise triumphant from the dirt, Williams's poet sits in the ditch, contemplating a handful of it.[32] As Peter Halter puts it, "whereas the futurists saw modern urban space as the epitome of collectivity and mass identity, Williams still retains the individual in a central role."[33] Williams's individual is vulnerable, and the poet of "Romance Moderne" can't fling himself to the stars he sees from the ditch, because these "green stars" are—we learn after the line break—"scrawny weed." This double vision between imaginative stars and the mundane ditch is formalized, then, in the enjambment of the poem, a technique that Williams will further develop in *Spring and All*.

In his early driving poems "The Young Housewife" and "Romance Moderne," Williams struggles to negotiate between a Romantic inheritance and modernist iconoclasm. In "The Young Housewife" the driver's mechanistic male gaze both relies upon and seeks to overcome the gendered division of labor that was central to Fordism. Yet seeking greater contact through driving seems to lead to femicide in "The Young Housewife," and results in explicit violence in "Romance Moderne," landing the poet in the dirt. As with Marinetti's "maternal ditch," sitting in the dirt becomes the birthing ground of modernism for bombastic, "*living* men" like Williams, a theme that returns, in somewhat inverted form, in *The Great American Novel*. As we are about to see, in that book it is oil and not mud that generates new words for Williams's poetic drive.

THE GREAT AMERICAN NOVEL

In *The Great American Novel,* first published in 1923 in Paris, Williams strains to find the energy for avant-garde literature. The novel's doctor-narrator draws upon various energetic sources, including cars and oil, an electric power plant, and a mother giving birth. Indeed, the poet himself becomes a distracted mother in this anti-novel, comically attempting to protect the claims of American modernism through tending to the labors of both actual mothers and machines. This tender mothering through machines stands in contrast to the dangers of the automobile so prominent in Williams's poetry. Yet, as we have just seen, even in his early poetry, Williams tells the origin story of his modernist technique through driving and crashing. Williams's petropoetics is therefore inherently ambivalent, as he seeks to harness oil and cars for modernist writing while worrying over the fragile and potentially destructive forms of self-possession that they afford.

The Great American Novel is, appropriately for its title, a kind of road novel that begins with interrogating the sources for modernist art. These sources include new words such as *petrol*, but such words cannot progress into a novel when their origin remains unexamined. "Progress is to get," writes Williams. "But how can words get.—Let them get drunk. Bah. Words are words. Fog of words. The car runs through it. The words take up the smell of the car. Petrol. Face powder, arm pits, food-grease in the hair, foul breath, clean musk. Words. Words cannot progress. There cannot be a novel."[34] Williams strains here after an organicist conception of language akin to Pound's ideogram, where words and characters are meant to have a necessary connection to the objects they signify. The smell of petrol coming from the car seems to attach itself to the word "petrol," but it is also mixed up with a host of other scents, all of which adhere to people, like "clean musk" and "face powder." Indeed, it is as though the products of mass culture both energize and distract the car in its search for a new language for modernist writing. Looking to cut through the accretion of signification that encloses it like a fog, the car searches out the energy of a power plant: "Turned into the wrong street seeking to pass the power house from which the hum, hmmmmmmmmmmmmm—sprang. Electricity has been discovered for ever. I'm new, says the great dynamo. I am progress. I make a word. Listen! UMMMMMMMMMMMM—" (*I*, 162). The plant seems to create new words with its primal hum, which trumps the sputtering energy of the car careening amidst "food-grease" and "foul breath."

The novel's search for its own energetic origins does not stop at the power plant, though, but turns to the generative power of mothers, asking, in effect, which is a better source for imaginative writing. Indeed, the very hum of machinery vies for supremacy with the screams of a mother in labor:

> The fog lay in deep masses on the roads at three A.M. Into the wrong street turned the car seeking the high pitched singing tone of the dynamos endlessly spinning in the high banquet hall, filling the house and the room where the bed of pain stood with progress. Ow, ow! Oh help me somebody! said she. UMMMMMM sang the dynamo in the next street, UMMMM. With a terrible scream she drowned out its sound. He went to the window to see if his car was still there, pulled the curtain aside, green—Yes it was still there. (*I*, 162)

The "UMMMM" and "hmmm" of dynamos grasping for a new language are meant to exceed the "fog" that Williams associates with European modernism: "But Joyce. He is misjudged, misunderstood. His vaunted invention is a fragile fog" (*I*, 168). The new words coming from machinery evince the powers of American innovation, but they are nevertheless drowned out by an even more primal scream—that of the woman in labor. Lisa Siraganian has compellingly linked Williams's novel to Progressive Era ideas about maternity, writing that "the woman matches and even exceeds the social and technological progress of modernity—we might even say that by giving birth, the maternal body turns into a symbol of progress."[35] The doctor seems uncertain, though, of whether the mother or machinery is a better symbol for progress. Indeed, it is as if maternal labors cannot help but remind him of his automobile, for while the baby is born and the mother is screaming for the doctor's help, he is checking on his green car.

Thirty-five years after its publication, Williams reflected that *The Great American Novel* was "a travesty on what I considered conventional American writing. People were always talking about the Great American Novel so I thought I'd write it. The heroine is a little Ford car—she was very passionate—a hot little baby."[36] In harnessing the energy of a hot little baby Ford, the novel's doctor-narrator becomes its ultimate mother. Sianne Ngai has encapsulated such maternal desire for commodities in a word: cute. As she writes, "cuteness solicits a regard of the commodity as an anthropomorphic being less powerful than the aesthetic subject, appealing specifically to us for protection and care."[37] The little car demands such care while it searches for its energy-mother amidst "the high pitched singing tone of the dynamos" and trucks "FULL of gas" (*I*, 172). Only the doctor, who is at once the author of the story, can fulfill this role. In this way, Williams fictionalizes himself as the mother of a cute modernism he imagines as "a hot little baby." As Ngai explains, "cuteness might be explicitly mobilized by the poetic avant-garde as a meditation on its own restricted agency."[38] Indeed, Williams must nurture his nativist, self-consciously American version of modernism, lest it be schooled by the likes of James Joyce and T. S. Eliot, or lest it become just another commodity amidst the array of American industrial products.[39] His conception of machine modernism is therefore inherently vulnerable, calling for his protection and care. As we are about to see, Williams's impulse to protect the hot little baby of American modernism will only become more acute as mass automobility comes to dominate the American landscape.

SPRING AND ALL

Williams's mothering of modernism in the experimental prose of *The Great American Novel* fed into the composition of his fourth book of poems, *Spring and All,* which was also published in 1923. Mixing poetry and prose, *Spring and All* constellates diverse things and people, often seen from the driver's seat, into a kaleidoscopic poetic collage. The book's poetic drive depends on the poet's social status as an upper-middle-class white doctor, which is apparent in how he poeticizes working-class women and African Americans. The doctor-poet figures the maladies affecting these people as an effect of the absence of capable drivers, while attempting to prove through his aesthetic achievement that he can fill this role. This is a highly tenuous solution, though, forging a petropoetics from the driver's seat while yearning to leave the ills of petromodernity behind. As we shall see, Williams did eventually turn away from automobility as a source for poetic inspiration later in the same decade.

In the imagistic technique of *Spring and All*, Williams found a poetic solution to the problem of contact with the surrounding world, which characterized his early driving poems. While in "Romance Moderne" the modern perspective from inside the car clashed with a Romantic outside, in *Spring and All*, as Roy Miki puts it, "the mind finds itself inside an outside, and when the driving begins, the driver enters the play of a doubleness: not only an inside experienced as an outside, but now as well an outside experienced as an inside."[40] In the book's first lines of verse, the ditch that the poet landed in in "Romance Moderne" has been transformed into muddy fields, a harbinger of spring:

> By the road to the contagious hospital
> under the surge of the blue
> mottled clouds driven from the
> northeast—a cold wind. Beyond, the
> waste of broad, muddy fields
> brown with dried weeds, standing and fallen
>
> patches of standing water
> the scattering of tall trees (*CP I*, 183)

Presumably the poet-doctor is driving to work during the influenza pandemic, while clouds "driven" by wind evoke a pathetic fallacy of the poet's movement being akin to the weather. Like Miki, T. Hugh Crawford links the poet's perspective to a kind of doubleness: "The opening poem of *Spring and All*—'By the road to the contagious hospital'—is a twofold paradigm . . . in which the narrator catalogs the symptoms of the coming spring as he witnesses them through the window of his car. Thus the automobile (and other transportation and communication technologies) not only lets physicians see things hidden from view but also constructs those objects as symptoms or details by bringing to bear the medical gaze as part of the theater of proof."[41] In the age of the house call, Williams found being a suburban doctor a mode of both intimacy and isolation, part science and part craft. Poetry had a similar status for him, as it meant attending to facts as well as harnessing the power of the imagination. Attending to ideas in things did not, then, mean slavishly giving things priority over the imagination, nor trying to subtract the poet's own personality from the world, as Eliot's version of modernism appeared to suggest one should.[42] Rather, the things outside the window reflects the poet's own auto-mobility.

This seeming autonomy of things becomes even more suggestive in "The Right of Way," which versifies the doctor's flickers of perception from behind the driver's seat. In this poem, the driver's kaleidoscopic perspective is inscribed through its lineation, where individual lines are syntactically linked together, while each asserts the priority of its own subject:

> In passing with my mind
> on nothing in the world
>
> but the right of way
> I enjoy on the road by
>
> virtue of the law—
> I saw
>
> an elderly man who
> smiled and looked away
>
> to the north past a house—
> a woman in blue
>
> who was laughing and
> leaning forward to look up

into the man's half
averted face

and a boy of eight who was
looking at the middle of

the man's belly
at a watchchain—

The supreme importance
of this nameless spectacle

sped me by them
without a word—

Why bother where I went?
for I went spinning on the

four wheels of my car
along the wet road until

I saw a girl with one leg
over the rail of a balcony (*CP I*, 205–6)

Here Williams develops his signature line breaks to stunning effect, so that myriad actors transform the driver's vision. This vision is premised on legally having "the right of way," which was affirmed by the police officer's permissiveness toward Williams's reckless driving in the *Autobiography* and is inseparable from his social standing. The poem's "radical discontinuity," as Jon Chatlos calls it, can cause us to ask whether it is the driver's mind, the right of way, the law, the boy of eight, or the woman in blue, that is the dynamo of the poem's progression.[43] There is a centrifugal logic to this movement, represented by the "four wheels of my car" and counterpoised by the "watchchain" holding the boy motionless. As in "The Young Housewife," the doctor's gaze, facilitated by driving, is explicitly sexual and potentially dangerous. His vision follows a line of sight until it encounters the broken line of a girl's leg hanging over a balcony. For a brief moment—as long as a short line—we are led to believe that the girl only has one leg, suggesting her vulnerability in relation to the spinning wheels of the man's car, until suddenly—at the next line—the leg is above the driver, tantalizingly secure in comparison to the driver's aimlessness. As Susan McCabe points out, "Williams here literalizes enjambment—a word that derives from the French 'jambe' for leg, thus linking his 'revolution in the conception of the poetic foot' to its metaphoric bodily significance."[44]

In "The Right of Way" the automobile is the vehicle for a free-associative play of materials, not least industrial ones. At the same time, the car demands an attentive driver, who provides an auto-mobile structure and measure. Indeed, Williams melds machine and human in the prose from *Spring and All*, where "the imagination is an actual force comparable to electricity or steam" (*CP I*, 207). Without the poet's imagination to order the energies of the machine age, human flourishing is threatened. In contrast to "The Right of Way," the poem that comes to be titled "To Elsie" dramatizes how "the pure products of America / go crazy" for want of any stabilizing perspective. These "products" include women workers:

> and young slatterns, bathed
> in filth
> from Monday to Saturday
>
> to be tricked out that night
> with gauds
> from imaginations which have no
>
> peasant traditions to give them
> character
> but flutter and flaunt
>
> sheer rags—succumbing without
> emotion
> save numbed terror
>
> under some hedge or choke-cherry
> or viburnum—
> which they cannot express— (*CP I*, 217)

With imaginations debased by consumer goods, these workingwomen are led astray into the bushes like "sheer rags." Yet the modern worldview of these workers is analogous to the frenetic perception these poems themselves put on display; is not the watchchain that catches the boy's attention in "The Right of Way" itself a kind of gaud for the imagination? The same forces that threaten the imagination also provide, in short, a model for how to constellate the diverse objects and experiences of modern life.

Indeed, part of the pathos of "To Elsie" is that the doctor is not saved from the poem's indictment against modern America, as Elsie is employed by "some doctor's family." The doctor-poet ends the poem by again lamenting the degraded condition of the imagination, which is now inseparable from driving:

> It is only in isolate flecks that
> something
> is given off
>
> No one
> to witness
> and adjust, no one to drive the car (*CP I*, 219)

The driving that constellated the "isolate flecks" of "The Right of Way" has here run amok. Yet the negative inflection of this poem's final line—"no one to drive the car"—at once reveals its opposite, since the doctor is not only witness to but also composer of the perspective offered on his characters' dissolution. In this way, *Spring and All* serves as proof that poetry can be driven in new directions by a capable modernist poet.

In the subsequent poem of the book, "XIX," Williams turns his gaze to "boys fifteen and seventeen" who are "drivers for grocers or taxidrivers / white and colored." While the "slatterns" of "To Elsie" have been sexually assaulted "under some hedge or choke-cherry / or viburnum," the boys of this poem "wear two horned lilac blossoms / in their caps—or over one ear," which they have "stolen"—"broken the bushes apart / with a curse for their owner" (*CP I*, 221–22). It is as though these drivers have stolen the very flowers of the young women whom Williams concerns himself with in "To Elsie." It is nevertheless jarring when the poet calls these boys "dirty satyrs," as both their driving and "vulgarity" mirror the poet's own lascivious gaze through the car's windshield. Does the dirtiness of these working-class satyrs refer not only to their brazenness but also to the fact that they are Black and white? These are the only non-white drivers I have come across in Williams's poetry, and his judgment of them foregrounds his own whiteness, which assures his "right of way." He writes derogatorily of the satyr drivers who "stand in doorways / on the business streets with a sneer / on their faces," prefiguring the more laudatory lines from Frank O'Hara's "A Step Away from Them": "A / Negro stands in a doorway with a / toothpick, languorously agitating."[45] O'Hara's lines serve as a send-up of the idea, which Williams's poem perpetuates, that a Black man is agitating simply by existing in public as a sexual being. Williams's satyrs also foreshadow the motorcyclists of Charles Olson's poem "The Lordly and Isolate Satyrs," which I discuss in the next chapter.

The conflict between commodities and art that Williams stages in *The Great American Novel* is resolved in *Spring and All* as a new perspective and form—a "new realism," as Charles Altieri would have it—where the driver's vision holds the scattered things (including people) of modern life together by the penetrating bricolage of a vexed poetic gaze.[46] This bricolage of commodities, people, and perspectives is a highly tenuous form of petropoetics, though, as the "no one" of the final lines of "To Elsie" suggests that the logic of automobility is beyond individual control. The doctor's ability to forge this petropoetics is, furthermore, predicated on having the "right of way" ensured by his social status; only a certain kind of poet (who himself calls the working-class drivers "a certain sort" [*CP I*, 221]) gets to see, and to drive, freely. Driving nevertheless becomes a creative liability for the doctor, and after *Spring and All*, Williams begins to move away from the tightrope walk of affirming imaginative art through machines. As we are about to see, he increasingly figures the automobile as stalled junk, available for poetic reflection but no longer the center of generative energy that it was for him in 1923.

"THE FIVE DOLLAR GUY"

Williams's short story "The Five Dollar Guy" was published in the inaugural issue of *New Masses* in May 1926. Like many of Williams's stories, it is framed as a doctor's visit to a patient. In this case, the doctor-narrator visits a mother to check on her third, newborn child. The woman relates how the attendant at the "filling station for the Mex Pet Gas and Oil Co." down the street has promised her a joyride in his Mex Pet oil truck, and that "the Boss down there" made sexual advances while she walked by one night with one of her children.[47] The anxiety over moral dissolution coupled to automobility that we saw in *Spring and All* returns in this story in a way that also calls to mind the gas station in F. Scott Fitzgerald's *The Great Gatsby*, published the previous year. Williams neglected to alter the name of the gas station and the boss in his story—Henwood—before publication and was charged with libel, a suit which he settled to the tune of $5,000, the equivalent of a year's salary.[48] This experience was part of a shift in Williams's attitude toward automobility, which he increasingly figured through traffic and wrecked cars both in his prose and poetry.

While, in "The Young Housewife," the poet fantasizes about a woman inside her husband's house, in "The Five Dollar Guy," the doctor-poet is himself inside a woman's home, bantering away about cars and (mostly imagined) sexual escapades. Rather than writing from the frenetic perspective of a driver as in *Spring and All*, the view from this story is contemplative, and it is a junked car that attracts the doctor's attention. The narrator begins the story philosophically, stating that "all the forenoon" he had been thinking of this: "To put down, to find and to put down some small, primary thing, to begin low down so that all the color and the smell should be in it—plainly seen and sensed,—solidly stated—with this we should begin to have a literature; but we must begin low. It is not to write intriguingly, to fabricate a fascinating tissue of words (so I had been thinking) but to get down to one word where that is fastened upon the object, and so to begin to write—some plain phrase: that would be story enough" (*FDG*, 19). As in *The Great American Novel*, Williams is preoccupied here with finding words that will allow for a direct contact with things. Yet words prove to be as low down and slippery as oil. When the young mother tells the narrator about the offer of a joyride in an oil truck, he replies that "it's a good thing to have a load of gas behind you when you go for a joy ride," which the woman laughingly interprets two ways. The narrator then looks out the window and reflects, "it flashed across my mind that here it was, the inexplicable, exquisite, vulgar thing—rarest of the rare in the imagination, the trodden and defeated atmosphere of perfection." The doctor sees a yellow bench in the yard, upon which lays a mongrel dog of the kind "loved by the poor" for having a "soft, delicate texture of richness" found nowhere else in their experience (*FDG*, 19). He then turns his attention to the rest of the yard: "At the back was a shack where one might shed chickens or, after them, a Ford. The Ford, flat-tired and written on the sides with witticisms half rubbed out, ROLLS ROUGH, the door hanging open, the hood of the engine flapping like a loose cap, the seat busted in and the stuffing showing—the Ford stood with the off wheels in the garden, sunken, abandoned." Everything in the yard, furthermore, "had been pushed sideways to the edges to make room in the center for—what? The ground was trampled. The dog was asleep" (*FDG*, 29).

Rather than providing "one word . . . that is fastened upon the object," the meanings of words proliferate in the story. Such semiotic play is fastened on the dilapidated Ford as the witticism "ROLLS ROUGH," which puns on the finery of a Rolls-Royce. Indeed, the folksiness of the Model T incited a plethora of nicknames besides the most famous one, "Tin Lizzy." As with the word "gas," the meanings of the word "pet" also proliferate in the story, referring at times to the Mex Pet truck, petroleum, actual pets, and (sexual) petting. While both the doctor and mother fantasize about joyrides, it is through attending to the "low down" "primary thing" of a broken-down Ford that "we should begin to have a literature." Modern American literature begins and ends for Williams with cars and oil. His auto-fictive narrator is attracted to a dilapidated Ford precisely because it can't go anywhere, can't become other things, yet the words inscribed on this low-down thing are themselves a slippery joke on automobility. To roll rough, to be vernacular, is here paradoxically to not roll at all, which seems a safe place to make "contact" with primary things. That such contact is inherently multivalent puts the lie to any organicist fantasy of a direct connection between words and things, since his petropoetics quite literally drives them apart.

This story seems to ask who, in the age of automobility, is not a five dollar guy? Indeed, the $5 that the boss at the filling station offers the mother to try and lure her inside is the same amount as the pay Henry Ford famously offered his factory workers in 1914 as part of an attempt to stem extremely high rates of worker turnover. Ironically, Williams did not earn

$5 but had to pay the five dollar guy $5,000 after publishing his story. As if to try to recoup this loss, two years later, Williams bought $5,000 worth of oil shares in Atlantic Refining, which he again lost in the crash of 1929.[49] The fortunes of oil and literature are, in short, intermingled for Williams. Writing directly about oil cost him dearly and may have inhibited him from expanding on the topic. In his subsequent poems, cars became much less prevalent, as he aimed to craft an imaginative vision beyond automobility. Even in "The Five Dollar Guy" it is not so much cars that lead to contact, as the most poignant connection is that between the doctor and the mother. The two seem to collude in nurturing modernist literature, which is written on the wall of a car that has run out of energy.

LATER POEMS

Williams's conception of driving, cars, and gasoline was transformed by the emergence of automobility as a mass phenomenon in the late 1920s. During the 1930s, Henry Ford also met intense public criticism for his violent union busting—overseen by the retired boxer Harry Bennett—that led to riots at the River Rouge Complex and strikes at Ford factories throughout the country.[50] The General Motors Corporation was equally anti-union, but after the dramatic sit-down strike of 1937, when workers occupied production plants for forty-four days straight, GM was forced to recognize the United Auto Workers, which was shortly followed by union recognition at the notoriously anti-union US Steel.[51] For Williams—who published in communist journals such as *New Masses* throughout the 1930s—the attraction of automobility as a vehicle for individual creativity waned markedly. Ironically, Ford himself displayed a similar skepticism toward mass automobility in the same period, opening Greenfield Village to the public in 1933 near River Rouge, where visitors could explore buildings and streets from an America before cars.[52] Williams's increasing alienation from mass automobility is apparent in *The Descent of Winter* (1928), as well as in later poems including "View of a Lake" (1935), "The Raper from Passenack" (1935), and "Sketch for a Portrait of Henry Ford" (1940). In these poems, gasoline is figured as having a suffocating effect on poetry, and mass automobility and its detritus are depicted as monotonous, degraded, and deadening.

In *The Descent of Winter,* Williams writes that "there is not excellence without the vibrant rhythm of a poem and poems are small and tied and gasping, they eat gasoline, they all ate gasoline and died" (*CP I,* 295). While eating gasoline kills poems, cars contribute to a deadening monotony. This Fordist monotony nevertheless leaves room for the kind of contact with mothers that we saw in "The Five Dollar Guy":

> Oh, blessed love, among insults, brawls, yelling, kicks, brutality—here the old dignity of life holds on—defying the law, defying monotony....
>
> Oh, blessed love—the dream engulfs her. She opens her eyes on the troubled bosom of the mother who is nursing the babe and watching the door. And watching the eye of the man. Talking English, a stream of Magyar, Polish what? to the tall man coming and going.
>
> Oh, blessed love where are you there, pleasure driven out, order triumphant, one house like another, grass cut to pay lovelessly. Bored we turn to cars to take us to "the country" to "nature" to breathe her good air. Jesus Christ. To nature. It's about time, for most of us. (*CP I,* 298–99)

Here an "old dignity" defies the same automotive "law" that was the engine behind "The Right of Way," a law that here signals not a generative, cruising point of view but rather "monotony." Whereas in "The Young Housewife" the poet can imagine the housewife's home as a distinct self-enclosed world, much like his car, in *The Descent of Winter* one house is like any other, with cars, ironically, offering a means of escape to "nature." This escape is fictional, though, holding up a separation between machines and nature that is elided by the "modern," where "there are no sagas—only trees now, animals, engines" (*CP I,* 302). Although, as we have seen, poems may themselves be engines, here engines have begun, with mass automobility, to deaden creativity. It is rather the "blessed love" of the "troubled bosom of the mother" that remains generative for the poetic imagination.

Even though gasoline and cars suffocate poetry, the narrator of *The Descent of Winter* still allows that car production can inspire great art: "Henry Ford has asked Chas. Sheeler to go to Detroit and photograph everything. Carte blanche. Sheeler!" (*CP I,* 307). Indeed, Charles Sheeler's photographs, and his subsequent paintings of Ford's River Rouge

Complex—completed in 1928—evince a cubist realism analogous to Williams's imagism. This excitement over Sheeler's professional success does not extend, though, to exalting car production or Henry Ford. On the following page of the book, the monotony of work in Fordism makes the United States akin to "a Soviet State decayed away in a misconception of richness. The states, counties, cities, are anemic Soviets. As rabbits are cottontailed the office-workers in cotton running pants get in a hot car, ride in a hot tunnel and confine themselves in a hot office—to sell asphalt, the trade in tanned leather" (*CP I,* 308). Such repetitive work and commuting are necessary in order to keep the roads paved, so that people can drive their "hot" cars to work, where they sell asphalt for more roads. The Ford, which was a "hot little baby" in *The Great American Novel,* is here enervating, producing heat only to keep the machinery of profit-making running. This development begs the question of what to make of modernist literature now that it is no longer a baby in need of nurturing.

Strikingly, in the one moment where the first-person poet explicitly emerges as driver in this book, it is grass that catches his attention:[53]

> I make really very little money.
> What of it?
> I prefer the grass with the rain on it
> the short grass before my headlights
> when I am turning my car—
> a degenerate trait, no doubt.
> It would ruin England. (*CP I,* 315)

The poet is still drawn to a peculiarly American complex of machinery coupled to poetry, the latter being invoked as "short grass" reminiscent of Whitman's *Leaves* but also of the grass "lovelessly" cut for pay earlier in the book. Since the poet isn't making much money, though, he is saved from the threat of selling out his art. Indeed, he appears proud here of his own nativist degeneracy, and his modest means distinguish him from the mania for possessions coupled to the monotony of suburbia, traffic, and offices. Rather than exuberant, driving here is melancholic.

This melancholic view of automobility is also intimated in "View of a Lake," which appeared in *An Early Martyr and Other Poems* (1935), and raises the question of what in Williams's imagist poetics remains, in the

Depression years when the once exciting advance of automobility has stalled or turned to junk. The poem begins on a highway below a recently blasted-away rock surface, which has left a "waste of cinders" strewn across the slope where

> stand three children
>
> beside the weed-grown
> chassis
> of a wrecked car
>
> immobile in a line
> facing the water (*CP I*, 380)

As in "The Five Dollar Guy," a wrecked car focuses the poet's vision, which is transposed to that of the children: "They are intent / watching something / below—?" (*CP I*, 380–81). The children's view extends that of the other drivers, who are fixated on the children much as they are all fixed on something below:

> Opposite
>
> remains a sycamore
> in leaf
> Intently fixed
>
> the three
> with straight backs
> ignore
>
> the stalled traffic
> all eyes
> toward the water (*CP I*, 381)

What is it that the children see? We know, at least, what they fixedly look away from: stalled traffic, highway construction, and the chassis of a wrecked car. The children's gaze may be the "primary thing" that captures the drivers' attention, not least because they are looking away from an automobility that has here stalled, and which is clearly connected to the waste, wires, and concrete flanking the highway. The "line" of this gaze has a similar logic to "The Right of Way," where the driver's view finally lands on a woman's leg. Yet in "View of a Lake" the driver's mechanized male gaze is now tempered by the views of others who turn away from automobility.[54]

There is another driving poem from *An Early Martyr* that melds the descriptive inclusivity of "View of a Lake" with the sexual charge of Williams's earlier poems, namely "The Raper from Passenack."[55] This is a relatively conventional narrative poem written in thirteen three-line stanzas, describing how a woman is driven home by the man who raped her, while she curses "all men," declaring that if she gets a "venereal infection," she "won't be treated" but would rather be found "dead in bed" (*CP I*, 386–87). This violent logic whereby rapists drive cars and their survivors are relegated to the role of passengers will return in Eileen Myles's first-person account of being gang-raped by "guys . . . who all owned cars." In contrast to Myles's story, "The Raper from Passenack" is told in the third person, and it is easy to imagine Williams turning a patient's traumatic account into fodder for this poem. Indeed, as Rachel Blau DuPlessis had pointed out in her creative criticism, this is precisely what happens in *Paterson,* where the "Beautiful Thing" at the center of the poem is a Black woman survivor of rape whom the poet-doctor treats.[56] Commenting on his reading at Wellesley College—a school for women—Williams told Edith Heal, "They were so adorable. I could have raped them all!"[57] As DuPlessis summarizes Williams's self-fashioning, "he is the doctor the poet the rapist these / are all identities he claims."[58] These identities place the imagined crushing of "The Young Housewife" under the wheels of the poet's car in an even more sinister light. For Williams, automobility, rape, and reporting are all prerogatives of the poet, and his poetic drive includes both the voices of survivors of rape and his own fantasy of being the rapist.

The tragedy of mass automobility reaches its culmination for Williams five years after *An Early Martyr,* when he writes "Sketch for a Portrait of Henry Ford" (1940):

> A tin bucket
> full of small used parts
> nuts and short bolts

slowly draining onto
the dented bottom—
forming a heavy sludge
of oil—depositing
in its turn steel grit—

Hangs on an arm
that whirls it at increasing
velocity around
a central pivot—
suddenly the handle gives
way and the bucket
is propelled through
space   .   .   . *(CP II,* 12–13)

As in "The Right of Way" and "View of a Lake," where the poet's automotive gaze follows a line of objects and others' gazes, "Sketch" likewise forges a tension between centripetal self-possession and centrifugal dispersion. But whereas in "The Right of Way" the poet's perspective remains intact as his car wheels continue aimlessly, joyously, spinning, here "the handle gives way" and the contents of the bucket "full of small used parts" goes flying off through "space." This flight seems to be the cost of maintaining an imaginative vision unreceptive to the views of others, as *The Descent of Winter* and *An Early Martyr* seek to be. Henry Ford's creation, we might deduce, is beyond his control, so that—as Mark Steven reads this poem— "an exemplary capitalist subjectivity [has been replaced by] the means of production."[59] In Williams's subsequent work, the poetic imagination will be freed from the pitfalls of mass automobility. Unfortunately, his imagistic rendering of those pitfalls, which was at its zenith with *Spring and All,* will likewise fall by the wayside.

In contrast to the vexed yet energized poetic drive of *Spring and All,* automobility becomes both monotonous and stalled in Williams's later work. In his epic poem *Paterson,* walking largely takes the place of driving as the means of personal poetic transport, while the few cars in *Pictures from Brueghel and Other Poems* (1962) are critically seen from without, not experienced from within. Following Perloff, I think that Williams's retreat from automobility was also an aesthetic retreat from the high-water mark of his earlier writing. If Williams's most successful works are inextricably coupled to automobility, then it is hard not to worry, as Anne Raine does over modernism in general, that our attachment to modernist aesthetics shows up our addiction to petromodernity.[60] Yet there is another generative impulse in Williams's work, namely maternity, which endures beyond his fascination with automobility.[61] In his struggle to complete *Paterson,* he even conceives of himself as a mother; "it's got to be born," he writes, "it's got to be pushed out of me somehow in some perfect form."[62] While my taste veers toward his earlier work fueled by automobility, *Paterson*'s influence on modern American poetry is hard to overestimate.

Williams's female poetic inheritors have been particularly attuned to the role of maternity in his work. In her 1980 lecture "Doctor Williams's Heiresses," printed as a limited-edition pamphlet that same year by Tuumba Press, Alice Notley confronts the gendered genealogy of Williams's work. Notley begins her lecture by imagining Williams as the poetic son of Emily Dickinson and Walt Whitman and then the husband of Gertrude Stein, with whom he has two sons of his own, Frank O'Hara and Philip Whalen. Williams also has an illegitimate son in this imaginative genealogy, Charles Olson, and Notley thereby prefigures the creative rivalry between Olson and O'Hara that is at the center of the next chapter. Wonderfully, Notley imagines O'Hara, Whalen, and Olson as the intersex parents of both herself and fellow poet Bernadette Mayer. Notley's lecture is in part a conversation with Mayer, whose letter to Notley from January 27, 1980, is included in the middle of the pamphlet. In Mayer's charming, rambling letter, she describes how she is pregnant and has a cold, and reflects on the authority that doctors have over women, while relating the story of how she rode around with Williams's complete works in the trunk of her car "because I always thought it was somehow necessary to have them there."

Williams's complete works in the trunk: ever-present and mobile, but also relegated to the role of disused passenger. Mayer's partner at the time, the poet Lewis Warsh, accuses her of a "lack of devotion to the books," but she asserts that "it was really just the opposite of that!" Although Mayer insists that driving around with Williams in the trunk is in fact an act of devotion, her devotion is clearly mixed with resentment. With a similar ambivalence, Notley addresses Williams while referring to her own depressive pregnancy in England: "In that bad time there was always you. To love as a poet & to love & hate as a man. Immobile pregnant & isolate & unhappy, I didn't need to read about your attractions to women other than your wife. Your reasoning seemed specious & was enraging." Notley couples Williams's sexual mobility to her own immobility as a pregnant mother isolated in a small town in a foreign country, as though Williams were both her poetic grandfather and her errant husband. As Julia Bloch, who introduced me to Notley's lecture, writes, "Notley's pregnancy here suggests the way feminist poetic critique looks toward a different future at the same time that it recasts the past in variant ways and puts pressure on the body as a textual medium as well as a site of genealogical inscription."[63] The same goes for Mayer's letter: keeping Williams's works safely stored in the trunk is like being pregnant with them, while intimating a feminist critique of their patriarchal contents. In Notley's pamphlet, two poet-mothers confront their vexed devotion to their poetic grandfather, who himself sought to inhabit the generative powers of mothers in his work. Perhaps, then, we should understand Williams's mothering as the poetic heir of Notley and Mayer's inspired correspondence, rather than the other way around.

2

FRANK O'HARA CRASHES CHARLES OLSON'S CAR

> I am for an art that tells you the time of day, or where such and such a street is.
> —CLAES OLDENBURG, *I Am for an Art*

> Sat in the Ford World Headquarters lobby, reading Olson.
> —RON SILLIMAN, *Ketjak*

ON SUNDAY, AUGUST 21, 1966, Edward Ruscha was driving a 1963 Buick LeSabre at 90 mph along Interstate 15 between Los Angeles and Las Vegas. At exactly 5:07 p.m., Mason Williams, who was in the car with Ruscha, threw a Royal 10 Typewriter out of the car window. Ruscha then circled back so that his other passenger, Patrick Blackwell, could photograph the typewriter's strewn remains, as well as the car and the three men involved in this murder of a typewriter. Blackwell's photos and their short, wry captions make up the artist's book *Royal Road Test* (1967), an early example of conceptual art and a commentary on the by then well-established association between driving and American literary production on the typewriter.

Kerouac's *On the Road* from the previous decade is the most obvious referent here. As David J. Alworth explains, "Kerouac typed the now-legendary manuscript as one enormous single-spaced paragraph on eight sheets of tracing paper, which he later taped together into a 120-foot scroll." Kerouac remarked that when the scroll was rolled out on the floor, it "look[ed] like a road."[1] Robert Rauschenberg and John Cage provide a striking analogue to Kerouac's manuscript in their *Automobile Tire Print* from 1953, which is a long paper scroll of a tire print, which looks like a brush stroke. By throwing a Royal typewriter out of the window of a car speeding through the desert, Ruscha and his fellow travelers are operating both within and against this cultural tradition where white men use cars and the road to make modern American literature and art.[2]

In the previous chapter, we saw how Williams's attempt to forge a poetic relationship with driving unraveled with the onset of mass automobility. Between 1929 and 1950, the number of registered cars in America more than doubled to 49.2 million.[3] As James Flink points out, the "passage of the 1956 Interstate Highway Act ensured the complete triumph of the automobile over mass-transit alternatives in the United States and killed off, except in a few large cities, the vestiges of balanced public transportation systems that remained in 1950s America."[4] By 1965 car production reached a historic peak of 11.1 million per year, while one-tenth of jobs were connected to the automobile industry.[5] Driving not only became the dominant way to get around during this period but was also central to the postwar economic boom.

In this chapter, I am going to focus on two post-WWII poets from successive generations, Charles Olson (1910–70) and Frank O'Hara (1926–66), who crafted related but distinct poetic drives in which typewriters and cars were central. Whereas Williams turned away from the social and ecological degradations of mass automobility, Olson and O'Hara forged their poetics in the teeth of postwar Fordism. They reveal in distinct and often contradictory ways the alienation and anxiety of precisely the white men who were the main beneficiaries of the golden era of American automobility. Pairing Olson and O'Hara makes apparent how throughout the postwar period, white men figured poetic authenticity in terms of driving, which inevitably became coupled with crashing and death. This poetic drive toward destruction is encapsulated in the ironic epigraph to

Ruscha's *Royal Road Test:* "It was too directly bound to its own anguish to be anything other than a cry of negation; carrying within itself, the seeds of its own destruction." What else could "it" be, if not the complex of men seeking self-possession through automobility, which could so easily lead to their destruction? We saw this dialectic at play in Robert Creeley's 1955 poem "I Know A Man" at the opening of this book, and in this chapter, it will reemerge in the crashed and damaged cars populating Olson's and O'Hara's poetry, as well as in O'Hara's film collaborations.[6]

In what follows, I show how Olson confidently couples masculine self-possession to Fordism in his poetics manifesto "Projective Verse" (1950), a coupling that becomes filled with anxiety in his dream poems. O'Hara inherits a poetics of breath and his signature "I do this I do that" style in part from Olson while also ironizing Olson's poetics of masculine authenticity. Andrew Epstein points out that O'Hara "never unequivocally worships the myth of the open road: he doesn't buy into (intellectually or physically) the romantic idea of escape via speeding cars down lonely highways of the vast American night, à la Jack Kerouac."[7] Indeed, O'Hara is the quintessential Manhattan flaneur, walking around the city both in his life and in his poems. But he also had a romantic idea about James Dean after he died in a car crash in 1955. As we shall see, O'Hara even couples his walking to the automotive traffic of New York City, which spurs his longing for connection with the 8 million people who live there. His poetry nevertheless turns away from what Marshall Berman has called an impersonal "expressway world" and toward a more intimate "shout in the street," a shout which would culminate in the protests of the late '60s, not least Stonewall.[8] As Berman puts it, "the streets erupted into American poetry at a crucial moment, just before they would erupt into our politics."[9] O'Hara's work seeks to make connections, then, across the social divides of Fordism; rather than pitting pedestrianism and driving against each other, he figures both as central to his poetics of transit.[10]

In exploring the nature of postwar automotive sociability, this chapter will also consider O'Hara's collaborations with Rudy Burckhardt and Alfred Leslie on experimental car films. Burckhardt's whimsical film *The Automotive Story* (1954), for which O'Hara played the piano music, foregrounds the historical contingency of mass automobility while anthropomorphizing cars in an attempt to make them personal and fun. O'Hara went on to write the subtitles for Alfred Leslie's *The Last Clean Shirt* (1964), where an interracial couple drives through Manhattan with a timer strapped to the dashboard. This film was made the same year as the passage of the 1964 Civil Rights Act, and it offers an opaque homage to the Civil Rights Movement while also suggesting the gap between aspirations for racial equality and the macabre reality of American race relations. O'Hara explicitly registers racist violence in poems that express a longing for contact with the whole city, in contrast to Olson's anxiety about Indigenous and Black mobility. Across work in different media, then, O'Hara forges a poetic drive where omnipresent traffic and the romance of the car crash index the seeming impossibility of sustained homosexual and interracial bonds in Fordism. The legacy of O'Hara's racial politics is mixed, though, as he often fetishized Black men in ways that are reminiscent of Williams's objectification of women in his driving poems.

OLSON'S LINE MANAGEMENT

Charles Olson's masculinist machine poetics is on full display in "Projective Verse," which is by many accounts the most influential North American poetics manifesto since WWII. It was first published in the relatively staid *Poetry New York,* then reprinted as a pamphlet by LeRoi Jones's avant-garde Totem Press, and finally canonized in Donald Allen's *The New American Poetry: 1945–1960* (1960). In his manifesto, Olson crafts a poetic drive that both relies on and seeks to distinguish itself from the Fordist assembly line, with its minute regulation of bodily movements. "Projective Verse" is focused on the machinery of the typewriter, a manual technology that Olson could imagine as organically connected to his own body. Yet by associating this typewriting with assembly-line production, he reveals the dialectical relationship between the myth of masculine self-possession and the alienation of mass production. "Projective Verse" provides a kind of instruction manual for how to write authentic poetry, but since this bid for authenticity relies on machinery, it ultimately attests—as we shall see in Olson's dream poems—to the fragility of masculine self-possession.

In the manifesto, Olson declares that his aim is to "get us, inside the machinery, now, 1950, of how projective verse is made."[11] According to him, by using a typewriter, the poet is no longer alienated from his means of production, and for the first time, he can have a direct encounter with his reader, unmediated by forms of poetic measure inherited from undemocratic traditions:

> It is the advantage of the typewriter that, due to its rigidity and its space precisions, it can, for a poet, indicate exactly the breath, the pauses, the suspensions even of syllables, the juxtapositions even of parts of phrases, which he intends. For the first time the poet has the stave and the bar a musician has had. For the first time he can, without the convention of rime and meter, record the listening he has done to his own speech and by that one act indicate how he would want any reader, silently or otherwise, to voice his work. (*Prose* 245)

For Olson, the typewriter allows men to take direct control over their means of poetic production. He couples this manual machine to an organic vision of the page as an open field, across which the poet's voice and breath—which he figures as specifically masculine—can extend. Ironically, it is the poet's authentic voice—that "place of origin" for both Whitman and Olson—that, through the machine, can now be transferred directly to the reader (*Prose* 245).

Olson imagines the poet as "the 'Single Intelligence'" and "the Boss of all," the boss, that is, of both syllables and lines, which are regulated by his own breath: "And the line comes (I swear it) from the breath, from the breathing of the man who writes, at the moment that he writes, and thus is, it is here that, the daily work, the WORK, gets in, for only he, the man who writes, can declare, at every moment, the line its metric and its ending—where its breathing, shall come to, termination" (*Prose* 242). The typewriter can be felt in Olson's many commas, in his capitalizations and italicizations, and in the starts and stops and ultimate rest that ends this percussive sentence. The poet's machine allows for the fiction that we are reading his respiration as he pushes back the roller of the typewriter and lets his breath expire at the end of the line. This direct control by the poet of his craft is an essential part of the difference between the projective and the "non-projective," with the latter consisting of inherited rhythms and materials, rather than those which the poet can, we are meant to believe, hold in his hands and shape to his own ends (*Prose* 239).

For Olson, the poet's bodily projection onto the typed page is inscribed through a taut poetic line that invokes the energies of assembly-line production. He quotes Creeley's statement that "FORM IS NEVER MORE THAN AN EXTENSION OF CONTENT" and Edward Dahlberg's that "ONE PERCEPTION MUST IMMEDIATELY AND DIRECTLY LEAD TO A FURTHER PERCEPTION," leading him to conclude: "So there we are, fast, there's the dogma" (*Prose* 240). He goes on to parse Dahlberg's statement with language that makes him sound like the boss of his own assembly line: "It means exactly what it says, is a matter of, at *all* points (even, I should say, of our management of daily reality as of the daily work) get on with it, keep moving, keep in, speed, the nerves, their speed, the perceptions, theirs, the acts, the split second acts, the whole business, keep it moving as fast as you can, citizen. And if you also set up as a poet, USE USE USE the process at all points, in any given poem always, always one perception must must must MOVE, INSTANTER, ON ANOTHER!" (*Prose* 240). The kinetic energy of Olson's poetic construct must hold itself taut to ensure its immediacy. As Libbie Rifkin has noted, "there's a certain Fordism in these injunctions, compromised only by their desperate tone."[12] Olson goes on to write, "contemporary workers go lazy RIGHT HERE WHERE THE LINE IS BORN" (*Prose* 242). His poet finds himself *on the line*, then, in several senses. First, he is putting himself at stake, attesting to his authenticity. This posturing, second, is inscribed in the poem's *line*ation, with the poet's breath as measure. Finally, as a "contemporary worker," the poet compares his work to that taking place on the *assembly line,* although his poetic utterances are produced by an organic measure rather than regulated time. This last part is crucial—in breaking from traditional meter, the projective poet is also breaking from measured time, but rather than becoming "lazy," this allows him to be more "taut."

Many critics, beginning with Rachel Blau DuPlessis, have shown how Olson figures physical immediacy in markedly phallic terms.[13] Michael Davidson points out, "it is clear that the body from which poetry is projective belongs to a male heterosexual whose alternating pattern of tumescence and detumescence, penetration and projection, dissemination and impregnation structures more than the poem's lineation."[14] Mark Byers has shown, furthermore, how Olson's phallic conception of "Projective Verse" was part of a larger turn to the liberatory potential of sexuality by leftist artists after the postwar development of an "administered world," as Max Horkheimer and Theodor Adorno put it.[15] Byers writes that "despite warnings from orthodox Marxists, by 1948 American painters and radical political theorists had begun to adopt the potent male subject as a substitute for conventional instruments of political change."[16] The affirmation of masculine autonomy was not limited to leftists, though. Cotten Seiler describes how "the reaffirmation of autonomous individuality, to which so many midcentury social critics, cultural producers, and representatives of the state directed their energies, doubled as a reaffirmation of masculinity."[17] As Seiler shows, driving became central to this postwar project of individual and national regeneration. On the one hand, Olson's management of his phallic poetic line arises as a protest against the alienation of Fordist line management. For Olson this protest was personal; in "The Post Office" (1948) he recounts how the modernization of the US postal service along Fordist lines led, ultimately, to the early death of his father, who worked as a postman.[18] Yet Olson's masculinist vision of individual and national regeneration was perfectly consonant with the aims of US cold war domestic policy. As DuPlessis explains, masculinist poets such as Olson offered "a critique of hegemonic maleness as it functions socially," while "at the same time" drawing "on ideologies of the center in order actively to resist the sense that textual females (or, indeed, real women) could themselves have a large stake in the gender shifts in male subjectivity occurring on the countercultural periphery."[19] Ultimately, Olson's "Projective Verse" uses what DuPlessis calls "outright phallicism as knowledge" in order to craft a form of literary authority that entailed excluding both poetry and people who were deemed "non-projective."[20]

Olson's phallicism as knowledge is inscribed in two dream poems where the poet struggles to enliven the detritus of mass automobility, in effect picking up where Williams left off. In the poems "The Lordly and Isolate Satyrs" and "As the Dead Prey upon Us," both of which Donald Allen included in *The New American Poetry*, the poet betrays his phallic envy for the power of motorcycles and cars. As Stephen Fredman points out, Olson was "a serious reader of Freud and Jung [and] believed that dreams supply essential psychic information that cannot be obtained by other means."[21] We can glean such psychic information from the following lines of "The

Lordly and Isolate Satyrs," where the poet is drawn to a motorcycle gang on the beach, whose machines become phalluses, and which appear to express the organic breath of "Projective Verse":

> Except for the stirring of the leader, they are still
> catching their breath. They are almost like scooters the way
> they sit there, up a little, on their thing. It is as though
> the extra effort of it tired them the most. Yet that just there
> was where their weight and separateness—their immensities—
> lay.[22]

The motorcycle gang's "immensities" enthrall the poet, and while their breath may have gotten away from them for a moment, they are "catching" it. Their attempt to "possess themselves" (*Poems*, 386) through machinery stands in contrast to the awed poet, who is simply comporting himself "as usual" while "the children were being fed pop / and potato chips, and everyone was sprawled as people are / on a beach" (*Poems*, 385). These isolate satyrs are separated, then, from the degradations of an implicitly feminized mass culture, while nevertheless harnessing mass automobility to make their quintessentially masculine countercultural stand.[23]

If, as DuPlessis has shown, "The Lordly and Isolate Satyrs" provides a dreamscape focused on "ambiguous Fathers" (*Poems*, 385), then "As the Dead Prey Upon Us"—which was previously titled "The Mother Poem" (*Poems*, 658)—couples mothers and automobility in ways that are reminiscent of Williams.[24] Early on in "As the Dead Prey upon Us" the poet is struggling with his unused automobile:

> I pushed my car, it had been sitting so long unused.
> I thought the tires looked as though they only needed air.
> But suddenly the huge underbody was above me, and the rear tires
> were masses of rubber and thread variously clinging together
>
> as were the dead souls in the living room (*Poems*, 388)

The poet is suddenly beneath his deflated machine, which he can't get started.[25] He had thought that it only needed air, similar to how his breath is meant to animate the typewritten page in "Projective Verse." But instead, he is confronted with both "the dead in ourselves" and the dead around him, including deadened workers (*Poems*, 388).

Indeed, it is as though "the dead" in "As the Dead Prey upon Us" are the proletarian underbelly of capital accumulation, whereas their living labor, in being objectified in commodities, has become so much dead labor now preying on them.[26] These dead workers, gathered in the poem's opening stanzas around Olson's mother in the living room, "are desperate with the tawdriness of their life in hell":

> I turned to the young man on my right and asked, "How is it,
> there?" And he begged me protestingly don't ask, we are poor
> poor. And the whole room was suddenly posters and presentations
> of brake linings and other automotive accessories, cardboard
> displays, the dead roaming from one to another
> as bored back in life as they are in hell, poor and doomed
> to mere equipments (*Poems*, 388)

The dead are as much the cogs of production as soulless consumers. This whole scene takes place, furthermore, while a movie is being projected in the room, with "some record / playing on the victrola," both of which are markers for Olson of a deadening commercial culture (*Poems*, 388). Indeed, he hated what in *Maximus* he refers to as "mu-sick," such as commercial jingles, and "the trick / of corporations, newspapers, slick magazines, movie houses," and lamented, "all is become billboards" and "even silence, is spray-gunned."[27] He therefore seeks to win autonomy from commercial culture through the self-possession machinery can afford, whether that of the typewriter or of the automobile. The return of the dead in "As the Dead Prey upon Us" attests, though, to the contradiction of attempting to forge masculine self-possession through Fordist machinery, which itself demands repetitive, deskilled, and deadened labor for its production.

Rather than inhabiting "outright phallicism as knowledge," the poet's phallic power is unraveling in "As the Dead Prey Upon Us," leading him to bolster his materials by extraneous means. A primitive vehicle suddenly appears in the poem, with a striking racial identity:

> O the dead!
>> and the Indian woman and I
>> enabled the blue deer
>> to walk
>
>> and the blue deer talked,
>> in the next room,
>> a Negro talk
>
>> it was like walking a jackass,
>> and its talk
>> was the pressing gabber of gammers
>> of old women
>
>> and we helped walk it around the room
>> because it was seeking socks
>> or shoes for its hooves
>> now that it was acquiring
>
>> human possibilities (*Poems,* 389)

The poet, along with his "Indian woman," is successful in getting this jackass of a deer moving, which "in the next room" begins talking "a Negro talk."[28] It is difficult to know how to parse the racial and animal politics of these lines. Is "Negro talk" an advance on the deer's abilities, suggesting a hierarchy of being from animals to Black people to whites? Is the "blue deer" itself a marker of Black culture, through jazz and the blues?[29] The poem continues:

> Walk the jackass
> Hear the victrola
> Let the automobile
> be tucked into a corner of the white fence
> when it is a white chair. Purity
>
> is only an instant of being (*Poems,* 389)

The poem tries to keep the white purity of the automobile separate from animals, Blacks, and their popular music. The deer and jackass have not broken down, though, as the poet's car has, which is revealed as threadbare compared to the at once natural and grotesque deer.

The automobile for Olson is—as with the motorcycles of "The Lordly and Isolate Satyrs"—a vehicle for masculine self-possession. But insofar as the poet's authority must be located in a machine, it is always already absent from him. His valorization of the typewriter is likewise a symptom of this loss of manly authority, which the machine is paradoxically meant to reinstate. As Rifkin puts it, there is something "desperate" about this reliance on machinery, which demands continual authorial vigilance in its operation. Olson's valorization of white automobility in contrast to animal blue and Blackness in "As the Dead Prey upon Us" is also a desperate bid to assert his poetry's separateness from mass culture (jazz, cinema, and advertisements) and exploitative production. That the exploited might themselves have a claim to authenticity without reliance on machinery is a source of vexed attraction for Olson. He conceives of the self-possessed individual as primarily white and male, and it is therefore little wonder that others (women, African Americans, Indigenous people, and animals) can only provide versions of authenticity threatening to that of white men, who were already threatened with becoming mere moving parts on the assembly line of the administered world.

TIME SIGNALS

While early modernists often made resisting clock time a hallmark of aesthetic novelty, postwar poets had a more ambivalent relationship to time, which they used to figure both alienation and immediacy.[30] Although neither Olson nor O'Hara worked on an assembly line, I want to suggest that the way they mark time in their poems is indebted to the regulated time of Fordism. Ford's assembly line incorporated the insights of Frederick Winslow Taylor's "scientific management," with its regulation of timed movements to increase productivity. With Fordism, precise time also came to determine the flow of automobiles outside the factory walls, whether through the timing of traffic lights or the transportation of people and products. Even office work would come to be structured by clocked efficiency, if less rigidly. The commitment of New American Poets such as O'Hara and Olson to poetic immediacy and nowness in contrast to monumentality and fixity should therefore be understood in relation to the timed existence of Fordism. By marking time in their poems, it is as if these poets are trying to poeticize Fordist precision on their own terms.

O'Hara's camp poetics have often been contrasted with Olson's masculinist projective verse, but as I will show, O'Hara's time signals are indebted to Olson.[31] Olson marks precise time in his car poems in a bid for masculine authenticity and immediacy that is in accord with his line management in "Projective Verse." His time signals are contradictory, though. As Adorno writes in *Aesthetic Theory*, "the substantive element of artistic modernism draws its power from the fact that the most advanced procedures of material production and organization are not limited to the sphere in which they originate. In a manner scarcely analyzed yet by sociology, they radiate out into areas of life far removed from them, deep into the zones of subjective experience, which does not notice this and guards the sanctity of its reserves."[32] The sanctity of Olson's reserves includes the personal poignancy of clocked time, which is in fact determined by Fordist regulation. Although O'Hara is commonly understood as inscribing quotidian immediacy through his time signals, by comparing his marking of time with Olson's, we can see how O'Hara ironizes the modernist struggle with time and machines. O'Hara's "I do this I do that" poetics is, then, partly a campy send-up of Olson's more desperate bid for timed presence.

There is a striking crossover between Olson's use of time signals in "As the Dead Prey Upon Us" and those for which O'Hara became famous. In Olson's poem, the poet is struggling to start his car, and time is slipping away from him:

> I shall get
> to the place
> 10 minutes late.
>
> It will be 20 minutes
> of 9. And I don't know,

without the car,

how I shall get there (*Poems* 390)

This passage is similar to the opening of O'Hara's most anthologized poem, "The Day Lady Died," which first appeared in *The New American Poetry:*

It is 12:20 in New York a Friday
three days after Bastille Day, yes
it is 1959 and I go get a shoeshine
because I will get off the 4:19 in Easthampton
at 7:15 and then go straight to dinner
and I don't know the people who will feed me. (*CP* 325)

In these passages O'Hara and Olson make use of time signals coupled to trains or cars to convey the pathos of an unknown outcome. Yet while in Olson's poem the struggle with a broken-down car is earnest, in O'Hara's poem the lunch poet's lack of knowledge about his dinner hosts borders on the ridiculous. Might it be that O'Hara, in the opening stanza of his most famous poem, is camping up Olson's inability to start his heroic car in "As the Dead Prey upon Us," while all this poet of Manhattan has to do is take the train?

"As the Dead Prey upon Us" was first published in 1957, so O'Hara could well have read it before composing "The Day Lady Died" in 1959. On April 12, 1956, O'Hara wrote to Kenneth Koch that he was reading Olson while in Cambridge for the Poets Theatre. O'Hara had befriended John Wieners there, whom he mentions in his letter immediately before parodying Olson:

I've also been reading some of Charles Olson's things, which are more attractive than most, tho' ve / ry   and quite sad-making it seems to me.[33]
                    Ez.

O'Hara appears to mourn Olson's inheritance of "Ez." Pound's poetics, which were a crucial inspiration for the *Maximus Poems,* although this filiation does not completely turn O'Hara off Olson. In his biography of O'Hara, Brad Gooch discusses how, "following his exposure to Wieners's emulation of Olson, and his own mimicry of 'projective verse' in 'To a Young Poet,' O'Hara began to use an open field more consistently."[34] Indeed, directly after writing his poem "To John Wieners" on May 12, 1956, O'Hara began spreading his lines across the page in an open field, rather than sticking to the left-hand margin (*CP*, 247). O'Hara also started marking precise time in his poems the same month he wrote to Koch about Wieners and Olson, which happens to be when Olson was composing "As the Dead Prey upon Us."

Although O'Hara wouldn't have read Olson's poem while he was composing it, he could have encountered instances of Olson's time signals in earlier work, such as the *Maximus Poems 1–10*, published in October 1953:

> they whine to my people, these entertainers, sellers
>
> they play upon their bigotries (upon their fears
>
> these   they have the nerve
> to speak of that lovely hour
> the Waiting Station, 5 o'clock, the Magnolia bus, Al Levy
> on duty (the difference
> from 1 o'clock, all the women getting off
> the Annisquam-Lanesville,
> and the letter carriers
>
> 5:40, and only the lollers
> in front of the shoe-shine parlor[35]

In line with his general sentiments about mass culture, Olson decries the despoliation of a moment in time by "these entertainers, sellers." Although O'Hara was much more enamored of popular culture, time signals become inseparable from the movement of buses, trains, cabs, and cars in the work of both poets. Indeed, it is as though in O'Hara's "The Day Lady Died," the poet becomes one of Olson's "lollers / in front of the shoe-shine parlor"— a twentieth-century loafer.[36]

O'Hara's "I do this I do that" style emerges in August of 1956 with "A Step Away from Them," four months after he had written to Koch about Olson. As David Herd observes, "the whole poem is framed, from one point of view, by the constraints of the working day. It is the poet's lunch hour. He has to get back. The clock is ticking."[37] The clocked time of work is also reflected by the traffic of the city: "It's my lunch hour, so I go / for a walk among the hum-colored / cabs" (*CP*, 257). This hum-drum imperative to enthusiasm in the midst of traffic is of a different order from Olson's heroic struggle with his car, a contrast evident in the tone of O'Hara's invocation of the typewriter on the back cover of *Lunch Poems* (1964): "Often this poet, strolling through the noisy splintered glare of a Manhattan noon, has paused at a sample Olivetti to type up thirty or forty lines of ruminations." Rather than inscribing a vigilant autonomy from commercial culture, O'Hara's casual typewriter is for sale. And while in "Projective Verse" Olson affirms his poetry as a site of traditional working-class labor ("the ear is purchased at the highest—40 hours a day—price") O'Hara's harried poetry is, by contrast, written during his leisure time, which is also full of shopping (*Prose*, 241–42).

In his posthumously published *A Frank O'Hara Notebook* (2019), O'Hara's friend and protégé Bill Berkson has written notes suggesting how O'Hara was inspired by Olson.[38] Berkson scribbles:

> FO'H and Olson
> O's 1956 poems "And the Dead Prey Upon Us"
>   —toward *Lunch Poems?*
> O's *Anubis*   his '56–'57 (to 1960?)[39]

Berkson links Olson's "As the Dead Prey upon Us" to O'Hara's *Lunch Poems,* while including reference to Olson's Anubis poem. Olson's "Anubis will stare..." is another dream poem, which immediately precedes "The Lordly and Isolate Satyrs" in his *Collected Poems.* Like the latter poem, it is also an exploration of phallicism in relation to driving, and includes the lines:

> Give over the wheel,
> if you ain't drivin'
> the buggy.

>   Anubis
> don't go for anything
> but Porsches. (*Poems* 383)

Being able to drive the car is again an imperative of masculine self-possession, now figured in relation to Anubis, the Egyptian god of death. "Anubis" was written in the spring of 1956, so Olson could be invoking James Dean's death in his Porsche the previous autumn, which I will soon return to. Berkson picks up on the theme of death on the following page of his manuscript, where he lists the deaths around O'Hara in 1956 that are included in "A Step Away from Them": V. R. Lang, John Latouche, and Jackson Pollock, who died in a car crash. Berkson also links O'Hara's time signals in "The Day Lady Died" to mourning: "Emily Dickinson's 'After great pain a formal feeling comes': a clue to Frank's turning to the numbers, 'It is 12:20 in New York a Friday / three days after Bastille Day, yes...' Nothing is more formal than numbers."[40] Berkson's notebook suggests, then, how both O'Hara and Olson invoke the numbers of regulated clock time as part of their reckoning with the dead of automobility, whether the victims of car crashes or deadening labor.

O'Hara was explicit about his debt to Olson in conversation with Edward Lucie-Smith:

> It seemed to me that the metrical, that the measure let us say, if you want to talk about it in Olson's poems or Ezra Pound's, comes from the breath of the person just as a stroke of paint comes from the wrist and hand and arm and shoulder and all that of a painter. So therefore the point is really to establish one's own measure and breath in poetry, I think, than—this sounds wildly ambitious since I don't think I've done it but I think that great poets do do it—rather than fitting your ideas into an established order, syllabically and phonetically and so on.[41]

Olson's conception of nonmetrical measure, which was central to the New American Poetry, provided O'Hara with the means of versifying personal experience through a syntax reeling beyond stable resting places. For both Olson and O'Hara, the poem was, at last, a go-for-broke event—the ground for projective experience. Yet O'Hara's reenactment of Olson's machine-time complex in his own register reveals the comedy of the modernist topos of man versus machine, which for O'Hara had already become a mainstay—rather than a radical critique—of modernity. As Mutlu Konuk Blasing writes, "when the connection between the values of aesthetic novelty and technological progress becomes increasingly clear, achieving a critical distance from a technology-driven culture requires a critical distance from modernist aesthetic values as well."[42] We can hear his pastiche of the modernist struggle with technology when he declares in "Memorial Day 1950" that "poetry is as useful as a machine!" (*CP*, 18). Rather than simply celebrating machine aesthetics, this sloganeering is tinged with a camp pathos portending death, as the machines in this poem become poetic catastrophes: "crashing in flames they show us how / to be prodigal" (*CP*, 18).

O'HARA'S CRASHING

O'Hara is known as the great flaneur of twentieth-century American poetry. He was also a driver, though, and like Williams wrote several poems from the perspective of the driver's seat. Yet many of his poems featuring cars and, especially his elegies for the actor James Dean, are fixated on crashing rather than driving. By foregrounding how driving can lead to crashing and death, O'Hara's elegies for Dean inherit the preoccupations of Creeley's "I Know a Man" while foreshadowing the pathos of his best-known elegy, "The Day Lady Died," as well as his own death after being hit by a dune buggy on Fire Island in 1966. In a certain sense, then, O'Hara realizes in his poetry the car crashes that Creeley and Olson intimate in theirs. Indeed, for O'Hara, postwar US prosperity is inseparable from "the enormous bliss of American death," which included the destruction of the Second World War but also domestic car crashes and racist violence (*CP*, 326).

Driving and crashing were central to both O'Hara's life and poetry. His uncle Joe Broderick died after crashing his truck into an elm tree near O'Hara's house when the poet was nine, a tragedy he refers to in "3 Requiems for a Young Uncle," which he wrote twenty years after the event.[43] Most of the biographical references to O'Hara behind the wheel are to him driving drunk in his hometown of Grafton, Massachusetts.[44] For instance, when Hal Fondren visited O'Hara in Grafton in September 1949, O'Hara abandoned him during a night out, appearing the next morning with "a black eye and blue bruises" after "wrecking his Aunt Grace's car" the night before.[45] Less menacingly, when O'Hara moved to Manhattan in August 1951, his friends celebrated his arrival with a drive to the Palisades Amusement Park in New Jersey, with O'Hara at the wheel.[46] As Jane Freilicher—who was in the car that day—put it, "we did a lot of driving around in the course of our friendship," leading Gooch to write that "it was as if once O'Hara got into his friends' car that day, he never stopped moving again—away from Grafton and toward his own version of bohemia."[47] Yet the car crashes of his youth would come to haunt his adult life.

O'Hara wrote at least two poems about driving on the Palisades Interstate Parkway, which was designed by Robert Moses, the man most responsible for turning New York City into an expressway after WWII.[48] The parkway was under construction between 1947 and 1958 and when it was finished it stretched forty-two miles between the George Washington Bridge—which connects upper Manhattan with New Jersey—and Bear Mountain in New York State. O'Hara's poems "Palisades" and "Bill's Body Shop" provide rare glimpses of this ambulatory poet at the wheel, though he appears skeptical and melancholic about "the expressway world" that Moses brought into being. The poems are likely from 1953, when O'Hara was having a relationship with Robert Fitzdale, who was living with Arthur Gold on Sneden's Landing, now known simply as Palisades.[49] The first part of the three-part "Palisades" reads:

> Driving in the morning to the city
> men building a new road
> we wait by them for the dynamite
> to raise earth and rock a short way
> slowly in the air, the dust
> after we go on to the bridge
> a reddish bloom on the hood.[50]

Much like in Williams's "View of a Lake," the driver in "Palisades" has to stop by dynamited rock, which here leaves a "reddish bloom on the hood" of the car. This floral image is expanded on in the final section of the poem, where the pedestrian poet has now left the car behind:

> A short walk from the car
> fragrant and wintry
> a white moon through twigs
>
> a minute or less to the house
> on the evening of the first day
> of all the leaves fallen
>
> onto the fields, lawns and road
> and a few into nests
> that can at last be counted[51]

Curiously, the poet is only in the car long enough for dust to settle before walking away. The walk between car and house takes—in an uncharacteristically suburban image—"a minute or less," a clocking that, as we have seen, is indicative of O'Hara's poetic pacing. The counting of minutes and leaves (read: poems) becomes melancholic in this autumnal ode, a mood that inflects the construction of the Palisades Interstate with a sense of loss.

"Bill's Body Shop" is also about losing a car, but this time the poet's car and his heart need a tune-up. If there is any doubt that in "Palisades" the poet is driving, in "Bill's Body Shop" he is clearly at the wheel. Here is the poem in its entirety:

> Oh snows of only two months ago!
> when will you fall back up into the sky
> and fall down again like an airplane?
>
> I put my passengers onto the plane
> and then drove back to Palisades in the car,
> the Palisades all hoary with the tears,
>
> and left a check with a note, Bill
> being out, "Fix up the car and fix up
> my heart, the thirty dollars is for that,"

> but the mechanics couldn't find the
> trouble, so how could they fix it up? Oh
> saffron snows! leaves tumbling, two months!
>
> and I never saw that car again, No,
> I don't remember the license number either.
> I remember the elephants passing, and snow.[52]

The first line of the poem plays on François Villon's famous refrain in "The Ballad of Dead Ladies" (1450): "But where are the snows of yester-year?"[53] Yet O'Hara is already nostalgic after two months! In surreal fashion, the poet wonders when the snow will fall back up, and airplanes fall down. The playfully tragic image of the plane with his friends on it falling is counterposed to the lonely driver who hopes that Bill's Body Shop will fix both his car and his heart for thirty dollars. The poet's cute note for the mechanic contrasts with Olson's heroic attempt to start his car in "As the Dead Prey upon Us." Strikingly, though, O'Hara's car can't be fixed either, and by the end of the poem, it is lost forever. Indeed, this car seems as fleeting as snow. The "note" left in this poem also suggests a tragic missed meeting, as in O'Hara's early "Poem" (1950), which begins, "The eager note on my door said 'Call me'" (*CP,* 14). Although in "Palisades" and "Bill's Body Shop" airplanes and cars can be poetic means of conveyance, poetry thrives in leaving them behind to encounter other absurdities, such as "elephants" or the myriad newspaper headlines, advertisements, and friends the poet muses upon during his walks through Manhattan.

While these driving poems are melancholic and foretell tragedy, it is with the death of James Dean at the end of September 1955 that car crashes became a recurrent fixation in O'Hara's poems. Dean died after crashing his 1955 Porsche 555 Spyder into another car on his way to the Salinas Road Race, which J. G. Ballard later called his best career move.[54] When he heard about Dean's death, O'Hara wrote the beginning of his poem "Four Little Elegies" in the sand at Water Island, which is connected to Fire Island, where O'Hara was himself killed in a driving accident eleven years later:

> 1. WRITTEN IN THE SAND AT WATER ISLAND AND REMEMBERED
> *James Dean*
> *actor*

> *made in USA*
> *eager to be everything*
> *stopped short*
>
> *Do we know what*
> *excellence is? it's*
> *all in this world*
> *not to be executed* (CP, 248)

The "excellence" of Dean's "made in USA" existence can't be realized in "this world" unless it is "executed," as though death and becoming fully American were one and the same. Through Dean's death, car crashes become metaphors of America's will "to be everything," so that self-realization and self-destruction seem indistinguishable.

In the later poem "For James Dean," O'Hara seeks to channel Dean's voice as his own poetic utterance:

> Men cry from the grave while they still live
> and now I am this dead man's voice,
> stammering, a little in the earth. (CP, 230)

The "stammering" of poetry in Dean's tongue vies with the "grave" cries of living men. After O'Hara published this poem in the March 1956 issue of *Poetry*, many people, including Paul Goodman and Bunny Lang, questioned the suitability of Dean's death as a subject for serious poetry. Yet as Gooch writes, "Dean became for [O'Hara] a screen actor version of the tragic lyric figure personified in literary history by Romantic poets who died young such as Keats and Shelley. The result was a deepening of O'Hara's poetic subject matter to take on the twin themes of love and death with a sentimental directness that set his work apart in style from that of Ashbery, Koch, and Schuyler."[55] For example, in part 4 of "Four Little Elegies," O'Hara again places himself alongside Dean in Romantic fashion: "I am among the noble / dead, the famous / most of the time" (CP, 251).

O'Hara was, of course, not alone in romanticizing Dean. In his essay "The Case of James Dean," published in the summer 1958 issue of *The Evergreen Review*, Edgar Morin sees the actor's life and death as a mythical rebellion against Fordist conformity:

> It is at this point in the Western middle-class world that adventure, risk, and death participate in the gunning of a motorcycle or a racing car....
>
> The automobile is escape at last: Rimbaud's sandals of the wind are replaced by James Dean's big racing Porsche. And the supreme escape is death just as the absolute is death, just as the supreme individuality is death.[56]

For Morin, death by car crash is the ultimate escape for isolated Americans. O'Hara's poems for Dean set the stage for such an assessment. Indeed, after meeting *Evergreen*'s editor, Donald Allen, in April 1957, O'Hara became Allen's "pass-key" to contemporary avant-garde culture, raising the possibility that O'Hara had a hand in the publication of Morin's essay.[57]

Too often, critics ignore O'Hara's preoccupation with car crashes and death, which is fundamental to understanding the pathos of his poetry. For example, in focusing on O'Hara's distraction and charm, critics such as Jasper Bernes and Peter J. Riley have read his poetry as a precursor to the service economy and flexible accumulation that emerged with post-Fordism. Riley cannily attends to how O'Hara's work at the Museum of Modern Art, as well as his poems, rely on a state of distraction, which has subsequently become a characteristic mode of work in advanced economies.[58] Similarly, Bernes reads O'Hara's poetics of personal attachments as prefiguring a service economy where acts of immaterial labor—such as those typified by attentive airplane hostesses—predominate. As Bernes puts it, "O'Hara's charisma is the charisma of the salesperson."[59] I agree with Benjamin Lee, though, that O'Hara's poetry "strain[s] to express something different from the language of advertising."[60] As Brian Glavey comments in his article "Having a Coke with You Is Even More Fun than Ideology Critique," reading O'Hara's poems "retrospectively as an anticipation of the strategies adopted by the new spirit of capitalism later in the twentieth century amplifies an important dynamic in O'Hara's poetry, but it does not adequately account for the way that the poetry explores the relation between the aesthetic and the political in its own moment."[61] Crucially, O'Hara cannot be reduced to a cheerleader for the variability of the ever new, because in his work, this newness is continually coupled to death. As Adorno writes in *Aesthetic Theory*, "the abstractness of the new is bound up with the commodity character of art. This is why the modern when it was first theoretically articulated—in Baudelaire—bore an ominous aspect. The new is akin to death."[62] O'Hara both embraces and ironizes the perpetually new, which is always on the verge of crashing. His poems are full of a whirlwind of enthusiasms and exclamation marks, setting a tone that has indeed become all but ubiquitous today. But for O'Hara the perpetually new is continually threatening to overwhelm the personality that is driven by enthusiasm. His poetic drive thereby reveals how the never-ending array of new styles, automobiles, and stars has an inherent tendency to crash and burn.

O'HARA'S TRAFFIC

After composing his elegies for James Dean, O'Hara's figuration of automobility becomes more abstract as he longs for intimate connection amidst the traffic of New York's 8 million inhabitants. His conception of sociability as traffic is of a piece, I would like to suggest, with his and Olson's time signals, as both poetic strategies seek to personalize the mass society of Fordism. But O'Hara's attempt to make his poetry into "a shout in the street," to use Berman's phrase, becomes more strained in the late '50s, as the street's social divisions become more palpable. His poetry of the street reveals, as Michael W. Clune writes, a desire to "enter into a direct relation with the *whole city*," but such a relation is of course impossible.[63] Indeed, his attraction to the whole city is—much like Whitman's in his own era—in part an index of the difficulty of sustained homosexual and interracial bonds in mid-century America. We can read this difficulty in several of O'Hara's poems written between 1958–1960, where the poet's longing for connection becomes tragic as sexual and racial violence seem to well up from beneath the city streets.

In the poems "Steps" and "Song," both from 1960, O'Hara uses traffic as a metaphor for modern life, which includes cruising for sex. The short poem "Song" opens with the lines:

> I am stuck in traffic in a taxicab
> which is typical
> and not just of modern life (*CP*, 361)

In what sense is being "stuck in traffic" typical for O'Hara? As in the opening of "The Day Lady Died," he is continually concerned with how he is going to get to where he's going. Getting to where he's going is also getting to particular people, but these people often remain anonymous: "I don't know the people who will feed me." This anonymity suggests sexual possibility, as in "Steps":

> and even the traffic halt so thick is a way
> for people to rub up against each other
> and when their surgical appliances lock
> they stay together
> for the rest of the day (what a day) (*CP*, 370)

Jumping into cars—and especially cabs—provides new ways for people to rub up against each other. Although traffic might leave one stuck, "what a day" it is when people's "surgical appliances lock."

While rubbing up against strangers seems like fun in "Steps," making connections with African Americans raises the specter of white supremacist violence. This comes across forcefully in "Rhapsody," written in 1959, where cruising for sex is coupled to lynching:

> 515 Madison Avenue
> door to heaven? portal
> stopped realities and eternal licentiousness
> or at least the jungle of impossible eagerness
> your marble is bronze and your lianas elevator cables
> swinging from the myth of ascending
> I would join
> or declining the challenge of racial attractions
> they zing on (into the lynch, dear friends)
> while everywhere love is breathing draftily
> like a doorway linking 53rd with 54th
> the east-bound with the west-bound traffic by 8,000,000s
> o midtown tunnels and the tunnels, too, of Holland (*CP*, 325–26)

The poet's "racial attraction" leads through the "door to heaven" to a "bronze" man in a "jungle" full of "lianas" that could, jarringly, just as soon be nooses. O'Hara's primitivizing fetishization of Black men in his poetry is well documented, and here it brushes up against anti-Black violence.[64] This poem evinces, as N. R. Lawrence writes, "O'Hara's determination to explore the forbidden terrain of interracial desire freely, to conflate the private space of longing with the public one of action."[65] Cruising for sex leads, in short, to a confrontation with Jim Crow America. Later in "Rhapsody," the poet catches a cab and "the Negro driver tells me about a $120 apartment / 'where you can't walk across the floor after 10 at night / not even to pee, cause it keeps them awake downstairs' / no, I don't like that 'well, I didn't take it.'" This "supper-club conversation for the mill of the gods" between the poet and his cabbie bespeaks both their difference—it is difficult to imagine O'Hara even considering an apartment where he couldn't walk around at night—and their commonality in transit (*CP*, 326). It is this implausible, poetic commonality that binds the poet to the city's 8 million, wherein deadly violence also lurks.

The city's "8,000,000" reappear in "Personal Poem" (written a month after "Rhapsody"), which revolves around a lunch with LeRoi Jones (later Amiri Baraka), who tells O'Hara that "Miles Davis was clubbed 12 / times last night outside BIRDLAND by a cop" (*CP*, 335). Davis had escorted a white woman to a taxi, when a New York City police officer assaulted him.[66] The poem ends:

> I wonder if one person out of the 8,000,000 is
> thinking of me as I shake hands with LeRoi
> and buy a strap for my wristwatch and go
> back to work happy at the thought possibly so (*CP*, 336)

Comradery between the white and Black poet is substantiated in a handshake, which for Paul Celan was a metaphor for the poem.[67] It is fitting that the white poet then goes off to buy a strap for his wristwatch, so that he can keep the time of his poems. Andrew Epstein reflects that "what touched off the disturbing incident in which Davis was beaten was the musician's daring to cross the racial divide in 1950s America, just as O'Hara and Baraka do in this poem."[68] It is this handshake, this poem, that attempts to forge a connection across the divide. This poetic connection is premised, though, on its opposite: the seeming impossibility of lasting interracial and homosexual bonds in this moment.[69]

Although O'Hara attempts to commune with the whole city in some of his poems, we can also see him turning away from the millions and toward the personal in the final lines of "Ode: Salute to the French Negro Poets," written in 1958:

> the beauty of America, neither cool jazz nor devoured Egyptian
>   heroes, lies in
> lives in the darkness I inhabit in the midst of sterile millions
>
> the only truth is face to face, the poem whose words become your
>   mouth
> and dying in black and white we fight for what we love, not are (*CP*,
>   305)

Here the millions of New York are "sterile," while "the only truth is face to face." The threat of "dying in black and white" "in the darkness" harkens back to the "blood" the poet must pay in exchange for his love's "shame" earlier in this poem, which intimates his mixed feelings about picking up Black men.[70] Connecting with strangers, whether in a cab or at the movies, might lead to poetry, but it can also—as with the lynch in "Rhapsody"—be deadly. Indeed, the threat of interracial death turns cinematic in "Vincent and I Inaugurate a Movie Theatre" (written in 1961), where "our country's black and white past spread out / before us is no time to spread over India," as Allen Ginsberg and Peter Orlovsky plan to do (*CP*, 399). It is interesting how the phrase "black and white" reappears in this poem, collapsing the difference between the aesthetics of cinema and the struggle over civil rights.[71] It is a mash-up that Yusef Komunyakaa plays on in his poetic response to O'Hara's racial poetics, when he writes that the James Dean film "*East of Eden* is / a compendium of light // & dark. Is this O'Hara's / Negritude?"[72] Komunyakaa suggests, in effect, that O'Hara's "Negritude" is only screen-deep, a problem to which I will return in discussing *The Last Clean Shirt*.

O'Hara's poetry is full of a longing for connection across the traffic of the city, which can lead—as with his fascination with Dean—to a romance with car crashes. More troublingly, his attempt to forge bonds in "black and white" can also lead to a romance with dead Black bodies. His coupling of Blackness with death grows out of his experience of witnessing Black death, both directly during World War II and through the media landscape of the civil rights struggle, including Billie Holiday's tragic demise.[73] By foregrounding Black death in poems that could fetishize Black men, the poet equates Black and queer vulnerabilities, mixing danger and desire. Such common vulnerability is belied, though, by the racist and primitivist imagery O'Hara uses to fetishize Black men in poems such as "Rhapsody." Indeed, his deadly attraction to and illicit identification with Black men is the mirror image of the racist sexual fantasies of white Americans during the lynching era, to which "Rhapsody" obliquely refers.[74] Some of O'Hara's poems participate in such racist fantasies, while he also asserts the dignity and civil rights of African Americans and explicitly affirms Black art in poems such as "Ode: Salute to the French Negro Poets." In contrast to Olson's white anxiety over a projected Black authenticity, O'Hara strives to forge interracial bonds "face to face," not least—as we shall see in *The Last Clean Shirt*—while driving.

PRESENTING JANE AND THE AUTOMOTIVE STORY

O'Hara was not unique in associating traffic with death. His New York School peers were also aware of the particularity of mass automobility in their historical moment, where New York City had become the center of modern art and culture after the destruction of the war, which many of them had taken part in. The postwar boom that buoyed their work was driven by automobile production, and so it is only fitting that they harnessed the energy of automobility in their work, which they could figure as fun, anxious, and deadly. These diverse valences of automobility are apparent in the experimental films on which O'Hara collaborated, where the stakes of poeticizing mass automobility and Fordism become acute. In Rudy Burckhardt's *The Automotive Story* (1954), the peculiarity of automobility is framed by the specter of horses, while cars nevertheless end up in the junkyard. Indeed, it is as though the fantastic nature of the postwar boom portends its own end. Let me begin, though, with an earlier short film, *Presenting Jane* (1952), which includes the only visual image of O'Hara behind the wheel that I have come across.

Frank O'Hara parking a convertible in *Presenting Jane*. (Harvard Film Archive)

Presenting Jane was directed by John Latouche and filmed by Harrison Starr in the summer after O'Hara arrived in New York City.[75] It stars O'Hara, John Ashbery, James Schuyler, and the eponymous Jane Freilicher, and it is inspired by Schuyler's script of the same title, though no audio was recorded while filming. In its opening scene, O'Hara parks Latouche's 1949 Buick Roadmaster convertible, and then a smoking Ashbery and anxious-looking Freilicher jump out of the front seat. Jane has the first line in Schuyler's script: "Critics promulg. I am filled with fear like a taxi."[76] Apparently, she was anxious about her upcoming debut solo exhibition at the Tibor de Nagy Gallery. After Ashbery and Freilicher exit the front seat, Schuyler gets out of the back seat of the convertible, carrying everyone's luggage, though he is also surrealistically watching the car from behind a white fence. The four-and-a-half-minute film ends with the three men witnessing Jane walking on the water of a lake as though she were Jesus. Karin Roffman writes in her biography of the young Ashbery: "When the film shoot ended, Harrison drove John and Jimmy back to New York City in his 1941 black Chevy Coupe. With Harrison occupied by his father, Jimmy suggested that he and John while away the hours in the car by collaborating on a novel. . . . They began *A Nest of Ninnies*, eventually published in 1969, in the car's comfortable back seat, setting the story in

Long Island and New York City simply because those were the places they passed on their way home."[77] As in Schuyler's script for *Presenting Jane*, Schuyler and Ashbery's novel begins with lines spoken by a woman anxious about cars: "I dislike being fifty miles from a great city. I don't know how many cars pass every day and it makes me wonder."[78] Two years later, Freilicher would find herself musing about cars in much the same way in *The Automotive Story*.

After being presented in *Presenting Jane*, Freilicher takes the role of narrator in *The Automotive Story*, a fourteen-minute black-and-white movie directed by the underground filmmaker Burckhardt. Freilicher's narration was written by Kenneth Koch, while O'Hara provided the soundtrack by playing Debussy, Poulenc, and Scriabin on the piano. *The Automotive Story* is a sort of mockumentary that offers a quirky take on the aesthetics of mass automobility in New York City in the mid-1950s. Just as O'Hara tried to find "one person out of the 8,000,000" to love in "Personal Poem," Burckhardt's film and Koch's script give personal significance to the endless traffic of cars surrounding them. Although traffic, as we have seen, can be deadly, in this film, forging a connection with automobiles becomes whimsical. Daniel Kane has shown how whimsy is central to Burckhardt and Koch's later film *The Apple* (1967), and a similar kind of "play, fancifulness, and drift" is at work in *The Automotive Story*, which draws us in with its cute, personable narration, only to prod us with the strange impersonality of mass automobility.[79]

The Automotive Story begins with a short monologue by Marge MacManus, played by Freilicher, who is seated in a living room, wearing all black and twirling a large white chrysanthemum. In a friendly, talk-show voice, she declares, "I'm going to ask you all a few things, and perhaps tell you one or two, about cars." She then picks up a piece of paper and recites a whimsical poem anthropomorphizing cars, which begins:

> In summer, autumn, fall and winter,
> Before the season itself is certain,
> The cars are out. Scouting the highways
> For adventure, pleasure and fuel.
> In the big city they line the curb like friends,
> Silently singing and motionlessly waving to one another.

Upon reading the last line, MacManus waves to the camera, as though she were also one of these waving cars. When she is finished reciting the whole poem, the camera shot jumps to a close-up of MacManus's face and she asks, "Who are these messengers? From where do they come? It seems so short a time has passed since we were alone with sails and with horses." MacManus then rests her chin in her hand and says, "Let's see. Let's see," leading to a crossfade to a pair of painted eyes on a billboard above a four-lane Manhattan street full of crawling cars and trucks, and O'Hara's piano playing begins.

The Automotive Story encompasses both the prehistory and imagined end of mass automobility during the apex of the Fordist boom, which it figures as mysterious and a lot of fun. The film mostly consists of various shots of cars in motion in Manhattan but also includes many close-ups of the fronts of cars as though they were people's faces—an association accentuated by the seemingly random insertion of close-ups of young women's faces at one point, who look directly into the camera and smile. As well as the fronts of cars, there are also close-ups of other stylish details, including the fantastic names of car models such as "Silver Streak," "Super Clipper," "Roadmaster," and "Dynaflow." While not quite as outlandish as Marianne Moore's suggestions for the name of a new Ford, these actual car names give a sense of what she was responding to. Evidently Burckhardt also thought these names sounded like poetry. An array of shiny new cars is followed by several shots of mangled fenders, including one upon which is written—much like in Williams's story "The Five Dollar Guy"—three evenly spaced words, "BAD LOOK OUT," comically suggesting that cars can be sinister as well as stylish and fun. We are then shown a sign for a business that provides "Auto Wrecking," followed by several shots of junked car parts and then dilapidated cars in a field. Burckhardt's editing, along with O'Hara's plaintive piano playing when we get to the junked cars, makes clear how the glory of those new, shiny Super Clippers and Roadmasters will nevertheless lead to an automotive grave.

In contrast to the life cycle of cars, the film presents an animal form of transport, namely a white horse, which emerges from a stable to pull a wooden wagon through the streets of Manhattan. After introducing us to the horse, the film then cuts back to MacManus in the living room, who is in mock tears. Kenneth Koch appears from behind the curtain to give her a tissue "courtesy of the studio." With feigned gravity MacManus says, "I don't know if you feel the way I do about horses, everybody." What is it that MacManus feels about horses? Daniel Bowman points out that "in 1899 there were over 21 million horses and other equines in the United States, compared to 3,200 registered automobiles . . . it was not until 1920 that the total number of motor vehicles in the U.S. surpassed that of equines."[80] MacManus appears to be crying over the emergence of a "horseless age" (to quote the title of the automotive magazine founded in 1895), evincing a nostalgia "for a more innocent, authentic, pre-industrial time."[81] *The Automotive Story* makes automobiles lifelike on the one hand, while on the other hand mourning the loss of actual animals on the road. In coupling horses and automobiles, the film harkens back to early automobility and its prehistory, thereby highlighting the fantastic historical contingency of postwar mass automobility.

Animals and cars are imbricated in more sinister ways as well. As Nicole Shukin has shown, the development of Ford's assembly line was inspired by the disassembly lines of the Chicago stockyards, which also provided the animal parts essential to the development of film stock. The Chicago stockyards were, furthermore, themselves rendered cinematic by popular tours, toward which viewers had visceral reactions. Shukin writes, "the physical response—the nervousness, laughter, or tears provoked by tours of animal disassembly lines—would also be a feature of cinema-going."[82] In *The Automotive Story*, MacManus's self-consciously cinematic tears gesture toward the violence inflicted upon animals in the development of both automobile production and moving pictures. The horse's whiteness, along with the white tissue that Koch hands MacManus and her white chrysanthemum, all function, though, to make this material history of mass automobility and cinema appear innocent, while nevertheless mimicking mourning. The whiteness of these objects contrasts, furthermore, with the nearly all-black automobiles in this black-and-white film. Cars are born and then die in *The Automotive Story*, not unlike how horses had to give way to the spread of mass automobility, which will in its turn also become history.[83]

Toward the end of the film, we see MacManus on the floor amidst sheets of paper while her voice-over haltingly yet enthusiastically declares, "Someone must be having a party! Having a party! Someone must be having a party tonight." With the word "tonight," the shot jumps to sets of headlights moving down a highway at night. MacManus continues, "oh, look at them coming to the party tonight." In a booming voice, she then declares, "This is *The Automotive Story*." The anonymity of endless car traffic is here given a personal and fantastic spin; all the cars driving at night are actually "going to a party," where we might imagine them meeting the avid partygoers making this film. Just as O'Hara hopes in "Personal Poem" that someone in the mass of people and traffic will be for him, MacManus improbably suggests that nighttime drivers are going to meet the makers and viewers of this film in celebration. Rather than alienating, mass automobility can—just as in some of O'Hara's poems—provide wonderful opportunities for connection. As we are about to be reminded, though, the fantastic nature of these connections often belied a more serious background, whether of animal disassembly, Fordist regulation, or white supremacy.

THE LAST CLEAN SHIRT

In 1964 O'Hara wrote the subtitles for Alfred Leslie's forty-one-minute film *The Last Clean Shirt,* which features video of a drive through Manhattan repeated three times. O'Hara's subtitles—often quotations from his own poetry—appear in the second and third repetitions of the drive. At the beginning of each loop, a silent Black doctor and driver, played by Richard White, straps a timer to the dashboard, while his white wife, played by Ruth Cazalet, blabbers in a made-up language. This interracial pairing gestures to the politics of mobility at the heart of the Civil Rights Movement, with its focus on bus boycotts and freedom rides. While the racial politics of O'Hara's poetry could be troubling, his views were consistently leftist, and he supported the Civil Rights Movement. For example, the year before working on *The Last Clean Shirt,* he solicited material for a special issue of *Kulchur* (no. 12, 1963) on civil rights, which included LeRoi Jones. In soliciting a contribution from Larry Rivers, O'Hara wrote on July 21, 1963, that the editors "are particularly interested in the problem of individual responsibility in relation to this crisis."[84] Due to his focus on individual responsibility, many critics have erroneously read O'Hara as apolitical. In an otherwise brilliant essay, Benjamin Friedlander writes that O'Hara "rejects politics, preferring the much-criticized personal solution."⁸⁵ O'Hara may well have preferred the personal solution, but rather than rejecting politics per se, questioning universalizing truths was a form of political engagement for him.⁸⁶ In a letter to Joan Mitchell from August 28–29, 1963, he writes that he missed the March on Washington on the 28th, when Martin Luther King Jr. delivered his "I Have a Dream" speech, but that he "did hear Charlton Heston and Burt Lancaster being interviewed on the radio, and Jimmy Baldwin too, and it all sounded very grand."⁸⁷ O'Hara had, in short, a long-standing interest in civil rights, while satirizing—much as Jones (Baraka) did—liberal pieties. This interest is mobilized in *The Last Clean Shirt* when a seemingly mundane drive through the city turns into a screen upon which questions of personal responsibility in relation to both the Civil Rights Movement and the Vietnam War are projected.

Each of the three loops of *The Last Clean Shirt* begins with an operatic woman's voice singing "The Present Crisis," a hymn based on James Russell Lowell's 1845 anti–Mexican War poem of the same title, which inspired the title of the NAACP's newsletter, *The Crisis,* and which King also quoted from in his speeches and sermons:⁸⁸

> Once to every man and nation, comes the moment to decide,
> In the strife of Truth with Falsehood, for the good or evil side;
> Then it is the brave man chooses, while the coward stands aside,
> And the choice goes by forever 'twixt the darkness and the light.

While these lines invoke an epic moral confrontation, there is no clear moment of decision in the cut-up of O'Hara's poetry that serves as the film's subtitles. Yet the film demands engagement from its viewers, as its repetitions and assemblage preclude easy consumption. Indeed, according to Leslie, people at the New York and London screenings of the film responded with "hissing, booing, slow clapping, and foot stamping."⁸⁹ For Olivier Brossard, the film poses a series of dire questions, centering on death: "Are we or the characters already dead, as the title to the film *The Last Clean Shirt* and the funerary hymn or other references to death might seem to suggest? And how can we avoid catastrophe?"⁹⁰ In answer to these questions, I want to suggest that O'Hara and Leslie crafted an ironic poetic drive that uses cut-up lines of poetry to obliquely address the nature of personal responsibility in relation to the social calamities of Fordism, war, and racism.

Beginning with the second loop of the film, O'Hara reassembles lines from his own poetry as subtitles as though they were so many parts on an assembly line. Instead of being subordinated toward a clear moral message, these lines become foreign and opaque in their new context. At the beginning of the second part of the film, where the subtitles refer to the wife's speech, these lines appear, some of which were included in promotional materials for the film:

> You don't say the victim is responsible
> for a concentration camp or a Mack truck.
> It's the nature of us all to want to be unconnected.
> I have the other idea about guilt.
> It's not in us, it's in the situation.

As if in answer to Adorno's statement that "lighthearted art is no longer conceivable" after Auschwitz, O'Hara couples the horrors of the Holocaust to the tragicomedy of getting run over by a truck.[91] A few years later, Leslie would incorporate these lines into his preparatory drawings for a series of paintings—*The Killing Cycle* (1967)—depicting O'Hara's own death by dune buggy. The desire "to be unconnected" emerges in response to such horrors, as well as to a more generalized alienation from Fordist society where, as we have seen, people are akin to traffic. Does the "guilt" of "the situation" also refer to white supremacy, as in James Baldwin's essay from the following year, "The White Man's Guilt"? O'Hara's mock existentialist statement, "I have the other idea about guilt. / It's not in us, it's in the situation," accords with the logic of the film, where individual responsibility is a kind of macabre joke, at once a product of, and an exception to, an assembly-line rationality that could lead to mechanized murder.

Further on in the second loop, the same subtitles are repeated, interspersed with new ones (in brackets are my own transcription of actions and sounds):

> It's the nature of us all to want to be unconnected
> [Suddenly the car radio turns on of its own accord and the couple

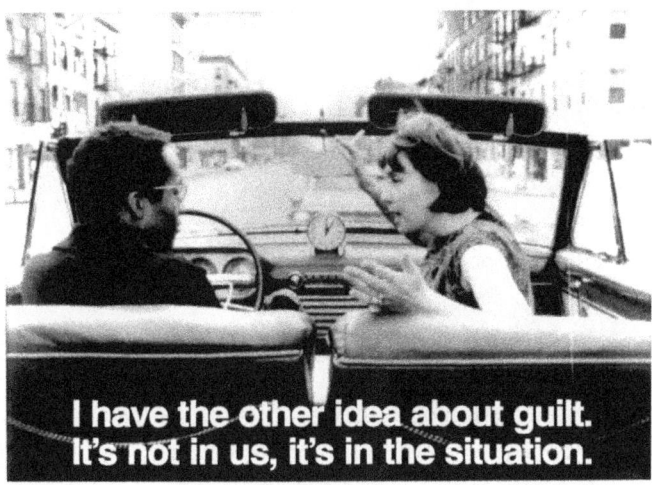

Promotional image for Alfred Leslie's *The Last Clean Shirt*. (Image courtesy of the Estate of Alfred Leslie)

    press its buttons until it turns off again.]
That's the real me speaking.
Not my scarier Proustian self.
And you should pull us all together . . .
like Humpty Dumpty
or a double carbonated bourbon
with a shot of vodka as a chaser
or something.
I didn't say I cared.
I didn't say I cared.
[Fire engine sirens begin.]
Who does?
Don't be silly.
Everyone thinks they're going up in these here America.
AND also—
If you're going to have one of those horrible attacks of guilt,
one of those horrible attacks of guilt,
you may as well . . .
you may as well be able to attach . . .
You may as well be able to attach it to something

>   like your mother or World War Two.
>   It isn't so bad then.
>   [Sirens end.]
>   I have the other idea about guilt.
>   It's not in us it's in the situation.
>   You don't say
>   that the victim is responsible for a concentration camp
>   or a Mack truck.
>   Breathing is not all about breath.

This mechanistic accretion of clauses concerning guilt sounds like a Freudian repetition of the repressed. This repetition serves nevertheless as a parody of the search for narrative truth, whether in "your mother / or World War Two," while leaving such primary explanations intact. The America in which "everyone thinks they're going / up," when "up" is here tellingly dropped down to the next line, suggests the contradiction of a national character that proposes individuals are both inherently free and united, like the pieces of pulled-back-together "Humpty Dumpty." As we have seen, there is no way to merge with the city's 8 million, and for so much of the population, "going / up" is a mere fiction. In "Rhapsody" this "myth of ascending" led "into the lynch," signaling how the American Dream is itself premised on white terror.

There is an uncanny match between the film's irreverent construction and its themes of civil rights and death. Each loop ends by playing the Honeyman's titulary song, "Brother Bill (The Last Clean Shirt)," where Charlie Otis describes how his brother Bill was found dead "in the back seat of an old abandoned Ford." A dead "brother" therefore haunts the Black driver, whose first thoughts in the third loop of the film are: "The pain. / I think continually. / And one Sunday I will be shot brushing my teeth. / I am ashamed of my country for being so entertaining." In having the driver think with his own poetry, O'Hara forges an identification between them. While the doctor isn't fetishized in the way Black men sometimes are in O'Hara's poems, his literal silence becomes a screen upon which O'Hara can project his own verse. One of the problems here, as Peter Stoneley points out, is how Blackness is "freed up for the white subject's fantasy, the original referent is erased and rendered irrecoverable in any other form."⁹² Just as with O'Hara's treatment of Blackness in his poems, the doctor's unembodied thoughts circle around death and brutality both domestically and abroad.

The Last Clean Shirt makes irreverent reference to violence, in the hope that its audience will confront contemporary catastrophes. One of these catastrophes was the Vietnam War, as Leslie made clear in an interview with R. C. Baker: "As the Vietnam War escalated, Leslie says, people saw 'an American soldier [on TV] firing an M-16 into a man's head' while voice-overs told viewers 'something entirely different, and the people believed it.' Leslie wanted *Shirt* to force the question 'What the fuck is going on?' because 'to most people, reality is nothing more than a confirmation of their expectations.'"⁹³ The film's casual references to violence confront its viewers with the deadly machinery behind American postwar ascendancy, not least in its destruction of Black and brown bodies. Such machinery is intimated by a barrage of nondiegetic car horns that greet the couple as the doctor makes a U-turn on Third Avenue, which was, as Daniel Kane points out, "an increasingly important if temporary site for a multiracial avant-garde."⁹⁴ Kane notes, "the appearance of a benign and safe interracial relationship is implicitly threatened by the welter of car klaxons overwhelming the woman's own babble."⁹⁵ The accord of the couple in the car is, then, as precarious as that of the multiracial avant-garde, both of which seem threatened by calamities such as the Vietnam War.

How, this film appears to be asking, are avant-garde artists to relate to their own moment? While O'Hara addresses the problem of immediacy through time signals in his poetry, in the film, Leslie uses an actual clock. At the beginning of each loop of the film, the doctor tapes a clock to the dashboard when he gets into the car, which records the length of the drive as ten minutes long. In considering the film's conception of time, Kane writes that

> O'Hara's impossible efforts to somehow enact the present moment, to embody that instant of time when "everything / suddenly honks: it is 12:40 of / a Thursday" are perhaps more able to be interrogated when text becomes film. Cinema only fully exists *in* the present, urged into being as it is through the whirr of the machine, the practically magical

projection of light. Film makes it corporeally evident "one second was never the same as the second before or after" [Gertrude Stein] even if—or, perhaps more appropriately, particularly if—what was being witnessed was the repeating mechanisms of a Chaplin skit or a road trip.[96]

Each second might be different, but here it is also repeated three times. The clock on the dashboard, then, foregrounds repetition, and an immediacy made available through mechanical reproduction. The film stages this repeated immediacy as a kind of joke, showing up any claim to unique presence, whether of the Pound-Olson tradition or of cinema. Ian White comments in the notes to the DVD of the film, "this is not absurdism for the sake of it, but marks something like the difference between the 'real' time of the single-shot structure and the artificiality of its recording, or 'film' time, such that time becomes like a poet playing the construction of himself."

As we have seen, for O'Hara, regulated time is part of the construction of poetic experience by Fordism. The film also obliquely links regulated time with the time of political action; in the "The Present Crisis," *this* is "the moment to decide," but what is this moment if it is a construction, which repeats itself like an assembly line? Instead of providing easy answers, or a program for action, Leslie and O'Hara demand critical reflexivity of their viewers, as Leslie's comments on the reporting of the war in Vietnam make clear. Precisely by making interracial accord look so easy and fun, *The Last Clean Shirt* suggests the difficulty of direct connection in the face of Fordist alienation, white supremacy, and war.

If poetry is to become "as useful as a machine!" it must seek to redetermine experience. O'Hara doesn't, I think, consider such redetermination an active possibility for his poetry, which mostly conceives of fulfillment negatively, through recognition of its limits. For example, *The Last Clean Shirt,* by cannibalizing his poems, uniquely registers how the self, mediated by technology, can never speak its own language. In being turned into subtitles, even O'Hara's own poems have become so much sloganeering! The possibility of transforming experience toward other ends resides, then, beyond the frame, with this film's enervated viewers.

The permeable frame of O'Hara's poetic drive is evident in one of his less well-known "I do this I do that" poems, "Song," which appeared in *Floating Bear*—the small magazine edited by Diane DiPrima and LeRoi Jones—in 1961, and where he writes of walking past wrecked cars:

> Did you see me walking by the Buick Repairs?
> I was thinking of you
> having a Coke in the heat it was your face
> I saw on the movie magazine, no it was Fabian's
> I was thinking of you
> and down at the railroad tracks where the station
> has mysteriously disappeared
> I was thinking of you
> as the bus pulled away in the twilight
> I was thinking of you
> and right now (*CP*, 367)

This poem's Whitmanesque personal address is at once wholly impersonal; its "you" could be a face on a movie magazine, Fabian, or anyone else in the traffic of 8 million New Yorkers.[97] Much like the famous ending of "The Day Lady Died," where "everyone and I stopped breathing" (*CP*, 265), a breathless finality closes "Song": "I am thinking of you / and right now." This "now" is both conditioned by the regulated time of Fordism and a bid for a life beyond it. In the end, everything goes: "The station / has mysteriously disappeared," "the bus pulled away," the poem is over. Despite or indeed because of its fictionality, the "you" of this poem's address is all the more real beyond the page.

While Olson sought to clock poetic presence through time signals, he also imagined that his own breathing would find its counterpart in that of the poem's reader, and in this way would extend beyond the page. Similarly, when O'Hara cuts up his own poetry for the repeated drives of *The Last Clean Shirt*, he makes apparent the mediation of his present by the societal surround of postwar Fordism, while leaving the question of personal responsibility open to his audience. Throughout his work, O'Hara shows us how "Everything/ suddenly honks," whether we are walking or crashing, and that the two can even go together, as they tragically did for him on Fire Island (*CP,* 257). Hearing something beyond this deadly music of automobility requires a form of poetic presence that he longs for but cannot fully realize in his own time, begging the question of what we will do with ours.

3

DRIVING THROUGH CATASTROPHE WITH EILEEN MYLES

> Gender is a place you have parked your car one day
> and one day only. That day is your life.
> —EILEEN MYLES, *Afterglow*

> Gender truth be told is always trans.
> —EILEEN MYLES, *Pathetic Literature*

EILEEN MYLES (B. 1949) is a transfeminist activist and poet whose work across different media has consistently coupled automobility to gender and, in the new millennium, to environmental catastrophe. In this chapter, I will explore how Myles's various engagements with automobility constitute a transfeminist petropoetics that confronts the petromasculinity and possessive individualism at the heart of white, masculine American road literature.[1] Myles began using *they/them* pronouns in 2016, not long after the release of their most ecologically charged work, *Snowflake / different streets* (2012).[2] Yet as early as their lecture "The Lesbian Poet" (1994), they express joy at being a man with a car, thereby reclaiming masculine forms of automotive embodiment as both trans and feminist. As the epigraphs to this chapter suggest, Myles uses automobility as a powerful vehicle for figuring the mobility—the transness—of gender. In their reflection on trans poetics, "My Boy's Red Hat," Myles writes that "gender and the self keep turning all the time. I think it's a kind of danger that moves us. Some people are capable of staying in their castle but for me they just aren't queer."[3] The dangers that Myles confronts vary throughout their career, from acts of sexual violence by men in cars in stories such as "Popponesset" and "Violence Towards Women" from *Chelsea Girls* (1994), to climate catastrophe in more recent poetry. Yet, following Frank O'Hara, for Myles the inherent dangers of automobility don't preclude fun. This mash-up of fear and fun is instantiated in their editing of the small magazine *dodgems* in 1977 and 1979, "where poems from different scenes metaphorically slam against each other like [dodgem] bumper cars," as Stephanie Anderson writes.[4] Or, as Myles puts it in the short video *Rambling* (2018), "The city is language.... There is so much collision, and I think that's how I learned to write."[5]

For Myles, being trans is inherently feminist: "I'm queer, and most recently I'm thinking of myself as a *they feminist*. I was formerly a *they lesbian* wanting to suture the two groups dykes and transwomen in particular since there's a growing sense in the trans community that lesbians and trans women are in opposition and I just don't think it's true. But I'm becoming more interested in attaching my transness to my feminism not my female body. I think the female body is every body's business."[6] Myles's feminism is trans because it is transversally open to everybody while also encompassing their own particular transitions from woman to lesbian to "they lesbian" to "they feminist." In this way, Myles's conception of trans accords with Susan Stryker's broad conception of transgender as "the movement across a socially imposed boundary away from an unchosen starting place, rather than any particular destination or mode of transition."[7] This coupling of trans with movement is central to Myles's poetic drive; as they also say, in *Rambling*, "I like to think, but not about where I'm going.... Often nothing happens when you stay still. I always feel like I write something out of a transition of some sort."

By foregrounding Myles's transfeminist petropoetics, I seek to bring the field of queer ecopoetics into conversation with petrocultures scholarship. With its focus on movement and its "playful emphasis on relationality as such," Myles's poetry displays many of the qualities that have come to define queer ecopoetics.[8] For Sarah Ensor, a queer ecopoetics is oriented toward relationality without a fixed object, as opposed to the environmentalist imperative to protect an already-defined environment or to consume less. Similarly, Timothy Morton, in arguing for a queer ecology, points out how "much American ecocriticism is a vector for various masculinity memes, including rugged individualism, a phallic authoritarian sublime, and an allergy to femininity in all its forms."[9] Although environmentalism can be culturally and ecologically conservative, books on ecopoetics by Lynn Keller and Margaret Ronda have sought to show poets' vexed imbrication with "nature's end" (to quote the subtitle to Ronda's *Remainders*), rather than arguing for the preservation of a pristine nature. By questioning the very category of nature, such ecopoetry is, then, in an important sense already queer or strange.[10] Indeed, as Hannah Freed-Thall points out, while queer ecology was once a "minor strain within literary criticism and environmental discourse [it has] increasingly become synonymous with ecological thought as such."[11] As we are about to see, Myles's transfeminist petropoetics extends queer ecopoetics to include trans reckonings with poetry's complicity with petromodernity.[12]

This chapter follows Myles as they transition from the role of traumatized passenger to that of guilty driver. In their work from the 1990s, being a passenger is associated with male violence against women, but in becoming a driver, Myles has to confront another kind of violence, namely the environmental consequences, as well as the racialized exclusions, of petromodernity. Myles's recognition of the violence inherent in driving leads not to immobility, though, but rather to acts of solidarity across boundaries—whether national, carceral, racial, gendered, or those between humans and nonhumans—that we can broadly think of as trans. As Nicole Seymour puts in in formulating a trans ecology, "one can transition in terms of gender and also move across geographical borders, but both processes may be difficult or even dangerous."[13] Trans is thereby more than a gender identity, in my reading of Myles, and includes various ways of inhabiting and contesting petromodernity's ever-shifting social and ecological contradictions. Myles's imaginative solidarity is especially apparent in the "LA/Driving poems" from *Snowflake / different streets,* which productively elide the boundaries between poet, pickup truck, animals, oil, and climate. Here the gadgetry of automobility becomes part of composing object-oriented poems that reflect on the environmental consequences of driving. The flow of things and perspectives in these poems, just like the flow of Myles's subjectivity and gender, mirrors the flow of fossil fuels from underground reservoirs to their gas tank, and the flow of driving itself. Myles's petropoetics of openness and flow is thereby part of the literal flow of oil and traffic, while at once critiquing the ecological and social violence of petromodernity. Similarly, their short road movie *The Trip* (2019), which I discuss at the end of this chapter, confronts some of the ways that white mobility has been premised on immobilizing Black and brown bodies, not least at the US-Mexico border. Myles's work across genders, genres, and forms of media asks us, ultimately, to live with the contradictions of a poetics that strives for a life and art beyond petromodernity, even if it means driving to get there.

CHELSEA GIRLS

As we have already seen, driving and masculinity co-constitute one another in American culture, forging an automobility that is often exclusionary of women and other minoritized groups. For example, Sal Paradise, the antihero of *On the Road,* consumes rides, women, and kicks with nearly equal fervor. While Paradise is mostly a passenger in the novel, this doesn't prevent him from treating the open road as his own. By contrast, in Eileen Myles's early writing, being a young female passenger leads to traumatic encounters with men who own cars. As Myles has said of this early writing, "trauma was the territory."[14] Later in life, though, they experience being a passenger in a way that is reminiscent of Paradise's best ride in the back of a pickup. In safely falling asleep while hitchhiking, Myles finally "felt like a man."[15] Myles's figuration of passengerhood thereby shifts across their career from a focus on trauma and survival to a transmasculine inhabitation of the open road.

Myles invokes their early experiences of passengerhood in their long poem "1993" from *School of Fish* (1997):

> My car
> breaks down

I return
to my
enraged pas-
sengerhood

under a blue
& Mackerel
sky, south
on 9.[16]

As with Olson's car in "As the Dead Prey upon Us," Myles's car breaks down in this poem, but unlike Olson, Myles does not offer a heroic reckoning with their machine. Yet the poet's breakdown in "1993" also leads to a state of abjection and a "return" to "my / enraged pas- / sengerhood." There is no explication in this poem of why the poet's passengerhood is enraged, but breaking the word into two after "pas" suggests both a return to what is "past" and the broken condition of being a "pas-senger." The poet appears to be either entering or leaving New York City on US route 9, where Myles had moved to become a poet in 1974 at the age of twenty-three. But their formative experiences of being a passenger occurred while growing up in and around Arlington and Boston, Massachusetts. By turning to their autobiographical novel *Chelsea Girls* (1994), we are able to understand the trauma of male sexual violence that lies behind Myles's enraged passengerhood, which sets the stage for their transfeminist reckoning with automobility.

In *Chelsea Girls* (1994), the character Eileen Myles is continually a passenger while growing up in a white working-class family in Arlington. Being a car passenger is, of course, part of growing up for most Americans, who generally can't legally drive until they reach the age of sixteen. But Myles also narrates being a passenger late into their teenage years. The vulnerability and disempowerment associated with this passengerhood comes across most forcefully in the short chapter "Popponesset," in which the character Eileen narrates being gang-raped at a party. This story, furthermore, is framed by the power politics of cars. It begins: "I guess I was about 18 and I was in a car driving down the Southeast Expressway towards Cape Cod. We had just had our Biology exam and I was immensely relieved. The sky was a pale blue like it is in late afternoon. I had a tall can of beer in my hand and it seems I see me in profile. How strange. I was riding in Louise's car, a black Mustang" (*CG,* 181). That Eileen is a passenger in Louise's car, rather than herself driving, foregrounds her lack of control over the events of the chapter. She becomes part of the story's scenery—"I see me in profile. How strange"—suggesting a traumatized disassociation from the events that she narrates.

"Popponesset" is only a few pages long, and Eileen only remembers fragments of the gang rape, which takes up less than a paragraph: "just a rhythm of many guys, I seem to remember all of them in there at once but that may have been a blur" (*CG,* 183). The next morning, she is hungover: "I had been raped, right? Even if I don't know exactly what happened. That's how I feel. A bunch of good-looking suburban guys, 18 or 19, same as me, who all owned cars, trashed me for two reasons: I was drunk, they didn't know me. I wrote my name on the sand with my toe. EILEEN MYLES. Yes, that's who I am. I rubbed it out with my foot" (*CG,* 184). The power and violence of Eileen's rapists becomes an extension of their car ownership, allowing them to take and "trash" her body, just like they might total a car. Eileen inscribes and then rubs out her name in the sand, connecting writing to both presence and erasure, a paradox I will return to.

"Popponesset" ends with Eileen again a passenger in the car. We have already been told that Louise's brother Eddy took part in the gang rape. As did Dave, "a therapist's son," who shames Eileen for being raped (*CG,* 183). The following night, the group are playing cards: "People were kind of taking care of me then. But Eddy, Louise's brother, just killed me. So righteous about what a bunch of little pricks they were. I went out with him a few times after that—we saw Vanilla Fudge. I wanted to see if his story would ever crack. Louise must've known he fucked me too. Once she pulled into a gas station in Lexington where Dave worked. She didn't warn me. *Louise.* Hi Dave. *Hey Louise.* He can't see you. I'm sure he doesn't even remember. Hey Dave! She got out of the car" (*CG,* 184–85). The gas station where Dave works becomes the ugly heart of Louise's complicity in Eileen's rape. Whereas Louise—who organized the party—and the guys who rape Eileen all drive their own cars, which they get in and out of at will, Eileen is trapped in the role of passenger. The best she can hope for is that the false facade of Eddy's control might crack. Much like the role played by the gas station in Williams's story "The Five Dollar Guy," the gas station where

Dave works localizes his predatory power and, by extension, Louise's complicity. It exerts a force field from which Eileen is unable to exit, even dating one of her rapists in an attempt to come to grips with what has happened.

Reading Myles alongside Walter Benjamin, Dianne Chisholm has shown how "the manifold 'girls' of *Chelsea Girls* form a constellation of lesbian images conjured from traumatic memory."[17] Throughout the book, we find "the untold stories of girls who have been 'trashed' by cultural authorities, or who trash themselves through various deployments of abjection, chiefly drug and alcohol addiction."[18] Myles has themself described their writing as "responding to the political environment, it's a distressed recording of the history of sexual violence on women, a map of mourning."[19] In another story from *Chelsea Girls*, "Violence Towards Women," we learn of Eileen's affection for Jane, a coworker at Boston's Little, Brown and Company, whom she also knew in high school. Jane "had been gang-raped one night and never seen again," leading Eileen to reflect that "I loved her because she had been raped and because she was tough and because she had a little girl and because she looked me right in the eyes and laughed at me, teased me as if I were a man" (*CG*, 136). Eileen and Jane's shared traumas bind them in memory, threading together otherwise disparate stories in the book. This thread also weaves through the chapter "Madras," where Jane's gang rape is described in more detail and where cars are again the vehicles for male violence: "A girl I know, Janey Coyne, got gang-banged outside of T & C. There were always girls puking and falling down and passed out in the ladies room. I remember Janey being a fucked up mess and she wore a ton of makeup. One night she left the place and got in a car with a bunch of guys she knew. Or she knew one of them. So they all fucked her. That was the last I saw of Janey for a long time" (*CG*, 83). In this traumatic weave, boys have a freedom of mobility not shared by girls, and getting into the wrong car can prove disastrous: "Now boys had cars, girls didn't. So you'd beg and beg for a ride" (*CG*, 83).

Myles earned their driver's license at age nineteen,[20] and as they write in "Madras," "a year or two after college I was driving a cab" (*CG*, 97). Becoming a driver does not immediately confer self-possession, though, and in "Madras," Eileen appears traumatized behind the wheel. On her twenty-third birthday, she picks up her old friend Tootsie hitchhiking on the side of the road; this is the same friend whom Myles describes a few pages earlier crashing into a deer in high school while Eileen is giving a guy a blow job in the back seat. Tootsie seems "alarmed" to see Eileen again, who for once feels she has "the upper hand" (*CG*, 98). But then Eileen narrates, "I instantly wished she was driving. I was terrified when people said airport and I had to go through that tunnel. My hands turned lily white with fear. I began to hallucinate. They turned into doves. I wasn't doing well" (*CG*, 98). The chapter ends when Eileen's friend "Gary came to New York several years later, maybe eight. He had looked me up. He was some kind of traveling salesman for cable teevee. It was good. They gave him a car" (*CG*, 98). Gary tells Eileen that he has heard that Tootsie is dead: "What a waste, he laughed" (*CG*, 98). Being "trashed," "wasted," and crashing leads in several instances to death in *Chelsea Girls*, deaths which constellate around Eileen's gang rape and make driving itself traumatic.

The stories of *Chelsea Girls* are more than merely personal; they make clear the material and social conditions that allow girls to be "trashed" by boys and men. Myles's whole literary project has persuasively been read by Maggie Nelson and Rosa Campbell as a reworking of the terms of a male-defined New York School, and a male-defined avant-garde poetics more generally. Whether inhabiting the position of a lesbian poet or that of a trans man in their work, Myles makes clear how insidious the exclusion of women and trans people from literary publics has been. The absence of sentimentality in *Chelsea Girls* serves, in effect, to make "links between sexual abuse and sexism," as Ann Cvetkovich writes, so that the seemingly personal is shown to be thoroughly social.[21] Four decades after the events narrated in *Chelsea Girls*, Myles's social position has changed, though. In their travel essay "Iceland" (2004), they find themselves in that country's remote West Fjords during the offseason and can't get a ride while stranded in a café, leading them to "ask the woman at the desk about men with cars."[22] Myles finally catches a ride with a truck driver who pulls up for gas. This ride turns out to be the high point of their trip to the West Fjords and is reminiscent of Sal Paradise's idyllic ride in the back of a pickup in *On the Road*.[23] The gas station in Myles's story, instead of foregrounding their position as a traumatized and immobilized passenger as in *Chelsea Girls*, is where they get a ride that leads to an awakening of embodied presence. Myles writes, "I even napped. In the bright lichen covered landscape

I bobbed and drooled. It sounds like a baby but I think I felt like a man. I think a man is safe like this in the world and a woman never is. So it was a masculine feeling when I woke up. I opened my eyes. And there it was again. Magnificent. A waterfall. And then he stopped."[24] For Myles, being safe as a passenger is an inherently masculine experience, and as we shall see, this also goes for their own driving as an adult.

Passengerhood can itself be conceived of as a position of power. In "The Metempsychosis of the Passenger" from his book *Negative Horizon* (2005), Paul Virilio writes of women being the original vehicles for masculine passengerhood. According to Virilio, masculine mobility is premised on the exploitation of women, then animals, and finally mechanized transport, by which men get to ride for free. As Mimi Sheller points out in her reading of Virilio, "This shifts our understanding of freedom of movement away from the usual liberal narrative, which begins with presumed rights-bearing individuals who exercise their freedom of movement. Rather than the assumption that all people enjoy equal mobility, we must begin our analysis from an account of profound inequality in which the freedom of mobility is at once an exploitation of others whose self-movement is coerced by bodily control and domination in the service of others."[25] While Virilio begins his theorization of masculine passengerhood at the dawn of civilization, when we start with the fact of automobility the terms change. Myles's account of automobility coupled to sexual violence demonstrates how male driving relies on the exploitation of female passengers, in effect flipping the terms of Virilio's analysis. Yet as we shall see, when Myles does finally become a driver in their work, they have to confront how their own mobility is, in Virilio's sense, a passenger of both the planet and incarcerated and immobilized bodies.

NOT ME AND MAXFIELD PARRISH

In Myles's poetry published in the 1990s, automobility is both an existential threat and a poetic possibility, as the poet struggles to queer the masculine-coded space of the car. When their poems begin to inhabit the driver's seat, the poet immediately has to reckon with the patriarchal dominance of both the American landscape and the inside of cars. In *The*

Real Drive, which was written from 1981 to 1985 and published as part of *Not Me* in 1991, the female driver in the poem "Mal Maison" roams the land as the poet's ultramobile alter ego. This projection of freedom on the open road contrasts with the poet's own lack of mobility in their New York apartment. In their subsequent collection, *Maxfield Parrish* (1995), the poet inhabits the driver's seat as a queer woman, leading to a confrontation with patriarchal violence on the road. The poet's car finally dies, alongside friends and other poets killed by drug overdoses and AIDS, underscoring the poet's struggle for survival. Rather than simply being liberatory, then, escaping passengerhood and becoming a driver leads in these poems to a more general reckoning with deadly inequalities.

Myles's book of poems *Not Me* was published as one of the first books in the Semiotext(e) Native Agents series and is commonly considered their literary breakthrough. The book is split into two sections, *Not Me* and *The Real Drive*. The title poem of *The Real Drive* takes place in a cab driving through New York City and is full of O'Haraesque fantasies of going to Europe. Yet it is in the following poem, "Mal Maison," where driving, rather than the experience of being a passenger, becomes associated with the freedom of the open road, albeit one delimited by the masculine dominance of the American landscape. The poem seems prompted by feelings of rejection and depression, but then makes a quick turn toward escapist reverie:

> and I'm memorizing
> in a movie script
> my other life . . .
>
> OK, I'm this
> woman, about
> 35—she's
> been somewhere
> else but now
> she's here.
> In a car, an unimportant
> American one, maybe
> blue-grey. And she
> drives around Michigan,

> maybe New Mexico,
> Arizona, selling,
> God, I don't
> know what she
> sells but she's
> me and I know
> all about her
> life, how
> she sells these
> things out of her
> car.[26]

Myles taps into a filmic road-trip romanticism here, but rather than being upwardly mobile, this other self who is driving across America is simply scraping by, selling things out of their "unimportant / American" car. There's a dour joy to this roaming, where the driver can feel their way forward without the humiliation that characterizes the earlier part of the poem. This "half- / bored" driver

> roams the plains
> of America
> and the painted
> desert & the mediocre
> cities of Illinois,
> etc. She's just
> moving her lips
> very softly
> I am not connected,
> I am not connected,
> very softly, laughing
> very softly occasionally
> oh, I am connected
> to everything,
> winks into the
> rear view mirror
> at her beautiful

> bland sardonic
> self, this American
> woman, endlessly
> riding like
> an astronaut
> inside the
> land (*NM,* 134)

The driver embodies a fantasy of freedom, where isolation—"I am not connected"—can be turned into the "sardonic" joy of a woman saying, "I am connected / to everything," while winking "into the / rear view mirror." These lines echo those from O'Hara and Leslie's road movie *The Last Clean Shirt,* where O'Hara's subtitles include the lines "It's the nature of us all / to want to be unconnected." Myles's driver appears to fulfill this dream of becoming unconnected, while at once making the quintessentially Whitmanian declaration "I am connected / to everything." Unlike Whitman, though, Myles is self-conscious about the fictiveness of posing as everyman, not least because their driver is a woman. I will return to the importance of *The Last Clean Shirt* to Myles's poetics, especially in relation to their own road movie, *The Trip.*

"Mal Maison" also contrasts the fantastic freedom of the woman driver with the masculine dominance of fixed spaces:

> The music
> in America,
> that junky
> scratchy
> music on the car
> radio, the
> endless miles,
> all the bad
> places to
> eat—greasy,
> meaty, tons
> of men—you'd
> think it was
> their country,

> the baseball
> fields, the locker rooms,
> war monuments, clubs,
> bars, the highways,
> the police department,
> it's strangely
> sinister to
> this woman,
> and she's wondering
> about that. (*NM*, 135)

Musing on bad road food leads directly to a description of all the spaces and institutions dominated by men, spaces which seem to stand for America itself. Masculinity appears as a "sinister" combination of private and public power; what happens in "locker rooms" and in "bars" and "clubs" and on "baseball / fields" is connected to the violence wielded by "police department[s]," a male violence that is memorialized and celebrated by "war monuments." Rather than confronting this "sinister" violence, though, the driver is simply "wondering / about that" while driving past.

Myles's driver in "Mal Maison" expresses her wondering through her mobile facial expressions, which contrast with the monumentalized heroics of male-dominated spaces: "Each facial / expression / shifts, the / car wheel / turns as / a leaf / falls / in New York" (*NM*, 137). Rather than the exclusionary weight of masculine presence and greasy, meaty food—and the violence upon which both are premised—the woman's face, the car wheel, and the leaf all shift and turn together. It is this "leaf"—Whitman's favorite term for the page of poetry—which connects the woman driving across America with the woman writing in New York City. This leaf is not unlike the leaves that Williams's driver crushes under his car while cruising past "the young housewife." Instead of the implied violence of that crushing, though, Myles's poem is full of cruising as wonder: "endlessly / riding like / an astronaut / inside the / land." Yet this fantasy of being an astronaut in space also speaks to the difficulty of actually moving freely across the American landscape as a woman.[27]

In Myles's subsequent collection, *Maxfield Parrish* (1995), the poet is no longer split between New York City and the American landscape, but instead fully inhabits the role of driver. Yet becoming a driver requires directly confronting patriarchal violence. The poem "En Garde" implores its readers:

>   Just
> think about
> how it's
> felt for
> me to
> be female
> in America.
> Or in
> this world.
> Any man
> would
> kill a
> man,
> certainly
> be exonerated
> in court
> for killing
> a man
> who was
> gay &
> came on
> to him
> that way,
> you know
> sexual.
>
> Every day
> I get
> treated
> that way.[28]

The poet asks her reader to imagine and, in effect, identify with her vulnerability and rage. In a striking reversal, she identifies not only with the victims of homophobic murder but also with murderous straight men offended by unwanted sexual advances from other men. The lesbian poet must herself rebuff unwanted advances from men "every day," leading perhaps to her own murderous fantasies.

In "En Garde" the poet's confrontation with patriarchal violence is located in her car, revealing the difficulty of inhabiting the authorial position of female driver:

> My tongue &
> lips are
> in America.
> So's my
> dog who
> I love.
> My car.
> That wreck,
> my ultimate
> female karma
> spilling over
> into the
> male space
> like acid[29]

With her beloved dog and "wreck" of a car, the poet sings her song in an America full of homophobic, killer men. Indeed, this poet's particular "female karma" presumably includes surviving the gang rape narrated in "Popponesset." In inhabiting the "male space" of the car, her karma spills "like acid," seeking to burn away the ghosts of male sexual violence. There is, though, a semantic ambiguity facilitated by the poem's punctuation and line breaks, where "that wreck" might refer both to "my car" and to "my ultimate / female karma," which is accentuated by the rhyme between "car" and "karma." Despite being wrecked by male violence, then, cars and karma can also come together to make poetry. The poem continues:

> if they
> had to

> be me
> for a
> moment
> the beauty &
> the beast
> they could
> read my
> face, they
> would know
> their place
> they would
> give me
> space[30]

The poet's double-edged experience of automobility as both beautiful and enraged demands "space" from men who have denied it to others. As in "Mal Maison," we are invited to "read my / face" as the leaf of the poem. The rhyming of "face," "place," and "space" creates an association between poetry and claiming space, while the poem's incredibly short lines seem to enact the difficulty of taking up space on the page as a queer woman.

Instead of vaunting self-invention through driving in *Maxfield Parrish*, Myles confronts self-destruction. Towards the beginning of "Looking Out, A Sailor," the poet declares, "I'm dying tomorrow // my car died tonight / a glorious explosion / then clunk" (162). The death of their car causes the poet to reflect on their own mortality and the deaths taking place around them:

> I remember the last
> night with my
> car. Came home
> & called the night
> watery grave. Didn't
> know why. Everyone
> dying around
> me now. But
> not yet,
> not me yet.[31]

This poem focuses on the Chicago poet Lorri Jackson's death by heroin overdose, but in referring to "everyone / dying" it also intimates the ongoing AIDS crisis. The line "not me yet" echoes the title of *Not Me*, highlighting how that book also refers to surviving catastrophe.[32] In memorializing Jackson, Myles inscribes a woman into a collective traumatic memory that might otherwise exclude her. As they complain in their 1994 talk "The Lesbian Poet," "the awesome mortality AIDS conjures up leaves fags ever more protective of their lineage" (*SoF,* 126), to the exclusion of lesbians.[33] Whether in *Chelsea Girls* or with the example of Jackson, Myles is at pains to make clear that the lives of women and lesbians are also endangered.

Toward the end of "Looking Out, a Sailor," the poet's "car dies / & I drive / on."[34] As Myles narrates in their novel *Inferno* (2010), their first car, while seeming to promise freedom and flight, simply became an encumbrance, and so they abandoned it:

> By 1990 everyone was dying. I had a big car—a long ugly LTD somebody painted with house paint. Fordie. Elinor [Nauen] gave her to me. I couldn't really drive. I drove Tom to the beach in it and I scared him on those big metal things in Brooklyn. I guess ramps? I had just gotten the dog. I was thinking we would move to San Francisco. The car starts breaking down I couldn't afford to fix it the dog was too young so I left the car on the street and stayed home. Elinor never forgave me. She walked past it every day till the city took it. She loved that car.[35]

In being named "Fordie," Eileen's car becomes a kind of great-niece to Stein and Toklas' "Auntie." Yet the freedom promised by driving proves elusive, and while Eileen lives on here despite all the deaths around her, her car does not. Indeed, the traumatic driving of *Chelsea Girls* returns in the poet's struggle to drive her Ford LTD in New York City, the trashing of which contrasts with the fantasy of mobility in "Mal Maison." In driving on without the car in "Looking Out, a Sailor," the poet attests to this tension between female mobility and the masculine-coded realm of driving, while suggesting that they will find other ways to continue their journey.

"THE LESBIAN POET"

In their May 1994 talk at the St. Mark's Poetry Project, "The Lesbian Poet," which was first published in *School of Fish* (1997), Myles provides a transfeminist figuration of automobility that differs from their earlier struggle to inhabit the driver's seat as a woman. Myles had not yet used the term *trans* to describe themselves at this point, yet in figuring themselves as a man with a car, they are nevertheless reckoning with their alienation from the women's movement. Indeed, in "The Lesbian Poet" Myles offers a telling contrast to other feminists such as Judy Chicago, who in the 1960s began painting stunning female imagery on car hoods. In 1972 Chicago's students, including Suzanne Lacy, created a twenty-four-hour land-art project entitled *Route 126* along the highway north of Los Angeles.[36] Lacy writes that Chicago's "only restriction" for the project was that the "performance or installation would be something recognizably feminine (or stereotypically so)." In the 1990s, Lacy would extend this tradition of feminist car art in her powerful work *Auto: On the Edge of Time* (1993–94), which used battered cars across several sites to raise awareness about domestic abuse. While Lacy's trashed cars recall the trashed girls and women of *Chelsea Girls,* Myles's increasingly palpable desire to leave womanhood behind altogether offers a poignant contrast to such radical feminist appropriations of automobility.

In "The Lesbian Poet" Myles explicitly inhabits automobility not as a woman but as a man: "Last summer I was standing alone on a hill with my dog and a car as an amazing shower of meteorites *flash flash* had stained the sky orange. It was so sensational and I was utterly alone with my animal. I knew I was a man. It was utterly clear, there was no thing of woman at all. I was standing in nature alone, this guy. It was a terrifically human feeling. Alone. Completely full" (*SoF,* 124–25). Myles inverts the terms of Chicago's and Lacy's staging of collective womanhood, becoming instead a lone man. Being a lone man nevertheless includes identifying with a lineage of male poets, all of whom Myles had met: "For many years my favorite poets were Jimmy Schuyler, John Wieners and Robert Creeley" (*SoF,* 127). After quoting Creeley's "I Know a Man," Myles invokes "Jimmy Schuyler counting counting then looking up at the sky in a quiet explosion. Pretty ejaculatory. I have to say I began to perceive a male shape, a conversation with God the Father. A conversation man to man" (*SoF*, 128). Fulfilling this conversation allows the lesbian poet to become "human" and "full" while being alone with their car and dog, in contrast to being the "no thing" of woman.

Myles's spirit communes with "God the Father," yet they also make clear the stakes of having a female body. While identifying with a male poetic lineage (as well as with Gertrude Stein and a long list of women contemporaries), Myles reminds us that their female body is excluded from this lineage:

> It strikes me that the act of creativity, male creativity is a conversation with a masculine God, a self-fulfilling act of male conception, something roomy. I know that I can't see like a man, fuck like a man, not exactly. His literature doesn't fit me. Nor should it. He makes art for different reasons from me. To perpetuate himself. To rewrite woman.
>
> If I were to start unwriting myself, Eileen Myles, I would begin with my name. That's the title of the poem, I own her. (*SoF*, 128–29)

In contrast to male self-perpetuation, Myles seeks to "unwrite" themself. Prudence Bussey-Chamberlain shows that in "The Lesbian Poet" "the transcendent and sublime is made impossible to women through danger."[37] As we have seen, that danger is associated in Myles's work with a passengerhood where Eileen is trashed, rubbed out, and here unwritten. Myles inserts a footnote after the word "unwriting," where they clarify that they mean an act of "shedding," of "consciously breathing *out*, exhaling, unwriting, so to speak. The huge fact of my body has all the momentum of literature" (*SoF*, 128). The fact of their femaleness resides, it would seem, most clearly *inside* their body and is associated with their menstrual cycle: "I began a practice of naming, owning, praying after that, liking every node and tube and squeaky tunnel in my female belly. I want it there, it's mine. My poem rumbles through it all, unbelievable, and as the month turns the poems get manic, crazy, weird, sullen and bloody, stay at home, the words I use narrate a female cycle, probably much more than a female orgasm" (*SoF*, 130). To shed "Eileen Myles" is akin to shedding one's uterine lining during a period, and both are a kind of exhalation, or "rubbing out."[38] If men have "rewrit[ten]" Eileen Myles, then the poet will shed her own name, while at the same time, paradoxically, "own[ing] her" and having her name become "the title of the poem." In reflecting on the rubbing out of "Eileen Myles" in the sand in "Popponesset," Myles states, "I've tasted enough to know that the primary fact of one's name is quite precious. It's the writer's body."[39] In "The Lesbian Poet" it is as though, to become literature, the "Eileen Myles" that has been trashed by men must be shed and rubbed out, and then be rewritten as poetry.

Myles also couples the politics of female embodiment to their car in their 1998 story "Heat," where their car troubles are narrated alongside the experience of being perimenopausal. They summarize the story in a 2014 interview with Morgan Parker while making a larger point about the marginality of aging female bodies:

> I had this essay in *Inferno* in *Iceland* that I could not publish because it was about the fact that I had this old, funky car that's air-conditioning and speed were fucked up, and it would speed up and slow down and there was something really wrong with the electronics of this car while I was going through menopause. And these two things were very funny and nobody would let me write about it. The piece finally ran in the shittiest little Bay Area gay newspaper and even they had to make a joke and the banner was like "raging hormones," I just wasn't allowed to be ... me?[40]

In "Heat," the poet's car troubles, which cause their car to uncontrollably accelerate, lead to a minor collision at a stoplight with a group of teenage girls in a shiny new car. Despite declaring in the story, "I don't like metaphor," the collision with these teenage girls becomes symbolic of the poet's transition into menopause, with both their body and their car experiencing hot flashes. In contrast to "The Lesbian Poet," where being with the car leaves "no thing of woman at all," the aging poet drives the car as a female in "Heat." Yet even here, they are not in control; "my car was driving me."[41]

In their later book *Skies* (2001), there is no longer any conflict between driving and gendered embodiment. Through inhabiting the driver's seat, the poet has found a way to perpetuate themself, to rewrite "Eileen Myles" as transfeminist petropoetry. Indeed, the poet's inhabation of the driver's seat leads to a reckoning with the environmental consequences of driving. At the end of the poem "My Light," poetry is itself complicit with petromodernity:

> I'm saddened
> the trees are electrified
> & the world surrounded with black tar roads
> winding our ball with sound
>
> My machine
> my light, my day
> my lady reddening by the pressure
> of the trees on her flesh
> stand up to her lads
> soon we'll be nothing but what surrounds. (134)

The roads surrounding the world "with black tar" also "sound" like poetry.[42] Indeed, there is an erotic pleasure in this surrounding music where "my lady redden[s]" while providing for an insistent self-possession that can "stand up to her lads." Nevertheless, this poem is laden with sadness over the electrification and tarring of the planet. Inhabiting the role of driver is a lonely journey in many of the poems in *Skies*. Echoing the "lone man" of "The Lesbian Poet," in the poem "Weather," the poet laments "being a woman who lived / mostly alone" (162), suggesting the cost of poetic self-possession through driving. The tension that Myles's work stages between poetic self-possession through driving on the one hand, and the planetary catastrophe wrought by automobility on the other, will only become more acute in subsequent work.

THE LA/DRIVING POEMS

In this millennium, Myles's driving poems have become more explicitly ecological, as they confront the environmental consequences of petromodernity.[43] In 2002 Myles began teaching at the University of California–San Diego, and as they detail in *For Now* (2020), the university bought them a house and a 1999 Ford Ranger (52). This is the pickup truck that they presumably drive in *Snowflake / different streets* (2012), where the poet's confrontation with oil and the climate catastrophe brought on by mass automobility takes center stage. This small book is really made up of two even smaller ones bound together and facing each other, so that when finishing *Snowflake,* the reader finds themselves at the end of *different streets* and has to turn the book around to read it from the beginning. In *Snowflake* there is a sequence of twelve short, numbered poems, which Myles "vaguely" thinks of as "the LA/Driving poems." These poems "were dictated onto a small digital recorder while I drove from San Diego to Los Angeles at twilight then night."[44] In recording their voice while driving, Myles retools Allen Ginsberg's method in *The Fall of America: Poems of These States, 1965–1971* (1972), where he records his voice on a tape recorder given to him by Bob Dylan, while riding as a passenger in road trips across America.[45] Myles is in the driver's seat in their poems, though. As they write in *Afterglow* (2017), "I like this new idea of talking to the road rather than singing about it. Rather than dangerously writing with a pad on my knee I pick up the slim Gumby-like recorder every once in a while."[46] The LA/Driving poems make clear the centrality of technology for Myles's process of composition, which in these poems includes making calls and taking photos with their flip phone, a product which had recently flooded the market.[47] As Stephanie LeMenager points out, "Southern California, with its sunshine and endless opportunities for self-extension via gadgetry, was, for the twentieth century, the location of the Nature of the Modern."[48] This self-extension through gadgetry has, of course, extended into the twenty-first century. As we have seen with other poets, such as Olson, self-possession through machinery is inherently destabilizing. Yet for Myles such instability is just as revelatory as it is anxious.

The LA/Driving poems reveal the transfeminist stakes of letting the camera and car be part of the process of composition.[49] In poems such as "#8 Car Camera," Myles reckons with the inherent directionality of these technologies, which the poet seems to distrust:

> my bullet regular
> my two-fisted slim little
> gun of a man

> now to touch a button
> and turn the entire outside of my
> car into a camera
> so that everything that's going
> on out there could be coming in
> could be held and recorded
> cause I don't want to point the camera
>
> I want it to be as open as I am
>
> what's moving *be* the thing
> that holds it all
> I think that dot is me
>
> ferris wheel, bridge, trusty grey & pink scarves
> of secondary color decorating
> the light blue but as we know
> darkening sky. (*S*, 34–35)

Driving is the motor of the poet's aliveness in this poem, while being a "gun of a man" appears both exciting and ominous. The line "I don't want to point the camera" harks back to this "gun," suggesting the violence implicit in a certain kind of directionality.[50] As Ian C. Davidson writes of another poem in this series, "inside and outside become part of the same experience, and we never forget that the speaking 'I' of the poem is navigating a metal projectile at speed down the road."[51]

Rather than simply gunning their metal projectile down the road, as masculinist writers have done, Myles aspires to use recording technology and their truck to craft a transfeminist petropoetics where the poet is themself part of an ecological flow that doesn't solidify a point of view. In *Rambling*, Myles uses a more comic image to illustrate this flow: "an image I've been obsessed with lately is like when you're in a pool and there's like a blow-up raft. And when you give it a little shove, just a tiny little shove, and then you watch it just move across the whole pool, like magic. And I kind of like that being the kind of level of rigor or craft that I put into a poem. You know, just a tiny shove, and then see what it does. You can kind of tell when a poem has finished when it's really stopped moving."⁵² The movement of the poem, then, is like magic, and it stops beyond a clear intention. The poem's flow across water is also cinematic. As Myles put it in an interview with Kaveh Akbar, "I am really interested in language that works like a camera, following the flow of these things rather than working one angle."⁵³ In this poetic vision, the poet follows and becomes part of a flow, rather than being its sole author. As Rosa Campbell elucidates, "#8 Car Camera" retools "Ralph Waldo Emerson's notion of the poet as a 'transparent eyeball,' a transcendent channel for sensory experience." Whereas Emerson's poet becomes "nothing" through vanishing into "Universal Being," Myles's poet remains a particular "dot" and is more interested in the transitivity of relating to "everything" than in being nothing.⁵⁴

Indeed, the LA/Driving poems reveal how driving provides for forms of authorial self-possession as well as modes of poetic inhabitation that decenter human intentionality. In "#9 Destroying Us" and "#10 Ball," the poet reckons with the way in which petroleum allows them to drive their car and to compose poems while its overuse threatens planetary destruction. Here is "#9 Destroying Us" in its entirety:

> I don't mean to romanticize
> this thing that's destroying
> us all
> I would happily drive
> more than two hours
> no
> I would drive . . .
>
> romanticize this thing
> that's destroying us
> I would drive
> a couple of hours
> for friendship. (*S*, 36)

Suddenly the poet seems ashamed for reveling in the affordances of automobility, which is bluntly referred to as "this thing." Rather than seeking to disengage from the sense of aliveness that the car provides, though, "#9" performs the compulsion to drive and write, by repeating the phrases "I would drive" and "romanticize this thing." That the initial qualifier "happily" has been removed in the second and third repetitions of "I would drive" suggests how the poet's enthusiasm for driving has been dampened by an awareness of environmental catastrophe.

Myles's driving poems acknowledge how oil is fundamental to getting around modern America, yet instead of seeking to unveil the reality of oil and climate catastrophe, these poems assume their constitutive presence. Myles further explores the complicity of poetry with petromodernity in "#10 Ball," here in its entirety:

> Is there anything about oil we don't
> know already
> like we're driving on our own limited past
> something that's ancient like the history of
> this ball we're driving these cars on
> the fluid of everything and everybody
> that ever was here
> we're draining that
> to just get around
>
> and it's nice that
> I could feel around in
> the dark to say
> these things
> to touch a button
> to make it light
> and then
> go out (S, 37)

One common response to skeptics of global warming is to show them the facts, while the opening of this poem seems to ask, what more do we really need to know? In this way, these lines also provide a criticism of the demand for more knowledge about and representations of oil that many petrocultures scholars have made. In "#10 Ball" the poet already knows everything about oil but is nevertheless compelled to drive, and here this driving appears as the occasion for the poem. Oil allows the poet to "say / these things" at the "touch [of] a button." This facility appears absurdly destructive, though, since "we're driving these cars on / the fluid of everything and everybody / that ever was."

Myles's confrontation with the all-encompassing fluidity of oil accords with that of another trans writer, Timothy Morton, for whom oil is a kind of "hyperobject." Morton writes, "Oil is the result of some dark, secret collusion between rocks and algae and plankton millions and millions of years in the past. When you look at oil you're looking at the past. Hyperobjects are time-stretched to such a vast extent that they become almost impossible to hold in mind."[55] Oil resides both here and now and in a prehuman past, and this awareness is weird for Morton, much as it is in Myles's poems. Furthermore, driving is a recurring scene of this weirdness for both writers:

> There you are, turning the ignition of your car. And it creeps up on you. You are a member of a massively distributed thing. This thing is called *species*. Yet the difference between the weirdness of my ignition key twist and the weirdness of being a member of the human species is itself weird. Every time I start my car or steam engine I don't mean to harm Earth, let alone cause the Sixth Mass Extinction Event in the four-and-a-half billion-year history of life on this planet.... Furthermore, I'm not harming Earth! My key turning is statistically meaningless. In an individual sense this turn isn't weird at all.[56]

Myles's poems also register this weird relationship between driving, history, and climate catastrophe. For Morton and Myles, driving on oil foregrounds the accumulated history that both moves us and is destroying the planet. Automobility, in its own right, makes apparent the elision of the autonomous individual into the human species in a way that is weird or, indeed, queer or trans. Morton asserts that "queer ecology must show how interconnectedness is not organic.... Instead of perpetuating metaphors of depth and authenticity (as in deep ecology), we might aim for something profound yet ironic, neither nihilistic nor solipsistic, but aware like a character in a noir movie of her or his entanglement in and with life-forms."[57] Myles's poetry is aware in this way, as it allows for an ironic intimacy with—rather than dismissal of—the catastrophe that is ourselves.

Yet Myles's driving poems are unlikely to satisfy readers looking for a trenchant critique of petrocultures. Although these poems reflect on, and even lament, the imbrication of their composition with fossil fuels, "#10 Ball" suggests that ultimately "it's nice" to be able to write in this way. Indeed, Myles's occasional oil poems foreground their own smallness in ways that are both queer and "cute" in Sianne Ngai's sense of the term. These poems can at once display aggression toward oil and a desire to protect their own smallness. It is as though Myles's poems need protection just as the Earth does, which is figured as a "ball" that humans are irresponsibly playing with, as though it were a toy. As we saw in chapter 1, for Ngai "cuteness might be explicitly mobilized by the poetic avant-garde as a meditation on its own restricted agency."[58] The cute poem cannot save the world, which itself becomes cute by virtue of its fragility. Just as Earth might be used as a toy, the upside-down halves and small size of *Snowflake / different streets* suggest that readers must play with it in order to read both sides. Rather than performing a heroic confrontation with oil, these poems attest to the everyday discomfort of having to depend upon it and the frustrating inability of poetry to change this.

In a later poem in *Snowflake,* entitled "More Oil," driving causes the death of a quintessentially cute animal while revealing the driving poet's own animality. Here it is not only the weird movement between scales that is trans, but also the movement between species:

> he was dead
> and not a particular
> rabbit
> his legs crossed
> like he was asleep
> and I hate us
> I hate our roads (*S,* 76)

While in "#9 Destroying Us" driving seems like a form of self-harm, in "More Oil" cars are responsible for killing a cute rabbit. In both poems, the poet stays in their car, while in "More Oil" they have internalized the mechanics of driving: "I don't run / I just pull over / listening to the fossil / fuel churning / in my guts" (*S,* 78). Myles's poetry is full of coffee, and they have written about writing on caffeine and sugar, so it is easy to hear a cute analogy here between the petroleum that fuels cars and the caffeine fueling many of Myles's poems. While this analogy might be cute, there is also something uncanny and frightening about the similarity between the "guts" fueling the poet, the car, and those of the dead rabbit. In this trans-species poem, not only cute, dead animals populate the roadside, but people are themselves casualties of driving. This weird identification between species is, furthermore—just like the weird awareness of species as such—facilitated by a deadly automobility.

If driving is quite literally a dead end, then so too are individual responses to climate change. *Snowflake*'s subsequent poem, "D. H.," dramatizes how such individual responses themselves appear cute in relation to the immensity of the problem. Here is the poem in its entirety:

> Politically speaking
> look at this
> a word at a time
> on my knee
> looking forward to a picnic
> with my friends
> in the afternoon
> in their car
> but no the climate is such
> that I never
> arrive
> stayed on the stair
> master
> one more time
> *I'm depressed*
> all my life
> enraged the man behind
> me as we plow
> into the brite grey light
> it's evening here
> bright as a flea
> as I enter the history

of intellectuals
who escaped *that*
to land in
this eternal
sun
burning what's left
of the earth
never meeting
anyone (*S*, 80–82)

In Myles's poetics of flow, "the climate is such" that we "never / arrive." Yet unlike Kerouac's *On the Road* and other more or less romantic representations of driving in American culture, the endless journey for Myles is beset by danger, whether for the planet or the trans driver. Staying at home, though, is just as depressing as staying on the road, since opting out of a picnic with friends won't prevent the Earth from burning. This predicament between endless movement and meaningless standstill is encapsulated in the image of the StairMaster, which works like the poem itself, where pushing down the next step is literally depressing. What is it that the poet has escaped? It seems they have been a plodding driver, ever enraging the man behind them. But escaping road rage does not save them from "burning what's left / of the earth / never meeting / anyone."

Rather than seeking to forever stave off the same trauma of catastrophe, Myles's driving poems live with it as a part-object that they continually relate to. In this way, their poems are both paranoid and reparative, to invoke Sedgwick's dichotomy. While these poems put "a playful emphasis on relationality as such"—as Sarah Ensor writes of queer ecopoetics—they also show how the interrelation of poetry, oil, and driving leaves no one's hands clean.[59] Playing with oil, which comes from dead life, also leads to death. The LA/Driving poems powerfully illustrate how driving and being alive have indeed become inseparable, but they also show how cars are part of killing rather than living. The poet cannot simply opt out of this predicament, though. To "enter the history / of intellectuals / who escaped *that*" offers loneliness rather than solace and does not mitigate the Earth's burning. Although these poems sometimes long to escape the trauma of climate catastrophe, they ultimately ask us to live with it as a constitutive part of our world and its poetry.

THE TRIP

Myles has always had an interest in poet's movies, and as early as 1977, they organized a recording of themselves and their friends reading poetry while high on speed in a laundromat in SoHo.[60] Reflecting on the relationship of their poetry to film, they write, "I wanted to make films, always did and poetry was a default profession."[61] Myles has been both behind and in front of the camera, and they make an appearance in Joey Soloway's television series *Transparent* (2014–19).[62] On the heels of the success of that series, as well as Soloway's adaptation of Chris Kraus's book *I Love Dick* (2016–17), which were both produced by Amazon Studios, Myles began work on *Chelsea Girls* for Amazon, but the project later fell through. In the wake of this setback, they teamed up with David Fenster to make *The Trip*, a seventeen-minute-long road movie, where Myles drives their Ford Ranger from Marfa to Alpine, Texas, along with their dog Honey and a group of papier-mâché puppets they created as a child. In *The Trip* Myles confronts US migration policy on the US-Mexico border, as well as mass incarceration in US prisons, suggesting how white mobility is predicated on immobilizing the dispossessed. *Trans* takes on another valence here, of moving across national and carceral boundaries, as well as of crossing the distinction between fantasy and reality.

Myles provides the voice-over in *The Trip*, which is inspired by earlier poetry movies such as Robert Frank and Alfred Leslie's 1959 film *Pull My Daisy*, which has voice-over by Jack Kerouac. Another important predecessor is Leslie and O'Hara's *The Last Clean Shirt* (1964), which was central to Myles's poetic development after moving to New York City. In a 2000 interview in *Provincetown Arts,* they describe the effect of first seeing Leslie and O'Hara's film:

> It was kind of like yippee! and kind of like sorrow, and it was profound and excited in that way that O'Hara's voice just shifts and shifts and shifts and keeps taking in everything and letting it out. When I saw that movie I thought, "That's it." That is, in the most classic sense, who O'Hara was, even what the New York School was. The poet was like this open car in the middle of the century, at some peak moments just saying, "Yes!" and catching the shape—moving through it all in a very excited way. People

who romanticize and imitate O'Hara mistakenly think that abundance gets to be what it's about—that mid-century excess and heroism and triumph, which it isn't.

History has continued. It's the '70s and the '80s and the feeling changes.[63]

The flow of Myles's work, their "taking in everything and letting it out," found inspiration and affirmation in O'Hara's road movie. Myles historicizes postwar exuberance much as Frederick Buell does in his essay, "A Short History of Oil Cultures; or, The Marriage of Catastrophe and Exuberance," where he argues that mid-century exuberance is premised on petroleum. For Myles this feeling has changed into something else after the 1973 oil shock and post-Fordist economic restructuring, which has led to increased precarity for many, not least marginalized groups, something I will return to in the next chapter. Myles nevertheless inherits from O'Hara's poetics an ethos of expansive inclusivity, evident in *The Trip*'s chatty excitement.

Like *The Last Clean Shirt,* Myles's film is concerned with racialized mobility, showing how white automobility immobilizes and ghosts brown and Black bodies. Their poem "December 16," which is both geographically and thematically related to *The Trip,* begins: "driving / through Tor / nillo & / I feel / all the / children / we can't / see / in his / America."[64] Tornillo, Texas, is a border town 160 miles northwest of Marfa by car, where thousands of migrant children were detained, reaching a crescendo during Donald Trump's first term as president. Since these children can't be seen, they haunt the poet's imagination, reappearing both in "December 16" and *The Trip* as the puppet Casper the ghost, who is on his way to study philosophy at Sul Ross State University in Alpine, which he informs us is "approximately 88 miles" from the Mexican border. When Myles's carload of puppets and dog get to campus, Casper makes a speech on the white steps of the university, which is named for a Confederate general (figs. 4 and 5). Casper's speech is also included as a poem in *a "Working Life"* (2023):

> I make common cause now
> with the slaves of the world, prisoners of our security
> state, and most abundantly

most locally today, America's prisoners of war,
not immigrants, illegals, aliens, but refugees—children
women and men in
jails and cages not far from here. A multitude, less visible
than a ghost,
more silent than a puppet. (28–29)

Casper invokes the victims of a white mobility that, since the Atlantic slave trade, has been predicated on the forced migration and detention of Black and brown bodies. Casper the white ghost "make[s] common cause" with "the slaves of the world," attesting to Myles's aspiration to be in solidarity with the victims of white supremacy. This aspiration was also apparent at the movie's New York City premiere at the Metrograph in August 2019, where Myles paired *The Trip* with a screening of the 1973 Black Power action movie, *The Spook Who Sat by the Door*. Myles hadn't seen the latter film before the screening, but they evidently sought to put their movie in conversation with the nascent Black Lives Matter movement.[65]

The excavation of the ghosts of white supremacy in *The Trip* is part and parcel of Myles's literally excavating their ghostly puppets, who have been stuck in a basket for the last sixty years. Aside from Casper, there is the puppet Oscar, who is based on Myles's dead father, and at one point, Myles talks with the puppets about all of them taking a trip to Buenos Aires to meet César Aira, author of *Ghosts* (1990). Having their puppets as passengers gives Myles a technology to think with, similar to the role of recording devices in *Snowflake / different streets*. Aside from the four human puppets, *The Trip* also features a papier-mâché crocodile—"Crocky"—who is voiced by John Ashbery singing portions of "Old Man River," the 1927 show tune narrated from the perspective of a Black stevedore on the Mississippi (*FN*, 69). Crocky begins singing as Myles drives by the local jail in Marfa, where the theme of incarceration is introduced. Later in the film, they enter Alpine after driving under a train carrying oil tanks, and Crocky has his second cameo, stating—after Myles has made a squeaking noise—that "I would like a little oil." It is the only explicit mention of oil in the film, which nevertheless ends in Sul Ross's parking lot, where Casper proclaims, "abolish all of it, the borders and the jails / and the police / state, open the door, R.I.P. / not rest in peace, but abolish the racist imperialist / patriarchy,

Eileen Myles with their puppets in *The Trip*. (David Fenster and Eileen Myles)

abolish it abolish it."[66] Casper repeats the phrase "abolish it" several times, until it begins to sound like he is saying, "a ball of shit," echoing the "ball" of "#10 Ball." Ultimately, "the racist imperialist / patriarchy" seems to threaten planetary destruction, while Casper's protest and Crocky's singing nevertheless rely on the oil fueling their road trip.

While Myles drives across genders in their poetry, in *The Trip* they drive past the enforced immobility of prisoners and migrants. As Jacqueline Rose points out, the policing of gender boundaries is of a piece with "the fear directed at migrants who threaten the world's illusory safety by refusing to stand still."[67] Myles's transfeminist petropoetics confronts, then, the boundaries between genders, as well as those between mobility and immobility. *The Trip* also cruises between the registers of serious political polemic and whimsy; that the puppets have been stuck in a basket for sixty years hints at the dire immobility experienced by many humans as well. As Eliza Steinbock writes, in trans cinema, a "shimmering boundary refuse[s] to settle embodied or cinematic images into the diction of true or false, fantasy or actuality."[68] It is on this shimmering boundary that a ghost who has been trapped in a basket is set free on a road trip to study philosophy, only to become a political soapbox for the prisoners of the world. One might be tempted to call this movie uncanny, but that would suggest a return of the

Casper on the steps of Sul Ross State University in *The Trip*. (David Fenster and Eileen Myles)

repressed. As with the oil in *Snowflake / different streets*, *The Trip* wears its shimmering boundaries on its sleeve. Insofar as the film is uncanny, it is so under the star of trans, where Myles confronts the politics of mobility that immobilizes migrants and prisoners while allowing for their own playful cruising with the ghosts of their past.

Myles's ghosts include their own poetic archive. In their 2020 book *For Now*, which is part of the Yale University Press series Why I Write, they discuss the sale of their manuscripts to Yale's Beinecke Library. This archive, while it comprises 108 linear feet of material, did not include original final copies of all their poems (which they had stored in a milk crate), nor a bin of valuable photographs, as these materials had all gone missing. Myles narrates at length the various scenarios that might have led to the disappearance of the milk crate and bin of photos, material which one archivist refers to as "the gusher," as though it were an oil well (*FN*, 57). The most convincing scenario that Myles describes is that the material was moved out of the unlocked covered bed of their truck one night by someone looking for a place to sleep or do drugs or have sex:

> I have one version of reality in which I parked the truck on 11th Street when [my girlfriend and I] came home from Montana. We definitely unloaded outside her apartment first but I think the box remained in the cab and also a big plastic bin of photographs. I thought who would steal this. And I also remember coming to the truck to move it that morning, some morning and the shock of its cab being empty. I don't know if this is true. You know when something terrible happens and you stand there in the wah-wah like the world keeps changing shapes because you can't believe it's gone. Is this a memory or a sensation of loss. A radiant hole? (*FN*, 54)

As we have seen, Myles's driving is inseparable from their becoming a poet—and, indeed, their professional literary success: their truck was bought for them by UCSD, and they bought their 2016 Prius with money from a Guggenheim Grant.[69] Their truck, though, is also the site of the disappearance of the manuscript material that had served as a guarantee of this success. Although the loss of this material is narrated in *For Now* as a personal tragedy, any bid for self-possession through automobility is always tenuous for Myles. Indeed, here their truck becomes its own kind of "shimmering boundary," making apparent the "wah-wah" of the world beyond individual intentionality.

In Myles's transfeminist petropoetics, self-possession is a fiction: "What I mean is that if the puppets are fiction and so is my dog then I can be fiction too. For one brief hairy moment it's not 'my writing' cause I'm not real, I'm alive. In my writing!" (*FN*, 71). The liveness of Myles's driving invigorates a writing that disappears the self, rather than seeking to perpetuate it. This *auto*-fiction is, indeed, "the horizon of the practice [of writing]. That out there. And even if the subject is 'me' it still feels that way. I'm gone. Necessarily" (*FN*, 67). When Eileen rubs her name out on the beach in "Popponesset," it is as though this fiction is for a moment obliterated, and we are uncannily confronted with the reality of trauma. Or as they put it in *For Now*, "I'm flat out on the beach of loss like a story I never understood until I got older" (*FN*, 60). Is this story of poetic self-development through catastrophes "a memory or a sensation of loss. A radiant hole?"

Catastrophe is the motor of Myles's transfeminist petropoetics, where "the world keeps changing shapes" by driving through it. The poet also changes shapes, as they transition from being a traumatized passenger to a driver confronting the planetary trauma caused by automobility. The traumatic "radiant hole" of Myles's poetic drive furthers O'Hara's undoing of the proprietary self-possession that Williams and Olson sought in the driver's seat. For Myles, taking up space on the road is an occasion for both joy and mourning, since their petropoetry seeks to be reparative of the climate crisis with which it is complicit. This inseparability of their work from climate catastrophe makes the latter appear both stranger and more real. Fossil fuels might be all-encompassing for us, but they are also transitory, not only in their burning but more broadly in their historical dominance. While Myles's poetry moves in part through fossil fuels, it also seeks to move beyond them, even if that means driving to get there.

4

NOT DRIVING WHILE BLACK
WITH CLAUDIA RANKINE

> How can I say this so that we can stay in this car together, and yet explore the things that I want to explore with you?
> —CLAUDIA RANKINE, Krista Tippett's *On Being* podcast

THE CONTRADICTIONS OF AUTOMOBILITY HAVE been particularly acute for African Americans. As the endurance of the phrase "driving while Black" attests, cars remain one of the primary sites for policing African American mobility. Yet driving has also provided Black Americans with a means of escape from the very forms of racial segregation that automobility has helped foster. In the introduction, we saw how cars were especially useful for escaping the segregated buses and trains of Jim Crow, and even for leaving the South behind altogether. Kathleen Franz writes that during the era of Jim Crow, "black narratives of progress used the automobile to insert African Americans into dominant discourses of economic prosperity, leisured mobility, and technological know-how."[1] As we shall see in this chapter, cars are also useful for leaving behind the poverty of the modern Black ghetto. Many Black writers have nevertheless questioned the association of automobility with progress, at times leading them to despair of achieving the American Dream. For example, Ron Stodghill wrote in *The New York Times* after attending a Black Lives Matter car caravan protest in Detroit, "it's our cars, hyped up in such American values as freedom, mobility and adventure, that reveal the falsity of these ideals, even in the basic routines of daily life. Think of Philando Castile in Minneapolis, Samuel DuBose in Cincinnati, Walter Scott in North Charleston, S.C.—just a few among the generations of Black men who were fatally gunned down by the police during traffic stops."[2] Indeed, if carrying through "the basic routine" of driving can still lead to deathly consequences for Black drivers more than a century after the advent of the Model T, then how much progress has actually been made?

Contemporary African American poets have addressed this question by making driving central to their confrontation with white supremacy. In his award-winning book *Heaven Is All Goodbyes* (2017), Tongo Eisen-Martin poignantly expresses the conflicted status of driving for Black Americans. His poems are full of drivers and cars, sometimes in mock-heroic postures, such as in the lines "A cigarette / A steering wheel / And a negotiation with the ruling class," from the poem "may we all refuse to die at the same time."[3] Eisen-Martin contrasts this mock-heroism with the violent restriction of Black mobility: "'They lynched his car too. Strung it up right next to him'" (*H*, 33). It seems that a Black man's car must, absurdly, be lynched alongside him, since it is the bearer of his personhood and a symbol of his striving for freedom. In his 2001 essay "Driving While Black," Paul Gilroy critiques the ways in which African Americans have used cars as status symbols, arguing that "the special seductions of car culture have become an important part of what binds the black populations of the overdeveloped countries to the most mainstream of dreams."[4] In Eisen-Martin's poems, though, Black drivers are battling for their very existence, rather than simply beholden to consumerist fantasies.

Although driving might provide for both mock heroism and absurd tragedy in Eisen-Martin's book, his title poem "Heaven Is All Goodbyes" couples driving to mourning and a restless, near-joyous futility. This is one of the few poems that bears thematic summary, in a book full of what Claudia Rankine has lauded as "tesseraic language" (*H*, i). In this poem, the poet and his brother are driving across the Midwest with "Father's ashes on the back seat behind two sons" (*H*, 29). They drive through an America colonized by "settlers," and where "everything south of canada is extrajudicial gun oil / And your local unemployment factory" (*H*, 28). As they pass through a segregated and impoverished landscape, the line "We don't know what else we good at besides this traveling" is repeated several times. This interminable traveling contrasts with another line—"Get out of the car against desperate white supremacy"—that is also repeated in different formulations (*H*, 29). Eisen-Martin's poetic drive in this poem reveals the compulsion to travel beyond the present situation, which is epitomized by the injustice of Black urban impoverishment in the rust belt. Is getting out of the car akin to fighting against white supremacy in this song of mourning and movement? Or is it that white supremacy is in fact forcing the brothers out of the car?

The apparent opposition between freely driving while Black and stopping the car to protest white supremacy—in other words, not driving while Black—speaks, in fact, to a continuity of experiences. When police and racists force African Americans to stop and get out of their cars, both moving and stopped cars become contested spaces. Indeed, gaining the freedom to drive and to stop for a meal or a place to sleep has been central to the struggle for Black mobility in the United States, giving rise to *The Negro Motorist Green Book* and other Black travel guides. Although the acute need for such guidebooks has abated, in the new millennium, African American writers use stopped cars to mourn the continued dangers of driving while Black, as well as the ecological consequences of a globalized mass automobility.

This chapter focuses on the poetic drive of Claudia Rankine (b. 1963), who, like Eisen-Martin, has subtly but compellingly used the automobile to mourn the repeated failures of progressive liberalism to achieve full equality between Black and white Americans. Rankine is best known for her trilogy of books, *Don't Let Me Be Lonely: An American Lyric* (2004), *Citizen: An American Lyric* (2014), and *Just Us: An American Conversation* (2020), with *Citizen* winning several awards and becoming a bestseller. *Citizen* also includes many of Rankine's scripts for the *Situation* videos she has created with her husband, the video artist John Lucas. While the first two books in the trilogy show how the automobile has been used as a weapon to kill Black men, in *Citizen* the *parked* car is also used to mourn the repetitions of anti-Black violence. Rankine's figuring of automobility at a standstill offers a poignant contrast to the coupling of movement, freedom, and progress that is central to the white mythos of the open road.[5] Ta-Nehisi Coates provides a similar reckoning with the failed promises of automobility in his best-selling letter to his son, *Between the World and Me* (2015). One of the main threads of Coates's book concerns the killing of his Howard University classmate and friend Prince Jones while in his car. As happens in *Citizen,* Coates responds to this tragedy by sitting silently in his car, where he reflects on the planetary death caused by white progress linked to automobility. Although Coates's letter is not poetry, by placing it alongside Rankine's prose poems and video scripts, we can see the significance of locating melancholic mourning within the stopped car. For these writers, the stopped car is, paradoxically, part of what Gilroy calls an African American "poetics of transit."[6] Their poetic drives encompass both the restricted freedom of movement on the open road and mourning songs that emerge while sitting still in automobiles.

MOURNING AMERICAN OPTIMISM

Before turning to Rankine's stalled poetic drive, it is necessary to frame it in relation to her larger project of mourning the unfulfilled promises of American democracy. Rankine's poetry is part of a long-standing "African-American genre of melancholic mourning" that stretches back to the Atlantic slave trade.[7] While she addresses this long history, her poetry specifically mourns the false promises of a postracial America that was supposed to have left behind struggles over Black life. The evocations of sadness, melancholy, and mourning in her work are also part of a larger conversation in Black studies over how to *affect*ively address ongoing histories of white supremacy. By foregrounding affective responses to everyday anti-Blackness, Rankine makes palpable the delimited horizon of post-Fordist struggles for racial equality after the heyday of the Civil Rights Movement. She shows how mourning the violence directed against Black lives—not least while driving—is an open, continual process, rather than a discreet event with a clear terminus. This mourning is also inherently political, as it draws attention to the reality of American racial inequality, while contesting political projects that seek to relegate racism to a past that no longer informs our present.

The wide reception of Rankine's work should be understood in relation to the Black Lives Matter movement, which has also addressed Black mobility. In 2012, Trayvon Martin was killed by George Zimmerman in Florida, sparking nationwide protests, and in 2014 protests over the police killing of Michael Brown in Ferguson, Missouri, brought international attention to the ways that largely white police departments can systematically oppress and exploit poor Black communities, often through traffic stops. As Julie Livingston and Andrew Ross explain, "The volume of stops swelled from the 1970s, as a result of the War on Drugs, and later in response to top-down pressure from local governments seeking to extract revenue from traffic fines and associated court fees. This invasive policing practice cast a long shadow over the civil rights landscape, consigning millions to jails and prisons, and resulting in the deaths of numerous Black drivers at the hands of trigger-happy officers."[8] The phrase "driving while Black" was minted in the 1990s to describe these discriminatory policing practices, which are not limited to traffic stops and stop-and-frisks. Indeed, Martin and Brown were killed while on foot, during the tenure of the first African American president, Barack Obama, underscoring the frustrated hopes of his presidency. In 2020 mass worldwide protests for Black life reemerged after George Floyd was murdered by Derek Chauvin in Minneapolis during the presidency of Donald Trump, whom Coates has referred to as "the first white president."[9]

Black Lives Matter developed on the heels of the Occupy movement, and both can be understood as responses to the 2008 financial crisis. Both movements are, furthermore, part of a post-Fordist social landscape where traditional forms of struggle, whether through unions or revolutionary political organizations, have largely been replaced by relatively spontaneous gatherings in the street and in squares, fueled by the prevalence of social media. These post-Fordist struggles are especially poignant for African Americans, who, in contrast to white Americans, were often excluded from the benefits of the postwar boom and were thereafter the population hit hardest by deindustrialization. As Thomas J. Sugrue has pointed out, "the great irony of postwar auto industry history was that just as blacks found themselves on the first rung of the ladder of economic mobility in the auto industry, that rung was cut away by decentralization and automation."[10] The post-Fordist underemployment of Black men led, predictably, to an increase in violent crime.[11] Rather than responding to this crisis with national social reform, politicians let fiscally strapped state and local governments resort to punitive measures, from traffic fines to prison labor, which could include making car parts and license plates.[12] It is therefore fitting that in the new millennium, demands to "defund the police" ring out against this landscape of cars and jails, continuing a centuries-long struggle for Black mobility.

For Rankine, along with other scholars of Black studies, confronting the everydayness of violence against African Americans calls for extended mourning or melancholy. In this way, the reality of white supremacy may gain recognition, both socially and psychically, leading to potential redress. Sigmund Freud famously conceived of mourning and melancholia as opposed psychological responses to loss. Mourning loss is, in his view, a conscious process allowing it to be worked through; a pathological melancholy or depression, by contrast, leaves loss unconscious, potentially leading to suicide. Freud states that mourning can be for "the loss of a loved person, or to the loss of some abstraction which has taken the place of one, such as one's country, liberty, an ideal, and so on."[13] Indeed, while there is no shortage of dead individuals in Rankine's trilogy, her work mourns the American condition more than any individual loss. As she writes in *Just Us,* "my optimism has been stolen by white supremacy," revealing how her loss of hope in equality itself requires mourning (*JU,* 327). In an interview with *Guernica,* she notes how "in *Cruel Optimism,* [Lauren] Berlant talks about things that we're invested in, despite the fact that they are not good for us and place us in a non-sovereign relationship to our own lives. And I thought, on a certain level, that thing that I am invested in that is hurting me would be this country [*laughs*]."[14] For Berlant, the social contract of Fordism and the post-WWII welfare state is no longer achievable by individual striving, and so the promises of this contract become cruel; this is especially the case for subjects who have precarious employment or are overworked. Rankine is, in many senses, mourning the elusive and exclusionary promises of American postwar prosperity, which have not led to racial equality.

In her essay "The Condition of Black Life Is One of Mourning," which was first published in *The New York Times Magazine* in 2015 five days after the Charleston church massacre where nine African Americans were killed, Rankine writes, "The Black Lives Matter movement can be read as an attempt to keep mourning an open dynamic in our culture because black lives exist in a state of precariousness. Mourning then bears both the vulnerability inherent in black lives and the instability regarding a future for those lives. Unlike earlier black-power movements that tried to fight or segregate for self-preservation, Black Lives Matter aligns with the dead, continues the mourning, and refuses the forgetting in front of all of us."[15] Rather than being a temporally discrete act, in the sense Freud had in mind, mourning becomes an open dynamic that refuses to forget the dead. Such mourning makes sadness and despair political rather than personal or pathological.[16] Melancholia can, by contrast, fuel reactionary politics. For instance, Tobias Hübinette and Catrin Lundström have coined the term "white melancholia" to connote the reactionary backlash of white voters to the apparent erosion of white hegemony.[17] White melancholic longing for the way things supposedly were is, then, the reverse image of Black mourning over an equality that never was.

Nevertheless, as though providing evidence of Freud's dichotomy between mourning and melancholia, Rankine's poetry succumbs, at times, to despair. Indeed, a keyword in the first book of Rankine's trilogy, *Don't Let Me Be Lonely,* is "sad." This book was published on September 1, 2004, two months before the reelection of George W. Bush as US president. In it the poet appears sick and lonely in a media landscape that includes the 1998 lynching by truck of James Byrd Jr. by three white men in Texas, the 1999 shooting of Amadou Diallo by New York City police, as well as the controversial 2000 presidential election. In addressing these events, Rankine uses language that foreshadows that of Black Lives Matter activists a decade later:

> I forget things too. It makes me sad. Or it makes me the saddest. The sadness is not really about George W. or our American optimism; the sadness lives in the recognition that a life can not matter. Or, as there are billions

of lives, my sadness is alive alongside the recognition that billions of lives never mattered. I write this without breaking my heart, without bursting into anything. Perhaps this is the real source of my sadness. Or, perhaps, Emily Dickinson, my love, hope was never a thing with feathers. I don't know, I just find when the news comes on I switch the channel. This new tendency might be indicative of a deepening personality flaw: IMH, The Inability to Maintain Hope, which translates into no innate trust in the supreme laws that govern us. Cornel West says this is what is wrong with black people today—too nihilistic. Too scarred by hope to hope, too experienced to experience, too close to dead is what I think.[18]

Under George W. Bush, "a real life can not matter," which provides a reversal and premonition of the slogan "Black Lives Matter." Christopher Nealon points out how *Don't Let Me Be Lonely* confronts this hopelessness "in a context where historical hope seems passé, and where its becoming passé is explicitly linked to its having ballooned into an empty spectacle."[19] He also notes how "IMH" sounds like "her deflated retirement account," thereby linking the spectacle of hope to financial speculation.[20] *Don't Let Me Be Lonely* ends with a kind of affirmation, though, imagining a poem, following Paul Celan, as a handshake, an encounter based on mutual recognition and a shared "here."[21] Yet as we saw with Frank O'Hara and LeRoi Jones's handshake, such moments of interracial accord can hardly be generalized to the whole population.

In order to appreciate the stakes of sadness and mourning in Rankine's work, it is instructive to consider two books published by Duke University Press in 2016, which make somewhat different assessments of how to reckon with the devaluing and capturing of Black life: Joseph R. Winters's *Hope Draped in Black: Race, Melancholy, and the Agony of Progress* and Christina Sharpe's *In the Wake: On Blackness and Being*. Sharpe and Winters share with Rankine and Berlant a critique of liberal narratives of progress, but whereas Winters advocates mourning and melancholy in confronting white supremacy, Sharpe wants to distinguish "Black being in the wake and wake work from the work of melancholia and mourning."[22] Sharpe asks, "even as we know that mourning an event might be interminable, how does one mourn the interminable event?"[23] Rather than seeing mourning as able to contest state authority, including the exclusionary politics of citizenship, Sharpe wishes to inhabit a position of "no-citizen," where there is "no state or nation to protect us, [and] no citizenship bound to be respected."[24] Rankine repeatedly cites Sharpe in *Just Us,* for whom the condition of "the hold" of forced movement and capture, as in the hold of the slave ship, makes *moving on* both profoundly precarious and contradictory. As Helen Gibson succinctly puts it, "moving while Black is tantamount to not moving."[25] In *Ordinary Notes,* Sharpe nevertheless rebukes Rankine for making a spectacle of Black death rather than staging the encounter of memorial and mourning, a critique which I consider unfounded in light of Rankine's attention to mourning.[26] In contrast to Sharpe's transnational and transhistorical figuration of the afterlives of slavery, Winters advocates "melancholic hope" as part of a concrete political project addressing racialized injustice.[27] Margo Natalie Crawford compellingly aligns Rankine with Winters: "Like Winters, Rankine is thinking about the agony of progress and melancholic hope. What kind of melancholic hope allows black melancholic subjects to move on with the awareness, not the denial, of the 'agony of progress?'"[28] As we have seen, Rankine's mourning is a response to her investment in America and her attachment to hope. But she is not as pragmatic as Winters, nor quite as pessimistic as Sharpe. Rankine's melancholic mourning occupies a middle ground between them; at once longing for hope while mourning its continual erasure. As Maureen Gallagher summarizes, "the melancholic mourning in *Citizen* is paradoxical: Both a central preoccupation and impervious to resolution; both circumscribed by the white gaze within media-driven narratives and also a form of resistance to white supremacy; both cataclysmic and woven into the fabric of everyday life."[29]

The subtitles of Rankine's trilogy also speak to her paradoxical mourning of the failed promise of America. On the one hand, *An American Lyric* and *An American Conversation* can be understood as affirming "America" and the full rights of citizenship for all its citizens, leaving unquestioned the exclusionary politics of citizenship Sharpe foregrounds. Also, by framing her book in terms of the US public sphere, Rankine appears to ignore the larger question of transnational Black identity. Another way to read Rankine's "America," though, is as a question or provocation that opens up toward the whole continent, even though its material is focused on the US. The title *Citizen* contains a similar ambiguity. As Maria

Windell writes, "what makes *Citizen* such an effective title for the book is the term's re-contextualization to African American experience: for many readers it is a Latina/o framework that signals 'citizen' as a fraught term and makes 'citizenship' visible as a contested category. *Citizen,* however, does not cite this re-contextualization."[30] In *Just Us,* Rankine grapples with the status of Latinx Americans in relation to African Americans. Is it the case, as her Afro-pessimist friend argues, "that Latinx and Asian people are the 'junior partners' in a white nationalist administration" (*JU,* 245)? Or is it that "true solidarity has personally been an oversight on my part as my gaze has been focused on the dead and targeted black people unable just to live, though this limited and targeted existence is also true for many Latinx people" (*JU,* 245)? Rankine writes that she "believe[s] antiblack racism is foundational to all of our problems, regardless of our ethnicity" (*JU,* 243). Yet this conclusion is troubled by the way that the title *Citizen: An American Lyric* suggests a series of struggles that has, as Windell suggests, affected many groups historically marked as non-white in the US, besides African Americans.

The subtitle of the two books in the trilogy that are presented as poetry—*An American Lyric*—also invokes the lyric tradition. In recent years, the status of "lyric" has been nearly as contested within poetics scholarship as citizenship has been contested in the world at large. Virginia Jackson has argued that literary scholars have inherited from New Criticism a transhistorical conception of lyric, where a wide variety of poetic forms have been cannibalized into an all-encompassing conception of lyric poetry. According to Jackson, this process, which she calls "the lyricization of poetry," has left us with a limiting framework within which to read so-called lyric poems, which have become synonymous with a short poem where we are meant to overhear a so-called speaker talking to themselves.[31] Using Jackson's framework, Kamran Javadizadeh has shown how Rankine revises the confessional lyric's focus on a personal experience coded as white, "repurposing its tropes of breakdown to animate her own representations of durably social—and not merely provisional or private—incoherence."[32] Anthony Reed also construes the subtitle *An American Lyric* against the tradition of lyricization, arguing that it is "insisting on a claim to 'lyric' that is nonuniversal and, insofar as America is a historical construction, nontranscendental—ergo 'postlyric.'"[33] Both "lyric" and "America" are contested terms precisely because of their idealization, with Rankine foregrounding instead their particularity and crisis, in effect "demand[ing]"—as Angela Huma puts it—"to be read, ironically."[34] In an important sense, then, the subtitle *An American Lyric* mourns the impossibility of a postracial poetry of subjective experience in America. Rather than being merely personal, her trilogy performs, as we are about to see, a fragmentary public that includes the positionality of its readers.

SITTING STILL WITH CITIZEN

Whereas *Don't Let Me Be Lonely* confronts isolation, depression, loneliness, and death, *Citizen* is made up of encounters between people, where racism stands in the way of mutual recognition. *Citizen* was published in 2014 and became associated with Black Lives Matter, thereby reaching an exceptionally wide audience for a book of documentary poetry. It explicitly addresses acts of everyday racism against Black Americans—what are often called microaggressions—as well as racial profiling by the police and the killings of Black men. The US edition from Graywolf Press is printed on glossy white paper with black text, and is full of high-resolution images, mostly from contemporary African American artists. Many of the experiences related in *Citizen* are based on those told to Rankine by her friends. She has stated that she imagines her readership as much like herself, educated, well-off, liberal.[35] This imagined readership is made up of people who might have felt confident they were part of a postracial American in the Obama era, where acts of racism, when they did occur, were supposedly committed by unenlightened *other* people. *Citizen* gains its pathos and force, though, by laying bare the racist assumptions and actions that emerge in everyday encounters between even liberal intellectuals. In this sense, it is a book, as Rankine herself has highlighted, about intimacy, or rather the intimacy of racism.

Rankine's interrogation of how Americans relate to one another extends to the public realm of automobility. In *Citizen* the Black driver on the road afraid of being stopped by police and the driver sitting still in a parked car both confront the restricted mobility of African Americans. While drivers habitually sit still whether they are parked or careening down a highway, in

Citizen such stillness becomes a means of mourning racism on the road and the failed promises of liberal progress. Rankine's song of mourning blossoms through a confrontation with the whiteness of automobility, which is at once a confrontation with the unfreedom of American free verse.

From its opening pages, *Citizen* suggests how the American system of automobility is a legacy of white supremacy. Aside from the evocative black hoodie on the front cover of the book, its first image is a photograph of a suburban intersection and a street sign bearing the name "Jim Crow Rd." In the background we can see large white houses and a white sedan in a driveway. From its opening pages, then, *Citizen* links whiteness and automobility, while placing the car in a history of racial oppression. As Rankine explains in a discussion with Berlant in *Bomb Magazine:*

> The first image in *Citizen* is a 2007 photograph taken in a suburban subdivision in Flowery Branch, Georgia, of Jim Crow Road. When I first saw the image I wondered if it was photoshopped, but it's an actual road curiously named after a James Crow (why not stick with James?), according to local lore. The photographer, Michael David Murphy, has a series entitled *Unphotographable,* in which he writes about photos that, unlike *Jim Crow Rd.,* he couldn't take for one reason or another—text stands in for the place of the image. In this case, his image stands in place of my text. The tangential relation of the images with the text, in a sense, mimics a form of "the public." They are related and can be taken in, but, at times, are hardly touching, or they come up in a different context elsewhere in the text, before or after they appear. *Jim Crow Rd.* comes after a piece about being in middle school. Presumably the school is on a road; here is another road. All these roads make up the country.[36]

The relation between Murphy's image and Rankine's text also applies to *Citizen* as a whole, where images and text form a constellation of difficult reckonings. This constellation of fragments, where images and text are "at times ... hardly touching," creates a kind of public, but one that is fundamentally fraught, and where touching or intimacy is precisely where racist aggression occurs. The American public, like the street Jim Crow Road, has a violent history of racial oppression inscribed within its encounters, which can burst forth at any moment and yet remain in a certain sense hidden from view, unphotographable.

Jim Crow Rd., Michael David Murphy, 2008. (Michael David Murphy)

Murphy's photograph suggests how the logic of Jim Crow has not fully abated from the American landscape, and might even emerge as a suburban response to the common practice of naming city streets after Martin Luther King Jr. and Malcolm X. Indeed, Walter Benjamin notes how street names have something to say about modern citizenship, becoming a sign of bourgeois equality, where any word can be elevated to "the noble status of a name."[37] In the modern metropolis, street names are, furthermore, ever shifting, making apparent the fortunes of power. Appropriately, Rankine and Berlant first met in a parking lot after a reading, and in their email conversation, Berlant offers an extended analysis of *Jim Crow Rd.*, stating, "I love what you say about street signs, that they always represent the lines that interconnect us in the space of the citizen (even when we are not citizens, presumably); also, they mark a fork in the road, a decision about the world. In relation to them, we are always in movement, even when we are also stuck."[38] Especially for African Americans, movement and stuckness can be the same thing. The very repetitiveness of the encounters or situations in *Citizen* enacts this stuck movement, while the reader, as though at a fork in the road, is left to ponder how things could be otherwise.

The dialectic of stuckness and movement that Rankine and Berlant recognize in *Jim Crow Rd.* is also central to a conversation in an automobile a few pages later in *Citizen*. This encounter begins where "you are in the dark, in the car, watching the black-tarred street being swallowed by speed."[39] Already in this scene-setting sentence, speed is swallowing Blackness, rather than providing for its freedom, in contrast to how speed has signaled freedom for many white writers. Here speed is something done to the street and to the driver, who watches, not something of which the driver is the agent. Someone is in the car with the driver, a man who complains about "the dean"—presumably of a humanities college with a creative writing program—who "is making him hire a person of color when there are so many great writers out there" (*C,* 10). The man's phrasing implies that great writers cannot at the same time be people of color. The line is especially charged because it also implicates the author of the book we are reading, who left her position as the Frederick Iseman Professor of Poetry at Yale University to become Professor of Creative Writing at New York University.

The passage continues with the driver's internal monologue: "Why do you feel comfortable saying this to me? You wish the light would turn red or a police siren would go off so you could slam on the brakes, slam into the car ahead of you, fly forward so quickly both your faces would suddenly be exposed to the wind" (*C,* 10). The driver longs for the violence of this possible exit from the everyday racism of America. But they remain in the car, as "you drive straight through the moment with the expected backing off of what was previously said." The driver has a "destination that doesn't include acting like this moment isn't inhabitable, hasn't happened before, and the before isn't part of the now as the night darkens and the time shortens between where we are and where we are going" (*C,* 10). Rankine's use of double negatives is both confounding and instructive. To not act like this moment is not inhabitable is to act like this moment *is* inhabitable. To not act like this moment has not happened before is to act like this moment *has* happened before, and is continuing to happen. Such moments are recurring but are also, by virtue of such double negatives, linked to a kind of erasure. The erasure, for example, of writers of color.

The passage ends on the following page with the driver sitting alone in their driveway, where the car's immobility becomes a means of mourning the damage wrought by racism and technological progress:

> When you arrive in your driveway and turn off the car, you remain behind the wheel another ten minutes. You fear the night is being locked in

and coded on a cellular level and want time to function as a power wash. Sitting there staring at the closed garage door you are reminded that a friend once told you there exists the medical term—John Henryism—for people exposed to stresses stemming from racism. They achieve themselves to death trying to dodge the buildup of erasure. Sherman James, the researcher who came up with the term, claimed the physiological costs were high. You hope by sitting in silence you are bucking the trend.
(C, 11)

After stopping the car, the driver continues to confront the question of how to arrive in the present experience of racism. They hope to evade the darkness of the night and let time "function as a power wash" so that it can clean off the uninhabitable moments "you" have had to inhabit. Stopping the car, sitting there in silence, becomes a way to exist beyond this moment. Sitting still reminds the driver of the medical term *John Henryism*, which is named after the folk hero John Henry, who was able to drive steel faster than a steam-powered rock-drilling machine. According to legend, Henry's victory over the new technology resulted in his death by heart attack. The attempt to outman machinery proves futile in the tale and its many song versions, which are often frenetic songs of mourning. Sitting still in the car is also an act of mourning, not only for what has just occurred but for what has occurred time and time again, and will continue to occur as "part of the now as the night darkens and the time shortens between where we are and where we are going" (C, 10). Yet, as John Henry's fate attests, there is nowhere to go, lest one be run over by technological optimism.

We have already seen how the marking of precise time in Olson's and O'Hara's poetry, as well as the clock on the dashboard in *The Last Clean Shirt*, confronted the regulated time of Fordism. For these mid-century poets, time signals served both as a bid for personal immediacy and a marker of alienation. The contradictory stakes of time are even more poignant for Rankine's driver, for whom time might function as a power wash against the cellular locking in of racism, becoming thereby the opposite of achievement, of clocked productivity. Sitting still in the car is an attempt to "buck the trend" of John Henry's deadly overachievement. In figuring time as a power wash that stops experience from being "locked in and coded," this passage lobbies for its own kind of erasure. Whereas O'Hara developed an ironic stance toward the authenticity Olson sought to inscribe through marking precise time, Rankine's time is here silent and potentially therapeutic and ameliorative. And yet, as Rankine puts it in *Just Us*, "once I confused the passage of time with change" (*JU*, 87). Progression between where we've been and where we are going is a trap in *Citizen*, keeping us locked in through inertia. In contrast to progressive time, which is the space within which racism repeats itself, Rankine imagines time when nothing happens as erasing racist erasure, as its possible undoing.

Rather than the cruel optimism of liberal progress, Rankine offers us here something akin to what Cornel West has called "the tragi-comic sense of life" (*JU*, 89).[40] The nearly comic image of time as a power wash, and the more or less counterfactual hope of "bucking the trend" of suffering the stresses of racism, evince a comic pessimism in Rankine's worldview and provide for a kind of ironic mourning. As part of this open dynamic of mourning, Rankine includes the audience in her work, so that the questions she asks about erasure and the possibilities of bucking this trend reach out towards "you." Rather than celebrating the escapist fantasy of white automobility, *Citizen* holds a mirror up to the reader, asking whether or not this is where we want to be, and where we are going. These questions are perhaps raised in the hope that the present will wash off, but also perhaps with the recognition that it won't, at least not while we are caught in the inertia of driving for freedom.[41]

The act of sitting still in the car is not unlike sitting still with a book, indeed, a book such as *Citizen*. The experiences of racism in *Citizen* endure through our reading, but therefore also have the possibility of being encoded otherwise. The book, the car, and *Jim Crow Rd.* can also function as stop signs, as one of *Citizen*'s readers, Johari Osayi Idusuyi, made apparent when she sat and quietly read the book in the audience of a Trump rally in 2015, the image of which received worldwide circulation, increasing sales of the book.[42] In confronting the nostalgic racism of Trump's "Make America Great Again" campaign, Idusuyi effectively channels the tradition of the sit-in protest, from the 1937 sit-down strike at General Motors to the sit-ins during the Civil Rights Movement, where activists often sat with books at segregated lunch counters. This lineage includes Rosa Parks, who famously refused to give up her bus seat for white passengers, initiating the Montgomery Bus Boycott, which Rita Dove memorializes in her 1999 book of poems *On the Bus with Rosa Parks*. Less well-known are the mostly

Black residents of Warren County, North Carolina, who in 1982 sat down in the road to block the delivery of six thousand truckloads of soil laced with toxic PCBs, a protest which gained national attention and led the civil rights activist Benjamin Chavis to coin the term "environmental racism."[43] Walter Benjamin, for his part, seems to anticipate such a tradition of sit-in protests when he imagines revolution as pulling the emergency brake on the train of historical development, in contrast to Marx's image of revolutions as "the locomotive of world history."[44] Rather than the speed and calamity of industrial economic progress, sitting still in and with *Citizen* invokes, then, another kind of progressive tradition: utilizing strikes and civil disobedience to try and stop the motor of petromodernity from running.

The virtues of sitting still in protest of white supremacy are not unambiguous, though, for African American drivers are also repeatedly stopped by police, sometimes with deadly consequences. For instance, Rankine and Lucas's video *Situation 8* includes dashcam footage of Sandra Bland being forcibly removed from her vehicle by a white police officer with a taser in 2015. Bland later died in police custody. Rankine's script for the *Situation* video *Stop-and-Frisk* poeticizes another driver's fear of such violence:

> I left my client's house knowing I would be pulled over. I knew. I just knew. I opened my briefcase on the passenger seat, just so they could see. Yes officer rolled around on my tongue, which grew out of a bell that could never ring because its emergency was a tolling I was meant to swallow.
>
> In a landscape drawn from an ocean bed, you can't drive yourself sane—so angry you are crying. You can't drive yourself sane. This motion wears a guy out. Our motion is wearing you out and still you are not that guy. (*C*, 105)

The pun in "you can't drive yourself sane" makes apparent how neither the car nor individual willpower will ameliorate the threat of violence hovering over Black drivers. It is also the case that "motion wears a guy out" so that the inertia of automobility again becomes a site of erasure rather than a means to freedom. Can we consider it progress that this "landscape [was] drawn from an ocean bed"? If so, it is glacial. In the phrase "still you are not that guy," the word "still" can be read as an adverb suggesting the duration of misrecognition. "Still" can also be read as an adjective, though, intimating how stillness might be the only means of not being erased for being the wrong guy.

While I have foregrounded the economic inequality that undergirds racialized American policing, Rankine is at pains to show how even upper-middle-class African Americans are not secure from harassment and violence. This reality is illustrated by the social position of the driver in the above passage, who is presumably a lawyer. Providing such accounts of racism suffered by upper-middle-class African American professionals drives home Rankine's oft-repeated point that white supremacy cannot be reduced to economic inequality. She recounts in her 2015 reading at Harvard University how she interviewed a Black lawyer friend about his experiences of being pulled over by the police. His white wife was with him during this recounting, and it struck Rankine that her friend had not previously told his wife about these experiences.[45] In *Just Us,* Rankine mentions how she and her husband, who is white, "many times driving in New York City and New Jersey ... were pulled over by police and asked how we knew each other" (*JU,* 79). This demand to justify being a professional interracial couple in the car in the twenty-first century throws into starker relief the performance of interracial accord in *The Last Clean Shirt* (1964), where the Black driver is a doctor. The racist acts Rankine describes are like a broken record, a discursive—which is not to say immaterial—tic that just won't let up, sometimes with deadly consequences. How and why, her works ask, does this tic persist?

Rankine's work gains part of its pathos from showing how wealth does not fully insulate African Americans from white supremacy. Yet she largely ignores the reality of class. As Kenneth Warren points out, *Citizen* illustrates the frustrations of achieving middle-class parity and the travails of upward mobility, rather than problematizing economic inequality as such.[46] Indeed, Rankine seems surprised when encountering a working-class, poor white student, who drives her from the airport to an event at a college in the Berkshires, a story that she recounts on an episode of Krista Tippett's podcast *On Being.* The young woman driving Rankine lives in a double-wide trailer, which Rankine has never heard of before. The woman explains how she must work over the summer, instead of visiting her sister in Washington, DC, as she usually does, because she needs about $300 to fix a crack in her double-wide. Rankine relates that she "spent part of the ride thinking should I just give her the $300 or what, you know, I didn't do that. But it was just, you know, a different reality." Rankine's own mobile life—which often causes her to reflect on the way that "space itself is one of the understood privileges of whiteness" (*JU,* 33)—relies here on being driven by a poor white woman, who must work to keep her mobile home warm instead of visiting family over the summer. Rankine reflects, "I'm often being driven by people who are not me. And I spend a lot of time thinking about 'How can I say this so that we can stay in this car together. And yet explore the things that I want to explore with you.'" Indeed, Rankine's exploration of American white supremacy is increasingly focused on discourse, as suggested by the subtitle of *Just Us: An American Conversation*. Tippett's podcast provides one of the rare instances, though, where Rankine intimates how free mobility, while being a privilege of whiteness, also depends on economic resources that don't neatly map onto racial inequalities.

Along with exploring the nature of free mobility, *Stop-and-Frisk* also talks back to the tradition of American free verse. In the script, "Yes officer rolled around on my tongue, which grew out of a bell that could never ring because its emergency was a tolling I was meant to swallow." This bell stuck in the driver's throat contrasts with the free verse emerging from the reader's throat in Whitman's *Leaves of Grass* (1855):

> Loafe with me on the grass.... loose the stop from your throat,
> Not words, not music or rhyme I want.... not custom or lecture, not
>   even the best,
> Only the lull I like, the hum of your valved voice.[47]

Loafing is a key term for Whitman, signaling a privileged occasion for human receptivity and the organic emergence of song free from social domination. Loafing is premised on the absence of work, and here this free leisure becomes song in loosing the stop from *your* throat, which of itself hums through a valved voice. Like Whitman's loafer, Rankine foregrounds stillness and receptivity as a privileged location of poetic utterance. But while Whitman's scene for poetic song is ecstatic, Rankine's passage is exhausted: "Yes officer." In contrast to the idealized free verse emerging from the throat of the loafing reader in *Leaves of Grass,* Rankine's Black driver is meant to swallow an unending toll, a sinister version of the kind of toll that drivers pay for using interstate highways.

This toll is also part mourning song. It is a hold stuck in the driver's throat, an enforced stopping, which reappears in Rankine's script for the *Situation* video *In Memory of Trayvon Martin.* In this script, years of anti-Black violence "accumulate into the hours inside our lives where we are all caught hanging, the rope inside us, the tree inside us, its roots our limbs, a throat sliced through and when we open our mouth to speak, blossoms, o blossoms, no place coming out, brother, dear brother, that kind of blue" (*C,* 89–90). The lynched Black body "caught hanging" might at once be a flowering tree, where "blossoms, o blossoms" emerge from an open mouth. This apostrophe to blossoms makes them a metaphor for poetry itself, "an image of beauty and new life that stands in for black creativity," as Maureen Gallagher writes.[48] Rankine's blossoms also call to mind Whitman's elegy for Abraham Lincoln, "When Lilacs Last in the Dooryard Bloom'd," where the tolling of bells meets the flowering of poetry: "With the tolling tolling bells' perpetual clang, / Here, coffin that slowly passes, / I give you my sprig of lilac."[49] Whereas Lincoln's coffin traversed the United States by train in the spring of 1865, Black lives must blossom, for Rankine, while holding on to the experience of erasure while driving—a toll stuck in their throat. As we have seen, the poetic pedigree of this erasure includes William Carlos Williams figuring Black drivers adorned with lilac blossoms as "dirty satyrs" loafing on street corners. Trayvon Martin was also simply walking down the street while talking on the phone, and Rankine's elegy ends with a request: "Wait with me. Wait with me though the waiting might be the call of good-byes" (*C,* 90). Rather than leave a phone call for what might be death—as it was for Martin—Rankine asks her "brothers" to stay on the line, to not hang up, to wait. It is through this waiting as wake that poetic utterance might blossom.

In comparing the sounds that are caught in the throat of Whitman's and Rankine's verse, we can see how the freedom of poetic expression remains unevenly distributed. The lawyer cannot let the emergency in his throat ring out, "because words hang in the air like pollen, the throat closes" (*C,* 156). Breathing is threatened in *Citizen,* suggesting Eric Garner's repeated statement "I can't breathe," the same statement later uttered by

George Floyd before he was murdered by Derek Chauvin. It is this repeated violence that the driver of the stopped car in the opening of *Citizen* hopes time will wash away. But instead, "that time and that time and that time the outside blistered the inside of you, words outmaneuvered years, had you in a chokehold, every part roughed up, the eyes dripping" (*C*, 156). This repetitive chokehold contrasts with Olson's and O'Hara's timed invocation of poetic breath, as well as Whitman's song emerging from a loose throat. Instead of white *free* verse, Rankine mourns the choking of Black life, figuring the limits of poetic utterance in unfree conditions.

Following Whitman, *Citizen* consistently addresses its readers as "you." Many of Whitman's poems imagine literally touching their readers, who are encouraged to think of his book as his own body. Not everyone, though, might be able to identify with Whitman's white, homosocial community. Indeed, in 2013, Timothy McNair, a master's student in music at Northwestern University, refused to sing Whitman's poetry because of his racist statements, leading to McNair not receiving his degree.[50] Rankine's address to "you" functions both similarly and differently from Whitman's. On one level, Rankine's "you" is generalizable, insofar as Americans have citizenship in common. But her "you" also begs the question of who has the rights to full citizenship and what those rights entail. She compels readers to locate their own social position in relation to the situations she narrates. As she put it in *Guernica*, "the second person for me disallowed the reader from knowing immediately how to position themselves."[51] *Citizen*, then, performs an openness to its readers—from Idusuyi to myself—who form the book's public, a public which the book itself seeks to mimic through its collage aesthetic where text, image, and video exist alongside each other without necessarily touching. In this constellation of *An American Lyric*, the (stalled) encounters of (un)free verse may bloom as a poetics of collective mourning.

SITTING STILL WITH TA-NEHISI COATES

In *Between the World and Me* (2015), Ta-Nehisi Coates foregrounds the centrality of the automobile to struggles over Black life in America in ways that are strikingly similar to *Citizen*. *Between the World and Me* is written as a letter to Coates's teenage son, Samori, about being Black in America, thereby providing an indirect homage to James Baldwin's earlier letter to a nephew, *The Fire Next Time* (1963). Coates grew up on the west side of Baltimore and attended Howard University in Washington, DC, where he also worked as a journalist. His book hinges on the killing of a Howard classmate, Prince Jones, by a police officer from the Prince George County Police Department in 2000. At the beginning of part 2 of the book, Coates recounts his own experience of being pulled over by a Prince George police officer. He writes to his son, "Shortly before you were born, I was pulled over by the PG County police, the same police that all the D.C. poets had warned me of. They approached on both sides of the car, shining their flashing lights through the windows. They took my identification and returned to the squad car. I sat there in terror."[52] Coates elaborates on the reasons for his terror, explaining to his son the violent history of the PG police, which led to the department being investigated by the FBI multiple times. He ends by reflecting, "these officers had my body, could do with that body whatever they pleased, and should I live to explain what they had done with it, this complaint would mean nothing. The officer returned. He handed back my license. He gave no explanation for the stop" (*BWM*, 75). In being stopped by the police for driving while Black, Coates experiences what the lawyer in *Citizen*—who drives with his briefcase open on the passenger seat in hopes of disarming the police—wants to avoid.

Coates links his own encounter with the PG Police to that of Prince Jones, who did not escape with his life. Jones was shot in his Jeep Cherokee by an undercover police officer posing as a drug dealer, who was trailing Jones across state lines, mistaking him for someone else. While Rankine's *Citizen* is especially concerned with interpersonal relations where white supremacy rears its head, Coates's book takes a larger view, detailing a history as old as the United States, in which the Black body has been repeatedly captured and killed, and where the American Dream has itself been built on the pillaging of Black lives. Coates is also clear that skin color will not save African Americans from being complicit in the devaluing of Black life: "I wrote about the history of the Prince George's County police. Nothing had ever felt so essential to me. Here is what I knew at the outset: The officer who killed Prince Jones was black. The politicians who empowered this officer to kill were black. Many of the black politicians, many of them twice as good [as their white counterparts], seemed unconcerned. How could this be?" (*BWM*, 83). In investigating the PG Police Department, Coates concludes that even the Black citizens of the county "viewed the destruction of the black body as incidental to the preservation of order" (84). Coates's awareness of the complicity of middle-class African Americans in the destruction of poor Black bodies unsettles Rankine's emphasis on the vulnerability of African Americans to white supremacy regardless of class.[53] Indeed, the high rates of violent crime in poor Black neighborhoods result in middle-class Black citizens being as vigilant against poor Black bodies as middle-class white citizens are.[54] This punitive response to poverty regardless of race leads Coates to the conclusion, in "The Case for Reparations," that reparations to African Americans for slavery, Jim Crow, and racist post-WWII federal housing policy would be a much more meaningful solution for structural inequality than police reform and affirmative action have been.[55]

Despite their differences of emphasis and genre, both Rankine and Coates make apparent how affluence does not insulate Black drivers from police violence. Coates illustrates this fact by recounting his visit to Jones's mother, Dr. Mabel Jones, who lives in a small, affluent gated community just outside of Philadelphia. Dr. Jones, who grew up poor in Louisiana, made a point of giving her two children all the luxuries she could afford, including gifting them each with new vehicles: a Mazda 626 for her daughter when she received her driver's license at age sixteen, and a Jeep Cherokee for the studious Prince on his twenty-third birthday. Dr. Jones tells Coates, "that was the jeep he was killed in" (*BWM*, 145). After leaving Dr. Jones's house, Coates finds himself in the same position as that of the driver toward the beginning of *Citizen:* sitting still in a car, mourning the vulnerability of Black life: "After I left, I sat in the car, idle for a few minutes. I thought of all that Prince's mother had invested in him, and all that was lost" (*BWM*, 146).

Sitting in the car, Coates mourns the death of his friend and reflects on what led Jones to Howard University. He thinks of their time there together, his own Homecoming return for a Howard football game, and the collective experience of Black Americans, which is "imbued by a power more gorgeous than any voting rights bill. This power, this Black power, originates in a view of the American galaxy taken from a dark and essential planet. Black power is the dungeon-side view of Monticello—which is to say, the view taken in struggle. And Black power births a kind of understanding that illuminates all the galaxies in their truest colors" (*BWM*, 149). Yet, as he makes clear, this Black power will not save African Americans from the ravages of the American Dream of whiteness, which is perpetuated by people whom he calls Dreamers, "those Americans who believe that they are white" (*BWM*, 6). This dream of whiteness is really a nightmare for Black people, and is fueled by cheap gasoline:

> Sitting in that car I thought of Dr. Jones's predictions of national doom. I had heard such predictions all my life from Malcolm and all his posthumous followers who hollered that the Dreamers must reap what they sow. I saw the same prediction in the words of Marcus Garvey who promised to return in a whirlwind of vengeful ancestors, an army of Middle Passage undead. No. I left The Mecca [of Howard University] knowing that this was all too pat, knowing that should the Dreamers reap what they had sown, we would reap it right with them. Plunder has matured into habit and addiction; the people who could author the mechanized death of our ghettos, the mass rape of private prisons, then engineer their own forgetting, must inevitably plunder much more. This is not a belief in prophecy but in the seductiveness of cheap gasoline. (*BWM,* 150)

The apocalyptic destruction of American optimism will not, Coates concludes, spare Black Americans. In the stillness of his car, he is, momentarily, on a "dark and essential planet" beyond Earth, from where he can see how cheap gasoline will make the Dreamers' plunder interminable, until even Earth is consumed by it. Coates shows how the vengeance of the oppressed that previous Black nationalists had imagined is, in the age of global climate catastrophe, too hopeful a narrative. Indeed, in Baldwin's *The Fire Next Time* from half a century earlier, the only automobile the author rides in belongs to Elijah Muhammad, illustrating how even the Nation of Islam could not escape the trappings of the American Dream.

Coates suggests how the modern geography of an America segregated by race and class depends on automobility, while also reflecting on how indiscriminate environmental destruction will be:

> The Earth is not our creation. It has no respect for us. It has no use for us. And its vengeance is not the fire in the cities but the fire in the

> sky. Something more fierce than Marcus Garvey is riding on the whirlwind. Something more awful than all our African ancestors is rising with the seas. The two phenomena are known to each other. It was the cotton that passed through our chained hands that inaugurated this age. It is the flight from us that sent them sprawling into the subdivided woods. And the method of transport through these new subdivisions, across the sprawl, is the automobile, the noose around the neck of the earth, and ultimately, the Dreamers themselves. (*BWM*, 150–51)

The automobile, which Jones died in, and in which Coates finds himself sitting, has carved up America between Black and white, between suburb and ghetto. Although Black experience might be something like a separate "dark and essential planet," it is nevertheless within the orbit of Earth, and will go down with it and the Dreamers. As Rita Dove puts it at the end of "Freedom Ride," her poem about the stalled hopes of the Civil Rights Movement, "where you sit is where you'll be / when the fire hits."[56] Yet Coates finds no succor or illumination in the coming of "the fire next time," as the most pressing threat of fire is no longer from urban riots but from global warming.

Coates can't do much else to confront climate catastrophe than drive away, however, in effect perpetuating the destruction he so eloquently enumerates: "I drove away from the house of Mable Jones thinking of all of this. I drove away, as always, thinking of you. I do not believe that we can stop them, Samori, because they must ultimately stop themselves. And still I urge you to struggle" (*BWM*, 151). While Coates struggles against the dream of whiteness, he can no more kick the habit of automobility than the Dreamers can; it is "the same habit that endangers the planet, the same habit that sees our bodies stowed away in prisons and ghettos" (*BWM*, 151). *Between the World and Me* ends not with a Black view from another planet but with a view of Black ghettos while driving, ghettos which have been defined by automobility: "I saw these ghettos driving back from Dr. Jones's home. They were the same ghettos I had seen in Chicago all those years ago, the same ghettos where my mother was raised, where my father was raised. Through the windshield I saw the mark of these ghettos—the abundance of beauty shops, churches, liquor stores, and crumbling housing—and I felt the old fear. Through the windshield I saw the rain coming down in sheets" (*BWM,* 151–52). Driving past urban poverty causes Coates to confront his own genealogy, much as Eisen-Martin does in "Heaven Is All Goodbyes." He cannot escape the fear for his body that living in the United States has instilled in him. While the automobile has served as a means of escape from the ghetto, and before that the segregated South, it was not able to save Prince Jones. Along with Prince, the Earth itself has become victim to a dream of whiteness fueled by automobility, a dream that Coates—like most other Americans, regardless of race—cannot easily free himself from.

While Rankine's "you" begs the question of who "you" are, "you" for Coates is first and foremost his own son, Samori. But there is something curious about Coates's "you," for isn't his book written for all of us? His more particular address to his son is therefore a kind of fiction, where his son stands in for anyone's Black son, echoing Barack Obama's statement that if he had a son, he would probably look like Trayvon Martin. As readers, we overhear Coates's letter, and it thereby has something in common with the lyric poem, where we are meant to overhear a speaker talking to themselves or addressing a significant other. Coates makes us aware of the deadly barriers between the larger "world" and his particular "me," while inviting us into intimacy with his family. As in Rankine's *Citizen,* where "we are traveling as a family" (133), Coates's letter stages familial intimacy in order to make his readers reflect on their position within the American Dream of whiteness. "Stay[ing] in this car together," as Rankine puts it in Tippett's podcast, thereby becomes a way for all of us to "explore" our relations with each other and the planet.

Rankine and Coates figure the automobile not as a means to freedom but as a site of restricted mobility and potential death for Black drivers. Rather than harnessing the speed of automobility, both authors at crucial moments show how sitting still in the car makes it a site of mourning over the violence continually perpetrated against African Americans. That both stopped cars and cars in motion require such stillness from their drivers foregrounds how neither stillness nor motion can allay the inertia of automobility. Mourning American optimism is, in short, constant. Indeed, these authors emphasize how the promises of automobility, and indeed optimism in social progress writ large, are not a truly democratic ground for citizenship. David M. McIvor writes that Rankine and

Coates reveal how "democratic optimism is cruel because it keeps individuals circling around the fantasy of generalized agency when the structural conditions of contemporary life radically preclude the realization of this dream."[57] Automobility is the hallmark of American fantasies of generalized agency, yet neither Rankine nor Coates can abandon their cars, pointing to how central it is to our current conception of American identity. These writers effectively use the (stalled) automobile to put in motion contradictions between progressive optimism and African American experience, making clear how neither driving while Black nor not driving while Black ensures the mattering of Black lives in the US.

Beyond the impasse of progressive visions of automobility, Rankine's poetry offers another kind of passage through the catastrophe of racialized violence. We can see this passage emerge between three of her car poems that take place in parking lots in *Nothing in Nature Is Private* (1994) and *Citizen*. Instead of relying on the ameliorative power of the passing of supposedly progressive time, Rankine in these poems opens a skeptical passage alongside American optimism, from which her critical poetic drive blossoms. Indeed, Rankine's implicit critique of progressive time encourages reading distinct moments in her oeuvre alongside each other, as opposed to foregrounding chronological development. That Rankine's poetic passage also calls to mind the Middle Passage, as well as racial passing, suggests how the catastrophe of white supremacy piles up before this poet who—much like Walter Benjamin's Angel of History—gets driven backwards into the future while passing over the wreckage of history.[58]

Before turning to *Nothing in Nature Is Private*, let us return to *Citizen*. In Rankine's script for the *Situation* video *In Memory of James Craig Anderson*, a truck takes center stage, echoing the killing of James Byrd Jr. in *Don't Let Me Be Lonely*. Anderson, age forty-eight, was murdered in 2011 by a group of white youth in Jackson, Mississippi, who beat him up before eighteen-year-old Deryl Dedmon drove over him with his pickup truck. Dedmon began his assault on Anderson—who had worked on the assembly line at the Nissan Canton plant in Mississippi for the previous seven years—in the parking lot of a Metro Inn at 5:00 a.m. on June 26, 2011. According to his killers, Anderson was trying to get inside his orange

Chevy Avalanche truck after locking the keys inside. Instead of helping him, the group of white teens murder him, with Dedmon running him over with his green Ford F-250 truck as he and his friends depart from the scene. The script begins: "in the next frame the pickup truck is in motion. Its motion activates its darkness. The pickup truck is a condition of darkness in motion. It makes a dark subject. You mean a black subject. No, a black object" (*C*, 93). In writing that "the pickup truck is a condition of darkness in motion," Rankine echoes the driving scene at the opening of the book where the passenger complains about his dean, and where darkness also defines the nighttime street. Now that darkness has contributed to a white youth harnessing automobility toward deadly ends: "Then the pickup is beating the black object to the ground and the tire marks the crushed organs. Then the audio, I ran that nigger over, is itself a record-breaking hot June day in the twenty-first century" (*C*, 94). Physical and verbal violence seem to emerge with the inevitability of days passing, rather than being decided by individual will.

The penultimate paragraph of this relatively short *Situation* script reads: "James Craig Anderson is dead. The pickup truck is a figure of speech. It is as the crown standing in for the kingdom. Who told you it was a crown? Did we tell you the pickup was as good as home? You are so young, Dedmon. You were so young" (*C*, 95). Why does Rankine address Dedmon? As Nikki Skillman writes, "We might expect Rankine to orient the animating potential of direct address toward Anderson, to bring the innocent victim (symbolically) back to life. But to face the attenuation of Dedmon's humanity in his act of racist violence (attenuation we come to hear ringing in the sounds of his name) and to summon him, as an avatar of white supremacy, from the realm of the unaccountable to the accountable, are more urgent aspirations of her address."[59] Directly addressing Dedmon is, moreover, a means of directly addressing *Citizen*'s readers, of calling us to account. In conceiving of the pickup as the crown of the kingdom, the script makes explicit its symbolic purchase in the United States and thereby begs the question of whether that United States is also fueled by "I ran that nigger over." Is not the whole country implicated in an atrocity carried out by such young people, carried out with the most potent symbolic vehicle of individual freedom in America, the automobile? They were handed the keys to the kingdom and used them to kill an autoworker who had locked his keys inside his truck.

The circumstances of Anderson's murder are reversed in an untitled poem from Rankine's first book, *Nothing in Nature Is Private,* where a white man who has locked his keys in his car asks for help:

> Passing, what I heard
> was the man asking,
> the white man asking,
> (as if he, the other
> were going nowhere)
> the white man asking
> for a minute
> of the other's time.
>
> It seemed that he,
> the white man,
> had forgotten and locked
> his keys in his car.
>
> Simply that he,
> the white man,
> had forgotten
> and was wondering,
> if he, the other, could,
> perhaps, get in, could,
> somehow, please, break
> in and get, please,
> the keys out of the car.[60]

The white man asks an "other" for help, presuming that the other man is not only "going nowhere" but also knows how to break into a car. While Dedmon and his friends treat Anderson as a criminal unworthy of living after locking himself out of his car, the white man in this poem seeks to avail himself of an other's presumed criminality to get into his own car. In contrast to *Citizen,* the poems in Rankine's first book are often told in the first person. In this poem, the poet is a witness to a halting conversation loaded with white presumption. Furthermore, the poet's "passing" invokes a history of racial passing, foregrounding how she manages to escape being interpellated by the white driver while overhearing his address to an other. This is a position of both power and vulnerability; for a moment, the poet can solitarily pass by, whereas the white man cannot gain access to his automobile. The poet's own lyric mutability signals a tenuous freedom—a passage—from which the mechanics of white supremacy can be criticized. This passage is at once the space from which Rankine's stalled poetic drive blossoms, interpellating us as readers into the constellation of a poetic public that includes experiences of immobility and violence, but also mourning and song.

In the last poem in *Citizen,* the poet dwells in this passage as the lesson of the book:

> I can hear the even breathing that creates passages to dreams. And yes, I want to interrupt to tell him her us you me I don't know how to end what doesn't have an ending.
>
> Tell me a story, he says, wrapping his arms around me.
>
> Yesterday, I begin, I was waiting in the car for time to pass. A woman pulled in and started to park her car facing mine. Our eyes met and what passed passed as quickly as the look away. She backed up and parked on the other side of the lot. I could have followed her to worry my question but I had to go, I was expected on court, I grabbed my racket.
>
> The sunrise is slow and cloudy, dragging the light in, but barely.
>
> Did you win? he asks.
>
> It wasn't a match, I say. It was a lesson. (*C,* 159)

The poet first wants to interrupt the breathing that leads to dreams, as if warning us that it is not yet safe to breathe or dream. She also wants to tell an assemblage of pronouns—which perform the constellated public of *Citizen*—that she doesn't know how to end. Her companion asks her to tell a story, and the story she tells is of sitting in the car waiting for time to pass. In contrast to the longing for ameliorative time in the driveway passage earlier in the book, here time passing becomes the space in which racism can make itself felt. Confronting racism is not a match on court—also suggesting a courtroom trial—with a definitive end, but rather a series of lessons.[61]

For Rankine, time seems to accumulate rather than ameliorate anti-Black racism, which repeats itself throughout history. This repetition is indeed what happens while the poet is waiting in her car at the end of *Citizen,* as another driver avoids parking her car in front of the poet's because—the poet is left worrying—of the color line. But "what passed passed." Likewise, the pun in the phrase "I grabbed my racket" makes apparent how the poet is left with the racket of this and so many other encounters where white supremacy has reared its head, echoing in hers. This is, in a sense, "the lesson" of *Citizen,* how the status of citizenship, and even the trappings of middle-class life in the US, cannot protect Black life. One of these trappings, the automobile—"the crown standing in for the kingdom"—continues to embody the contradictions of progressive optimism, as its promise of individual autonomy and mobility remains both a dream and a nightmare for Black drivers.

CODA

THIS BOOK OPENS WITH Robert Creeley's iconic driving poem "I Know a Man." Since we don't actually get to "know" the men in this poem, though, its title is ironic, intimating how these men know themselves and each other as little as they know the road ahead: "Look / out where yr going." Half a century later, this ending reads as a warning about the logic of petromodernity, where we careen our cars through climate catastrophe and automobility's inequalities, unsure of where we are going and seemingly unable to stop but for moments of mourning and, perhaps, poetry. We know so much, and many of us drive to know more, but we cannot meaningfully confront the planetary destruction wrought in no small part by automobility. And yet, as Min Hyoung Song argues in *Climate Lyricism* (2022), perhaps poetry can help train us to attend to the everyday, both in its pleasures and its violence and injustices, in ways that are needed to collectively address our present.

Poetic Drive has explored some of the ways that American poets have attended to the double bind of automobility, where driving provides for new freedoms while both depending on and perpetuating alienation and violence. At times this dialectical poetic drive comes—as it does with Rankine—to a standstill. Indeed, driving, crashing, and stopping are some of the ways that the contradictions of automobility are figured in the poetry I have been discussing. While the chapters of this book have progressed chronologically, poet by poet, the stakes of the contradictions of automobility are heightened when we think across periods and poets. Take, for example, Eileen Myles, who survives being raped by "guys... who all owned cars" before fully inhabiting the driver's seat themself. Myles's poetic and personal struggle with patriarchy and second wave feminism is also a confrontation with the tradition of American driving poems inaugurated by Williams's mechanized male gaze. Reading Myles after Williams helps focus a troubling question, which can be posed like this: Should we imagine Williams as himself a rapist—"I could have raped them all!" he said of his audience at Wellesley College—or instead as in proleptic solidarity with Myles when, in "The Raper from Passenack," he recounts the "insanely cruel" (*CP I,* 386) experience of a survivor of rape? This nameless passenger's "hatred of all men" (387) is turned on its head by Myles over half a century later in "The Lesbian Poet," where they experience the "terrifically human feeling" of being "this guy" with a car, echoing the language they used to describe their own rapists. In a sense, Myles inhabits in their own oeuvre the gap that also exists between their work and Williams's, where driving can be sexually predatory but also liberatory. In contrast to Williams's imagism, Myles's transfeminist petropoetics is not won at the cost of objectifying women. Instead, Myles shows us how driving is both a source of poetry and destroying the planet. Their profound ambivalence about driving also reflects back onto Williams's work, helping us see his poetic self-fashioning as a predatory driver and, paradoxically, as the doctor-confidant of the very women threatened by such driving. Little wonder, then, that Bernadette Mayer chose to drive around with his poems in the trunk, as an act of both demotion and devotion.

Even before Mayer and Myles, Frank O'Hara had begun reworking Williams's poetic drive toward his own ends. While Williams moved away from driving as a vehicle for his poetry with the onset of mass automobility around the Great Depression, O'Hara's poetics of presence emerges in the teeth of post-WWII Fordism. Rather than being a mere flaneur, O'Hara crafts his poetry of urban experience through inhabiting driving, traffic, and crashing. His invocation of automobility is nearly always tinged with irony, though, in contrast to Charles Olson's vexed attempt to keep his poetic car from running out of breath. This irony includes the celebration of interracial and homosocial bonds that remained inhibited by postwar racism and homophobia. O'Hara's poetics of Fordism is at once, then, a poetry of the impossible. Rather than being resolved by the passage of time, this impossibility is even more poignant in the work of Rankine in our own century. For Rankine and other African American writers such as Tongo Eisen-Martin, Ta-Nehisi Coates, and Wanda Coleman, the promised freedoms of automobility are at once a trap or hold, which can lead to death for Black drivers. How do we measure the distance between O'Hara's poeticization of James Dean's death by car crash, his own death by dune buggy, and the ongoing killings of Black drivers by the police and white supremacists? Indeed, the existential angst in Creeley's "I Know a Man" sounds quaint in comparison to the fear experienced by many Black drivers.

Rather than provide definitive answers to such questions, I have sought to illuminate the contradictions that they make apparent. In this spirit, I will finish by considering two contemporary queer poets of color whose poetic drives restage those in this book: Jericho Brown and Vickie Vértiz. Brown's Pulitzer Prize–winning book *The Tradition* (2019) includes several interconnected poems entitled "Duplex," which is his name for a poetic form that he imagines as "gutting a sonnet."[1] The final poem of Brown's book, "Duplex: Cento," begins:

> My last love drove a burgundy car,
> Color of a rash, a symptom of sickness.
>
>> We were the symptoms, the road our sickness:
>> None of our fights ended where they began.[2]

The poet's lover's "burgundy car" is also the poet's body, which, as many of the poems in this book attest, is sick with HIV. This sickness isn't merely personal, though, but rather the road is itself a sickness, with the car its rash or symptom. Sickness is also a metaphor for love, including that of an "awful" father, who is the poet's "first" and "last love."[3] This poem ends where it began and is itself a repetition of the book's first "Duplex," which includes the lines "My last love drove a burgundy car // My first love drove a burgundy car" and begins and ends, "A poem is a gesture toward home."⁴ First and last loves repeat themselves in a car that drives, like the poem, toward home. Brown spills the guts of this poetic drive into cascading lines that repeat their differences, singing the stalled and directionless car as a beautiful catastrophe. Yet he repeatedly reflects, "I didn't want to leave a messy corpse," as though his loves were a string of murders.⁵

The book's title poem, "The Tradition," makes clear that these messy corpses are Black men like "John Crawford. Eric Garner. Mike Brown." These men murdered by police are like flowers who "seemed to bloom against the will / Of the sun, which news reports claimed flamed hotter / On this planet than when our dead fathers / Wiped sweat from their necks."⁶ He may be repeating the love of his forefathers, Brown suggests, but the temperature has changed, the earth is heating up. Indeed, in "The Tradition," Black blossoms share the fate of all life: "Where the world ends / everything cut down." These flowers cut down at the end of the world contrast tragically with Gary Snyder's "Mimulus on the Road to Town," which, as we saw in the introduction, "never die." Brown's Black flowers, by contrast, are a harbinger of "everything" that could become a corpse by the roadside of petromodernity. Indeed, the poet's own body merges in these poems with those of other Black men, the car, and even the planet, which are all made sick by our love of driving.

Vickie Vértiz also foregrounds the coupling of cars and bodies in the title of her 2023 award-winning book *Auto/Body*. The book has three sections, entitled "Alternator," "Distributor" and "Transmission," and many individual poem titles are simply the year, make, and model of a car, making this perhaps *the* book of American poetry about automobility. In "'69 Chevy Impala" the poet recounts being a child in the car with her father, who is stopped at a red light, honking at women as they pass:

> I tell him to stop. Slink into the back seat
> cover my face with my hands. We're all in the car wit
> h him. Chuy repeats what I said in a whiny voice.
> Our baby brother is asleep.⁷

Despite being upsetting and mortifying, her father's behavior is framed as a lesson. The poem begins, "What I learned from my father's honking is that / women on the street are just like everyone's / mom," and ends with the lines

> He teaches me to look out, to give men nasty looks,
> but also that fools can honk at anything in a skirt and get to drive away. That sounds good to me: do whatever you want,
> go whenever you want. And no one tells you shit.[8]

Neither the poet, her siblings, her mother, nor the people outside the car, can stop her father from sexually harassing women with his car horn. Yet the poet learns from these women how "to give men nasty looks," while her father's behavior fosters a desire to defy men and to become her own driver. In her endnote to the poem, Vértiz writes that her "father was always buying old cars" and fixing them up to "look good" and "hunt in. The problem was that every single car he ever owned was busted, not unlike his intentions. I want to make something, anything else out of that."[9] It is as though Vértiz were yet another of Williams's heiresses, learning to drive with her father's legacy in the trunk.

Much like Myles, Vértiz uses the car to stage struggles over gender, power, and mobility, not least across the US-Mexico border. Her stopped car also calls to mind Rankine's many stopped cars, showing what driving and not driving can mean for a queer Latina. In the poem "Dictation," her brother Chuy hides from the Immigration and Naturalization Service in his black Mustang that is parked in the garage. As with the darkness of the stopped car in the driveway in *Citizen*, Chuy "was in the dark, in plain sight for we who can see. He sat in his car for hours and hours, waiting for our guests to leave."[10] Time passes in the stopped car, but it is no more ameliorative here than in *Citizen*: "Chuy waited so long that he turned into a Mustang. A workhorse, especially on Sundays."[11] Like John Henry, Chuy works to fight off the threat of erasure, of not being recognized as an American citizen, only to become a machine himself.

Vértiz and Brown are part of a rich history of American poets reckoning with the social, ecological, and aesthetic stakes of automobility. As we have seen, the myriad parts of the system of automobility—from gas stations and traffic to passengers and drivers—are, much like the page or screen, their own social forms, and invite both poetic inhabitation and contestation. Indeed, many of the poems and films examined in this book emerge through the automobile, and when poets and their collaborators confront the affordances and exclusions of automobility, they are often exploring the stakes of poetry itself. In *Auto/Body* Vértiz asks, "What does it feel like to drive my father's car?," a question to which her book offers several answers.[12] *Poetic Drive* has sought to answer a similar question: What does it feel like to drive a poem? While I have shown some of the ways that American poets have answered this question during the age of automobility, it will remain open for as long as driving defines our lives and, by extension, American poetry.

NOTES

INTRODUCTION

1. Creeley, *Collected Poems*, 132.
2. There is, indeed, a book entitled *Drive, They Said: Poems About Americans and Their Cars*, edited by Kurt Brown.
3. M. Davidson, *San Francisco*, 64; Altieri, "Unsure," 164. In line with my own reading, David J. Alworth considers "I Know a Man" "one of the strangest and most complicated responses to what has come to be known as American automobility" (*Site Reading*, 74).
4. M. Davidson, *San Francisco*, 64.
5. Aside from the books I will discuss below, see, in order of publication date, Dettelbach (1976), Lewis and Goldstein (1983), Scharff (1991), Primeau (1996), Casey (1997), Lackey (1997), Miller (2001), Paes de Barros (2004), Wollen and Kerr (2004), Mills (2006), Slethaug and Ford (2012), Primeau (2013), Pearce (2016), and Barndt (2018). Gijs Mom considers "autopoetics" (*Atlantic Automobilism*, 141-48), but this term mainly encompasses novels for him. Mom, in effect, follows the conclusions of "Jens Peter Becker [who] in his analysis of American autopoetic literature found surprisingly few poems in which the car played a carrying role" (*Atlantic Automobilism*, 509). Nevertheless, Mom repeatedly refers to writing by William Carlos Williams and Gertrude Stein in *Atlantic Automobilism* (2015) and *Globalizing Automobilism* (2020).
6. Brigham, *American Road Narratives*, 4.
7. In *Narrating a New Mobility Landscape* Vogel discusses poetry of the open road, but almost exclusively before the advent of mass automobility, and not in relation to driving. In *Cartographies of Empire* Tucker-Abramson provides a wide-ranging analysis of the global genre of the post–WWII road novel, but does not consider poetry.
8. Ballard, "The Future of the Car," 103. Notably, Ballard foresees the emergence of self-driving vehicles.

9. Berman, *All That Is Solid*, 328.
10. Brigham, *American Road Narratives*, 4.
11. Seiler, *Republic of Drivers*, 14.
12. On oil and privatized mobility, see Huber, *Lifeblood*, x.
13. Urry, "'System' of Automobility," 27.
14. The examples that I've found include Marianne Boruch's captivating essay "Poets in Cars." Stephen N. Brown writes interestingly of early middle-class car poetry, while making erroneous claims about the lack of cars in modernist poetry. For a compelling reading of Indigenous Canadian poetry in relation to automobility, see Deena Rymhs, *Roads, Mobility, and Violence*.
15. Goldstein, *Poetry Los Angeles*, 131.
16. Goldstein, 143.
17. Ronda and Turner, "Introduction."
18. For a useful overview of the history of the term *Fordism*, see Link, *Forging Global Fordism*, 3–8.
19. Qtd. in Flink, *Automobile Age*, 47.
20. Harvey, *Condition of Postmodernity*, 135.
21. Watten, *Constructivist Moment*, 106.
22. Denning, *Cultural Front*, 28.
23. In Rainey, Poggi, and Wittman, *Futurism*, 51.
24. In Rainey, Poggi, and Wittman, 49, 425.
25. Malm and Zetkin Collective, *White Skin, Black Fuel*, 403.
26. See image in Smith, *Making the Modern*, 54.
27. In Rainey, Poggi, and Wittman, *Futurism*, 119.
28. In Rainey, Poggi, and Wittman, 125. Bold in original.
29. Cecire, *Experimental*, 45; Yu, "Modernist Poetry and Race," 99.
30. Cecire, *Experimental*, 45.
31. D. H. Lawrence, *Studies in Classic American Literature*, 152.
32. D. H. Lawrence, 153.
33. Knapp, *Literary Modernism*, 20.
34. Watten writes, "it is a provocative question to ask, but it must be asked, whether there is an automobile in Ezra Pound's *Cantos*. There are wandering buses and at least a jeep or two, but no cars" (*Constructivist Moment*, 139).
35. On *Ballet Mécanique*, see Pound, "Workshop Orchestration."
36. Pound, *Machine Art*, 72.
37. Pound, 73–74.
38. Pound, 80.
39. Pound, 76.
40. Stein, *Autobiography*, 152.
41. Stein, *Lectures in America*, 177.

42. Watten, *Constructivist Moment*, 119.
43. Meadowsong, "Auto-biography."
44. Stein, *Autobiography*, 173.
45. Stein, *Useful Knowledge*, 78.
46. Stein, *Geography and Plays*, 392. On Stein's car poems for the *AFFW Bulletin*, see Fouirnaies, "'We Go.'"
47. Watten, *Constructivist Moment*, 123.
48. Williams, *Embodiment of Knowledge*, 63.
49. Moore, *Reader*, 220-22.
50. See Seiler, *Republic of Drivers*, 52-54.
51. Seiler, 51.
52. Seiler, 48.
53. Sheller, *Mobility Justice*, 51.
54. Cummings, *Poems*, 246.
55. Giucci, *Cultural Life*, 171.
56. See chapter 2 of Brigham's *American Road Narratives*, chapter 4 of Seiler's *Republic of Drivers*, Bay's *Traveling Black*, and Sorin's *Driving While Black*.
57. Seiler, *Republic of Drivers*, 133-34.
58. Sorin, *Driving While Black*, 262.
59. Ellison, "Cadillac Flambé," 449.
60. Qtd. in Clarke, *Driving Women*, 44.
61. Burns, *Unforgivable*.
62. Gilroy, "Driving While Black," 99.
63. Sorin, *Driving While Black*, 272; Levin, "US Police."
64. Rankine, *Just Us*, 33. Subsequent quotations from this work will be cited parenthetically in the text as *JU*.
65. Packer, *Mobility*, 211.
66. Brigham, *American Road Narratives*, 8.
67. Sheller, *Mobility Justice*, 1.
68. Myles, *Chelsea Girls*, 184. Subsequent quotations from this work will be cited parenthetically in the text as *CG*.
69. Coleman, *Wicked Enchantment*, 16.
70. Coleman, 16.
71. Coleman, 16.
72. Comer, "Revising," 362.
73. See Mickelson, *City Poems*, 85-91, for a reading of Coleman's stories and poems in terms of urban crisis and mobility.
74. Yau, "Wanda Coleman."
75. Coleman, *Wicked Enchantment*, 16.
76. Coleman, 16.

77. LeMenager, *Living Oil*, 6.
78. Ghosh, "Petrofiction," 30. See also Kate Marshall's critique of Ghosh's more recent demand for novels about climate change, in *Novels by Aliens*, 5–9.
79. Yaeger, "Literature," 306. It is worth noting that Fredric Jameson warns, in *The Political Unconscious*, of "the sterility of such classificatory procedures, which may always, it seems to me, be taken as symptoms and indices of the repression of a more genuinely dialectical or historical practice of cultural analysis" (79). Yaeger speaks to this difficulty in her piece's sole footnote.
80. Szeman, "Literature and Energy Futures," 324.
81. LeMenager, *Living Oil*, 80.
82. The critique of reading for a textual unconscious was perhaps made most strongly by Stephen Best and Laura Marcus in their introduction to the special issue of *Representations* that they edited on "Surface Reading."
83. Sedgwick, *Touching Feeling*, 130. Szeman meets this critique head-on in his chapter "Towards a Critical Theory of Energy," where he writes that "energy is not just another topic to animate the kind of critical paranoia challenged by Eve Kosofsky Sedgwick, which depends 'on an infinite reservoir of naïveté in those who make up the audience for these unveilings.' In truth, what the emergence of energy in the field of the human sciences demands is not just a slight amelioration of critical vocabularies, a nip-and-tuck addition of energy to the discourses we already have, but a *wholesale refashioning of these vocabularies and their presumed objects of study*" (29). Rather than reckon with the critical limits of paranoid reading, Szeman doubles down here, in effect asking us to become even more paranoid given the gravity of his object of study.
84. Ronda, *Remainders*, 6.
85. Seymour, *Bad Environmentalism*, 7.
86. Mendelson, *W. H. Auden*, 197.
87. For a helpful overview of the development of ecopoetics scholarship, see Keller, *Recomposing Ecopoetics*, 9–19.
88. Schuster, *Ecology of Modernism*, 168.
89. Ross, *Fast Cars*, 19.
90. Unrau, "'Tend the rusted steel,'" 21. I prefer this multivalent definition of petropoetics from Unrau's dissertation to the one that she provides in her subsequent book, where "petropoetics denies the significance of energy intimacy" (*Rough Poets*, 9).
91. Ronda and Bagdanov, "Energy Ecopoetics," 261.
92. For more scholarship on Canadian petropoetics, see Rauscher, "Canadian Petro-Poetics," as well as the special issue of *Canadian Literature* on "Poetry and Extraction" (2022), edited by Karpinski and Unrau.
93. Keller, *Recomposing Ecopoetics*, 24.

94. Keller, 24.
95. Irmscher, "'Sharing with the Ants,'" 380.
96. Rubenstein and Neuman, *Modernism*, 54.
97. Bishop, *Poems*, 125; Rubenstein and Neuman, *Modernism*, 55.
98. Lowell, *Collected Poems*, 378.
99. Lowell, 377.
100. On Lowell's whiteness, see Javadizadeh, "Atlantic Ocean." For a more detailed and sympathetic reading of "For the Union Dead," which also considers its critique of automobility, see LeMahieu, "Robert Lowell."
101. Ladd, *Autophobia*, 4.
102. Snyder, *Turtle Island*, 95.
103. Snyder, 103.
104. M. Davidson, *San Francisco*, 109–10.
105. Snyder, *Turtle Island*, 77; M. Davidson, *San Francisco*, 110.
106. Ronda, *Remainders*, 67–69. I also agree with Timothy Gray, who has shown how Snyder's book, rather than being hectoring, relies on humor and nuance for its success. See Gray, *Gary Snyder*, 281.
107. Snyder, *Danger on Peaks*, 32.
108. Snyder, *Turtle Island*, 63.

1. WILLIAM CARLOS WILLIAMS DRIVES A "HOT LITTLE BABY"

1. Mariani, *William Carlos Williams*, 98, 104; Williams appears to misdate the acquisition of his first car to 1911 in *Autobiography of William Carlos Williams*, 127. Along with Mariani, Williams's son Eric also dates Williams's acquisition of his Ford to several years later (Eric Williams, "Cars," 1).
2. On the discrepancies in Williams's memory regarding the Armory show, see Mariani, *William Carlos Williams*, 785–786n100.
3. Williams, *Paterson*, 211.
4. Flink, *Automobile Age*, 216–20.
5. Scholars have made conflicting assessments of the arc of Williams's poetic career in relation to technology. Cecelia Tichi argues, "Williams never abandoned his poetics of kinetics and efficiency. He became, on the contrary, increasingly explicit about machines made of words in the decades following the 1920s" (*Shifting Gears*, 287). By contrast, Perloff contends that his later "poems turn their back on the very principles that made Williams a central figure in twentieth-century poetics," and she suggests that he retreated from imagist principles due, in part, to the increasing dominance of mass-media

images (*Radical Artifice,* 58). Documenting this stylistic shift, Henry M. Sayre observes that "the aesthetics of the machine" are "finally antagonistic to at least a part of his sensibility" ("American Vernacular," 328).
6. Williams, *Collected Poems,* 2:62–63. Subsequent quotations from this work will be cited parenthetically in the text as *CP II.*
7. Flink, *Automobile Age,* 28.
8. Seiler, *Republic of Drivers,* 43.
9. Eric Williams, "Cars," 1.
10. Seiler, *Republic of Drivers,* 45.
11. Williams, *Autobiography,* 307–8.
12. Mariani, *William Carlos Williams,* 183.
13. Seiler, *Republic of Drivers,* 36.
14. Seiler, 36–37.
15. Wells, *Car Country,* 174–75.
16. Flink, *Automobile Age,* 188.
17. LeMenager, *Living Oil,* 69.
18. Schuster, *Ecology of Modernism,* 162.
19. Williams, *Collected Poems,* 1:264. Subsequent quotations from this work will be cited parenthetically in the text as *CP I.*
20. Duffy, *Speed Handbook,* 140.
21. Duffy attends to how "the apparently mundane act of looking either from the vantage point of a moving car or out of a car window became in the early twentieth century a characteristic gesture of a radical reevaluation of human looking aided by technology" (161). This crucial insight into the relationship between looking and driving is at the heart of my own reading of Williams's modernist breakthrough.
22. LeMenager, *Living Oil,* 73.
23. In Rogers, *Voices and Visions.* Perloff first elaborated this assessment in *The Poetics of Indeterminacy: Rimbaud to Cage* (1981), where she writes of *Paterson*: "The poet who began by saying that 'The word must be put down for itself, not as a symbol of nature but a part, cognizant of the whole,' who praised Gertrude Stein 'for her formal insistence on words in their literal, structural quality of being words,' has now turned, whether unwittingly or with the caution that may have come with age, to what is for him the alien rhetoric of Symbolism" (149–50).
24. DuPlessis, *Genders, Races,* 33.
25. Kinnahan, *Poetics of the Feminine,* 65.
26. Williams, "Belly Music," 63.
27. Williams, 63.
28. Adorno, *Aesthetic Theory,* 33. On Williams's anxiety about the relationship between technology and culture, see Steinman, *Made in America.*

29. In Rainey, Poggi, and Wittman, *Futurism,* 50.
30. In Rainey, Poggi, and Wittman, 51.
31. In Rainey, Poggi, and Wittman, 53.
32. For an incisive reading of "Romance Moderne," which places the futurists' misogyny and the end of Williams's poem alongside Mina Loy's contemporary feminist satire of futurism, see Kinnahan, *Poetics of the Feminine,* 58–63.
33. Halter, "Visual Arts," 43.
34. Williams, *Imaginations,* 159–60. Subsequent quotations from this work will be cited parenthetically in the text as *I*.
35. Siraganian, *Modernism's Other Work,* 104.
36. Williams, *I Wanted to Write,* 39.
37. Ngai, *Our Aesthetic Categories,* 60.
38. Ngai, 97.
39. In his *Autobiography,* Williams writes of *The Waste Land:* "I felt at once that it had set me back twenty years, and I'm sure it did. Critically Eliot returned us to the classroom just at the moment when I felt that we were on the point of an escape to matters much closer to the essence of a new art form itself—rooted in the locality which should give it fruit. I knew at once that in certain ways I was most defeated" (174). On Williams's nativism, see Michaels, *Our America,* 72–85.
40. Miki, "Driving and Writing," 114.
41. T. Hugh Crawford, *Modernism,* 89.
42. See Eliot, "Tradition and the Individual Talent."
43. Chatlos, "Automobility and Lyric Poetry," 150.
44. McCabe, *Cinematic Modernism,* 128.
45. Williams, *CP I,* 222; O'Hara, *Collected Poems,* 257. Subsequent quotations from this work will be cited parenthetically in the text as *CP*.
46. Altieri, *Art of Twentieth-Century,* 11.
47. Williams, "Five Dollar Guy," 19. Subsequent quotations from this work will be cited parenthetically in the text as *FDG*.
48. Mariani, *William Carlos Williams,* 254–55.
49. Mariani, 270, 297.
50. See Watts, *People's Tycoon,* 444–62.
51. See Kennedy, *Freedom from Fear,* 308–15.
52. For an incisive discussion of how Greenfield "renders the past incoherent" (159), see Smith, *Making the Modern,* 144–55.
53. Perloff shows how some of the prose in the book describes "what is evidently [seen from] the window of the poet's moving car" (*Poetics of Indeterminacy,* 146), though there is no explicit first-person driver there.
54. "View of a Lake" has been overlooked by critics in much the same way that the three ragged children in it look intently away from automobility. For

example, Mariani claims that Williams "knew that the images in a poem like 'View of a Lake' were nearly random lens shots, chance images thrown off at odd moments and not serious attacks on the structure of the poem" (*William Carlos Williams*, 368). And although Lawrence Buell has lauded Williams as a poet of an "unofficial countryside" of abandoned industrial places where nature has reasserted itself, he nevertheless considers this poem a mere "five-finger exercise compared to *Paterson*" (*Writing for an Endangered World*, 112).
55. In "Politics of Description" Robert von Hallberg has shown how description, rather than ideological grandstanding, was its own kind of inclusive politics for Williams in the 1930s, an inclusivity that was already apparent in *The Descent of Winter*.
56. DuPlessis, *Pink Guitar*, 63.
57. Williams, *I Wanted to Write*, 95.
58. DuPlessis, *Pink Guitar*, 63.
59. Steven, *Red Modernism*, 130.
60. See Raine, "Modernism, Eco-Anxiety."
61. The tension between maternity and automobility that is central to Williams's early writing can also be found in other work from the period, most notably perhaps Diego Rivera's Detroit Industry Murals (1932–33), where a child enclosed in the ground like a seed is shown to be the generative origin of Ford's assembly line. These murals have a striking synergy with Frida Kahlo's focus on maternity in her paintings; she suffered a miscarriage while in Detroit with her husband (see Smith, *Making the Modern*). John Steinbeck's *The Grapes of Wrath* (1939) is another example of road literature that foregrounds maternity, not least in its startling final scene.
62. Williams, qtd. in Dennison, "Childbirth Metaphor," 229. Dennison's article explores the significance of the maternity metaphor in *Paterson*.
63. Bloch, "Alice Notley's Descent," 9. See also her discussion of Notley's lecture in chapter 4 of *Lyric Trade*.

2. FRANK O'HARA CRASHES CHARLES OLSON'S CAR

1. Alworth, *Site Reading*, 78–79.
2. See Terranova, *Automotive Prosthetic*, 51–55.
3. Flink, *Automobile Age*, 359.
4. Flink, 372.
5. Bonneuil and Fressoz, *Shock of the Anthropocene*, 164.

6. For an expansive account of cultural engagements with car crashes, see Vidal, *Death and Desire.*
7. Epstein, *Beautiful Enemies,* 88.
8. Berman, *All That Is Solid,* 329.
9. Berman, 320.
10. In thinking about the relationship between pedestrianism and automobility, I have been influenced by Jennifer Wenzel's nuanced discussion of it in her chapter "Between Petro-Magic and the Pedestrian; or, Thinking Progress Backward" from her unpublished manuscript, "Beyond the Fossil-Fueled Imagination: How (and Why) to Read for Energy."
11. Olson, *Collected Prose,* 241. Subsequent quotations from this work will be cited parenthetically in the text as *Prose.*
12. Rifkin, *Career Moves,* 52.
13. DuPlessis, "Manifests."
14. M. Davidson, *Guys Like Us,* 33–34.
15. Horkheimer and Adorno, *Dialectic of Enlightenment,* xii.
16. Byers, *Charles Olson,* 58.
17. Seiler, *Republic of Drivers,* 78–79.
18. See Olson, "The Post Office," in *Collected Prose,* 217–236. See also Duncan, "Frank O'Hara Drives," 81–88.
19. DuPlessis, *Purple Passages,* 116.
20. DuPlessis, 112. Despite the exclusions of "Projective Verse," Joseph Pizza has shown how Olson and Creeley made an analogy between the role of breath in their poetics and in jazz, especially bebop (*Dissonant Voices,* 23–56). Pizza also makes clear how African American poets, including those in the Black Arts Movement, made use of "Projective Verse" in both their "typographic practices" and "performance styles" (3). Female poets and critics such as Rachel Blau DuPlessis, Susan Howe, and Kathleen Fraser also put "Projective Verse" to their own uses, while critiquing its masculinist ethos. See Fraser, *Translating the Unspeakable,* 174–200 and O'Connor, "Renovating the Open Field."
21. Fredman, "Contemporaries," 181.
22. Olson, *Collected Poems,* 386. Subsequent quotations from this work will be cited parenthetically in the text as *Poems.*
23. Olson's poem anticipates Kenneth Anger's groundbreaking homoerotic short film *Scorpio Rising* (1964). One of the motorcyclists featured in the film has a shrine to James Dean in his bedroom and models himself on the dead actor, a connection Anger accentuates by splicing in footage of Dean. Dean died the year before Olson wrote "The Lordly and Isolate Satyrs," and so it is plausible that Olson's poem is responding to the masculine bravado, angst, and mortality embodied in the cult of Dean.

24. See DuPlessis, *Purple Passages*, 112–13, for an extended discussion of father imagery in "The Lordly and Isolate Satyrs"; and Hickman, "Death in Life," 211, for an extended discussion of the mother imagery in "As the Dead Prey upon Us."
25. Compare to "Letter 22" of *The Maximus Poems*, where the poet is having "Trouble / with the car" (100).
26. "Capital is dead labour which, vampire-like, lives only by sucking living labour, and lives the more, the more labour it sucks" (Marx, *Capital*, 342).
27. Olson, *Maximus Poems*, 14, 6.
28. In the earlier version of the poem published in Allen's anthology, the deer is taken into "the kitchen," further suggesting its subordinate status (*New American Poetry*, 28).
29. It is noteworthy that in his long poem "Second Avenue," O'Hara also exoticizes Black people as "blue," yet in more laudatory terms: "Blue negroes on the verge of a true foreignness / escape nevertheless the chromaticism of occidental death / by traffic" (*CP*, 141).
30. On clocks in modernist literature, see Tung, "Clocks."
31. For comparisons of Olson and O'Hara, see Belgrad, *Culture of Spontaneity*, 254; Epstein, *Beautiful Enemies*, 79; Perloff, *Frank O'Hara*, 16; Silverberg, *New York School*, 47–48.
32. Adorno, *Aesthetic Theory*, 34.
33. In Schneiderman, *'this pertains to me,'* 14.
34. Gooch, *City Poet*, 302.
35. Olson, *Maximus Poems*, 14–15.
36. Paul Blackburn furthers this topos in his poem "Shoeshine Boy" (1963), which links the time signal to the subway, Wall Street, and pretty girls (Huttner, "'Possibility of Song'").
37. Herd, "Stepping Out," 83–84.
38. I first published this argument in 2016 in "Frank O'Hara Drives Charles Olson's Car" without knowledge of Berkson's notes, which were published three years later.
39. Berkson, *Notebook*, 183.
40. Berkson, 252.
41. O'Hara, "Interview with Frank O'Hara," 17.
42. Blasing, *Politics and Form*, 12.
43. Gooch, *City Poet*, 21.
44. Gooch, 113.
45. Gooch, 143. See Hal Fondren's full recollection in Calhoun, *Also a Poet*, 54–58.
46. Gooch, *City Poet*, 189–90.
47. Gooch, 190.

48. See Berman, *All That Is Solid*, 290-312.
49. O'Hara, *Poems Retrieved*, 226; Gooch, *City Poet*, 241-46.
50. O'Hara, *Poems Retrieved*, 119.
51. O'Hara, 119.
52. O'Hara, 120.
53. Translated by Rossetti in his *Poems*, 279.
54. Vidal, *Death and Desire*, 82.
55. Gooch, *City Poet*, 269.
56. Morin, "Case of James Dean," 10.
57. Richard Howard, qtd. in Gooch, *City Poet*, 316.
58. Riley, *Whitman, Melville, Crane*, 173-78.
59. Bernes, *Work of Art*, 25.
60. Lee, *Poetics of Emergence*, 29.
61. Glavey, "Having a Coke," 1003.
62. Adorno, *Aesthetic Theory*, 21.
63. Clune, *American Literature*, 64.
64. See Nielsen, *Reading Race*, 155-57; and Stoneley, "O'Hara, Blackness."
65. N. R. Lawrence, "Frank O'Hara," 99.
66. See Lehman, *Last Avant-Garde*, 193-95, for a full account of the incident.
67. In considering O'Hara's "Ode: Salute to the French Negro Poets," N. R. Lawrence asks, "if, in Paul Celan's formulation, there may be no fundamental difference between a poem and a handshake, what is the nature of this particular grasping of hands, and what lines do they reach across—racial, national, linguistic, sexual?" (86). This handshake will return in my discussion of Claudia Rankine.
68. Epstein, *Beautiful Enemies*, 201.
69. In a scathing reading of this poem's racial politics, Aldon Lynn Nielsen writes that "part of the terror of 'Personal Poem' is our understanding that the very placid surface offered to the 8,000,000 is in part underwritten by authority's battery of Miles Davis" (*Writing Between the Lines*, 225). Much as Billie Holiday's death lays the ground for "The Day Lady Died," Davis's bruised body lies under "Personal Poem."
70. For a discussion of O'Hara's cruising for Black men in the cinema, see Jack Parlett's chapter "Frank O'Hara's Moving Pictures," *Poetics of Cruising*, 119-50.
71. See Goble, "'Our Country's Black and White Past.'"
72. Komunyakaa, *Everyday Mojo Songs of Earth*, 97.
73. Benjamin Friedlander has shown how the gruesome murder of an African American mess cook on New Guinea, when O'Hara was stationed there during World War II, had traumatic resonances throughout his poetry ("Strange Fruit").

74. On the connection between lynching and white Americans' "wildly distorted fear of interracial sex," see the Equal Justice Initiative's report *Lynching in America*.
75. In 2017 the film was presented at Harvard University's Woodbury Poetry Room by John Ashbery's biographer, Karin Roffman, who had unearthed *Presenting Jane* a few years earlier: https://www.youtube.com/watch?v=F9VXLK1uJRs.
76. Qtd. in Roffman, *Songs We Know Best*, 206.
77. Roffman, 210.
78. Ashbery and Schuyler, *Nest of Ninnies*, 9.
79. Kane, "Whimsy."
80. Bowman, "Horsepower" 5.
81. Bowman, 4.
82. Shukin, *Animal Capital*, 101.
83. O'Hara also appears fascinated with horses in poems such as "Naptha," "Having a Coke with You," and "In Memory of My Feelings."
84. O'Hara, Letter to Larry Rivers.
85. Friedlander, "Strange Fruit," 129.
86. Lytle Shaw shows how "O'Hara could enter into a paradoxically public discourse from a position often misunderstood as private" (*Frank O'Hara*, 6). Consider also Baraka's statement that in contrast to Kenneth Koch and Kenward Elmslie, "Frank at least had a political sense" (qtd. in Gooch, *City Poet*, 425). For a discussion of O'Hara's racial politics, see also Gooch, 424–27.
87. O'Hara, Letter to Joan Mitchell.
88. See King, *Papers*, 417n2.
89. Qtd. in Kane, *We Saw the Light*, 95.
90. Brossard, "*Last Clean Shirt*."
91. Adorno, "Is Art Lighthearted?," 251.
92. Stoneley, "O'Hara, Blackness," 511.
93. Leslie, "Octopussarian Drugstore Cowboy."
94. Kane, *We Saw the Light*, 98.
95. Kane, 97.
96. Kane, 108.
97. Donald Allen notes that "Fabian" was only added to the poem after O'Hara crossed out "Eddie Fisher," who was the most successful pop singles artist of the first half of the 1950s and also had his own TV show (*CP*, 548). For other readings of this poem, see Perlow, *Poem Electric*, 156–59; and Parlett, *Poetics of Cruising*, 146–48.

3. DRIVING THROUGH CATASTROPHE WITH EILEEN MYLES

1. See Daggett, "Petro-Masculinity."
2. While I refer to the biographical Eileen Myles using *they/them* pronouns throughout this chapter, I stay true to the text of *Chelsea Girls* in referring to the character Eileen Myles with *she/her* pronouns when discussing that book. I also gender "the poet" speaker differently in Myles's poems, depending on context and chronology. For a discussion of the genders of Eileen Myles, see Rosa Campbell, my, and Jack Parlett's "Eileen Myles Now," 867–68.
3. Myles, "My Boy's Red Hat," 177.
4. Anderson, "Shiny Collisions," 925.
5. In McMullen, *Rambling*.
6. Myles, "Oath."
7. Stryker, *Transgender History*, 1; Myles's conception of trans is also in accord with Jack Halberstam's, for whom the term signifies "a politics of transivity" that "puts pressure on all modes of gendered embodiment and refuses to choose between the identitarian and contingent forms of trans identity" (*Trans**, xiii).
8. Ensor, "Ecopoetics of Contact," 152.
9. Morton, "Guest Column: Queer Ecology," 274.
10. See Seymour, *Strange Natures*.
11. Freed-Thall, *Modernism at the Beach*, 5.
12. In employing the phrase "transfeminist petropoetics," I am following Hume and Rahimtoola's call to elaborate a trans poetics, although I am aware of the inherent limitations of doing so as a cis man. For an overview of the burgeoning field of trans poetics, see Peterson, "Trans Poetry."
13. Seymour, "Trans Ecology."
14. Myles and Nelson, "Eileen Myles in Conversation," 895.
15. Myles, *Importance of Being Iceland*, 44.
16. Myles, *School of Fish*, 92. Subsequent quotations from this work will be cited parenthetically in the text as *SoF*.
17. Chisholm, *Queer Constellations*, 43.
18. Chisholm, 117.
19. Myles, "Painted Clear, Painted Black."
20. Myles, email to Joel Duncan, May 2, 2021.
21. Cvetkovich, *Archive of Feelings*, 33.
22. Myles, *Importance of Being Iceland*, 44.
23. In contrast to Sal Paradise, Eileen Myles is alone in the back of the truck. For an insightful discussion of the contrast between male homosocial bonding in

On the Road and female independence in Joan Didion's road novel *Play It as It Lays* (1970), see Alworth, *Site Reading*, 86–91.
24. Myles, *Importance of Being Iceland*, 44.
25. Sheller, *Mobility Justice*, 49.
26. Myles, *Not Me*, 132–33. Subsequent quotations from this work will be cited parenthetically in the text as *NM*.
27. Myles has stated, "when I was a kid more than anything in the world I wanted to be an astronaut" (*Skies*, 212).
28. Myles, *I Must Be Living Twice*, 156.
29. Myles, 157–58.
30. Myles, 158.
31. Myles, 163.
32. On Myles's survival of the housing crisis and the AIDS pandemic in this poem, see Knittle, "'Unruly Vernacular Riverfront,'" 427.
33. For an insightful analysis of Myles's problematic figuration of this exclusion, see Parlett, *Poetics of Cruising*, 12–15.
34. Myles, *I Must Be Living Twice*, 168.
35. Myles, *Inferno*, 259.
36. See Kraus, *I Love Dick*, 134.
37. Bussey-Chamberlain, *Queer Troublemakers*, 119.
38. For another, more detailed description of menstruation, see Myles, *Cool for You*, 87–89.
39. Myles, "Eileen Myles: The Art of Poetry."
40. Myles, "Interview with Eileen Myles," 189.
41. Myles, *Importance of Being Iceland*, 271.
42. See also Myles's driving poem "Uppity" in *Skies*, 95.
43. Myles has also become a climate activist, most prominently in protesting the destruction of their beloved East River Park on the Lower East Side of Manhattan. See Holman, "Class, Crisis"; and Knittle, "'Unruly Vernacular Riverfront'."
44. Myles, *Snowflake / different streets*, 84. This is a reference to the *different streets* section of this work. All subsequent quotations will refer to the *Snowflake* section and will be cited parenthetically in the text as *S*.
45. See Perlow, *Poem Electric*, 206–23.
46. Myles, *Afterglow*, 55.
47. Myles, email to Joel Duncan, March 3, 2021.
48. LeMenager, *Living Oil*, 76.
49. Myles also has earlier camera poems that—as Maggie Nelson has shown—posit their "speaker as a camera and the poem itself as a snapshot or collection of snapshots" (*Women*, 197).
50. The gun in "#8 Car Camera" can usefully be compared to the gun in "Road Buddy" from *Skies*, 189–90.

51. Ian C. Davidson, "Mobilities of Form," 554.
52. In McMullen, *Rambling*.
53. Myles, "'She was dying.'" Myles posted a driving photo to their Instagram account on March 2, 2021, that illustrates the tension between intentionality and flow that "#8 Car Camera" turns into poetry (Myles, "Already leaving"). It is a blurry photo taken while leaving their second home, in Marfa, Texas, at dusk, reminiscent of how "#8" ends with "the light blue but as we know / darkening sky." In the photo, light from the dotted streetlights extends and blurs into that of the setting sun, while also reflecting across the windshield and the hood of the car. It is as if the car is part of a directionality determined by light and, by extension, the taking of the photo itself, rather than the other way around. These lights carrying the car forward down the slim road echo, furthermore, Myles's short lines stretching down the page. As they write of their poetic line in "The Lesbian Poet," "The flickering lights of the fading lines re-erupting one quarter inch down, unpredictable, rude" (*SoF*, 126). Scrolling though Myles's Instagram feed, many of their photos are blurry or taken from strange angles and are in this way "unpredictable." Such photos perform their occasional nature, thereby becoming—like Myles's poetry—part of a larger experience of flow. A flow where the camera or cellphone, like the poet in their car, is literally a dot on a digital map.
54. Campbell, "So-Called New York School," 160.
55. Morton, *Hyperobjects*, 58.
56. Morton, *Dark Ecology*, 8.
57. Morton, "Guest Column: Queer Ecology," 279.
58. Ngai, *Our Aesthetic Categories*, 97.
59. Ensor, "Ecopoetics of Contact," 152.
60. See Kane, *Do You Have a Band?*, 188–90.
61. Myles, *For Now*, 43. Subsequent quotations from this work will be cited parenthetically in the text as *FN*.
62. Myles's poetry also appears in the feminist Californian driving movie *Grandma* (2015) starring Lily Tomlin, whom Myles solicited for material for *dodgems* decades earlier. See Anderson, "Shiny Collisions," 931–34.
63. Myles, "Never Real, Always True," 25.
64. Myles, "December 16."
65. See Horkley, "Double Bill."
66. Myles, *a "Working Life,"* 29.
67. Rose, "Stuart Hall," 51.
68. Steinbock, *Shimmering Images*, 17.
69. Myles, email to Joel Duncan, March 2, 2021.

4. NOT DRIVING WHILE BLACK WITH CLAUDIA RANKINE

1. Franz, "'Open Road,'" 133.
2. Stodghill, "Black Behind the Wheel."
3. Eisen-Martin, *Heaven Is All Goodbyes*, 34. Subsequent quotations from this work will be cited parenthetically in the text as *H*.
4. Gilroy, "Driving While Black," 90.
5. I am here invoking Walter Benjamin's famous formulation of the truly historical image as "dialectics at a standstill" (*Arcades Project*, 463). *Just Us* is also concerned with mobility justice, largely in relation to airplane travel.
6. Gilroy, *Darker than Blue*, 27.
7. Ramazani, *Poetry of Mourning*, xii.
8. Livingston and Ross, *Cars and Jails*, 8.
9. Coates, *We Were Eight Years*, 341.
10. Sugrue, "Driving While Black."
11. Clegg and Usmani, "Economic Origins."
12. Livingston and Ross, *Cars and Jails*, 38.
13. Freud, "Mourning and Melancholia," 243.
14. Rankine, "Claudia Rankine on Blackness."
15. Rankine, "Condition of Black Life," 33.
16. See Cvetkovich, *Depression*, 115–53.
17. Hübinette and Lundström, "Three Phases of Hegemonic Whiteness," 431–33.
18. Rankine, *Don't Let Me Be Lonely*, 23.
19. Nealon, *Matter of Capital*, 148.
20. Nealon, 149.
21. Rankine, *Don't Let Me Be Lonely*, 130.
22. Sharpe, *In the Wake*, 19.
23. Sharpe, 19.
24. Sharpe, 22.
25. Gibson, "Joyriding," 5.
26. Sharpe, *Ordinary Notes*, 32–36.
27. Winters, *Hope Draped in Black*, 16.
28. Margo Natalie Crawford, "Melancholy," 804.
29. Gallagher, "Didactic," 52.
30. Windell, "Citizenship in *Citizen*."
31. Jackson, "Lyric," 833. For a prominent defense of lyric poetry, see Culler's *Theory of the Lyric*.
32. Javadizadeh, "Atlantic Ocean," 483.
33. Reed, *Freedom Time*, 108.

34. Hume, "Toward an Antiracist Ecopoetics," 105.
35. Rankine, "Making of *Citizen.*"
36. Rankine, "Claudia Rankine" [Berlant interview].
37. Benjamin, *Arcades Project,* 522.
38. Qtd. in Rankine, "Claudia Rankine" [Berlant interview].
39. Rankine, *Citizen,* 10. Subsequent quotations from this work will be cited parenthetically in the text as *C.*
40. See also Winters, *Hope Draped in Black,* 23.
41. My use of inertia is informed by Jennifer Wenzel's "attention to the inertia that automobility produces *in the form of mobility*" ("Foreword," 23, footnote; emphasis added).
42. Bennett, "Being Private in Public," 378.
43. See Nyberg, "Homing Change."
44. Benjamin, *Selected Writings,* 402.
45. Rankine, "Making of *Citizen.*"
46. Warren, "Rankine's Elite Status."
47. Whitman, *Poetry and Prose,* 30.
48. Gallagher, "Didactic," 60. There are more pessimistic readings of these blossoms as signaling "complicity and surrender" (Rashid, "Lucille Clifton's," 74), where "loss is so overwhelming to the speaker that she becomes incapable of uttering, or claiming, a place and home for herself" (Hume, "Antiracist Ecopoetics," 99).
49. Whitman, *Poetry and Prose,* 460.
50. See my discussion of this event in "Review of *Whitman Noir.*"
51. Rankine, "Claudia Rankine on Blackness."
52. Coates, *Between the World and Me,* 75. Subsequent quotations from this work will be cited parenthetically in the text as *BWM.*
53. For a critique of Coates and Black Lives Matter for not fully taking account of the implications of class, see Clegg, "Black Representation."
54. See Clegg and Usami, "Economic Origins."
55. Coates, *We Were Eight Years,* 163–208.
56. Dove, *On the Bus,* 77.
57. McIvor, *Mourning in America,* 167.
58. See Benjamin, *Illuminations,* 249.
59. Skillman, "Lyric Reading Revisited," 439.
60. Rankine, *Nothing in Nature,* 11.
61. On the didacticism of *Citizen,* see Gallagher, "Didactic."

CODA

1. In Candace Williams, "Gutting the Sonnet."
2. Jericho Brown, *Tradition,* 72.
3. J. Brown, 72.
4. J. Brown, 18.
5. J. Brown, 72.
6. J. Brown, 10.
7. Vértiz, *Auto/Body,* 9.
8. Vértiz, 9.
9. Vértiz, 72.
10. Vértiz, 55.
11. Vértiz, 55.
12. Vértiz, 63.

WORKS CITED

Adorno, Theodor W. *Aesthetic Theory*. Translated by Robert Hullot-Kentor. University of Minnesota Press, 1997.
Adorno, Theodor W. "Is Art Lighthearted?" In *Notes to Literature*. Vol. 2. Edited by Rolf Tiedemann. Translated by Shierry Weber Nicholsen. Columbia University Press, 1992.
Allen, Donald, ed. *The New American Poetry: 1945–1960*. 1960. University of California Press, 1999.
Altieri, Charles F. *The Art of Twentieth-Century American Poetry: Modernism and After*. Blackwell, 2006.
Altieri, Charles F. "The Unsure Egoist: Robert Creeley and the Theme of Nothingness." *Contemporary Literature* 13, no. 2 (1972): 162–85.
Alworth, David J. *Site Reading: Fiction, Art, Social Form*. Princeton University Press, 2016.
Anderson, Stephanie. "Shiny Collisions: Editing as Serious Humor in *dodgems*." *Women's Studies* 51, no. 8 (2022): 925–44.
Anger, Kenneth, dir. *Scorpio Rising*. 1964.
Ashbery, John, and James Schuyler. *A Nest of Ninnies*. 1969. Carcanet Press, 1987.
Baker, R. C. "The Octopussarian Drugstore Cowboy," interview by Alfred Leslie. *The Village Voice,* November 16, 2004. https://www.villagevoice.com/2004/11/16/the-octopussarian-drugstore-cowboy/.
Baldwin, James. *Collected Essays*. Library of America, 1998.
Ballard, J. G. "The Future of the Car." *Drive,* no. 19 (1971): 102–9.
Barndt, Susan McWilliams. *The American Road Trip and American Political Thought*. Lexington, 2018.
Bay, Mia. *Traveling Black: A Story of Race and Resistance*. Belknap Press, 2021.
Belgrad, Daniel. *The Culture of Spontaneity: Improvisation and the Arts in Postwar America*. University of Chicago Press, 1998.
Benjamin, Walter. *The Arcades Project*. Translated by Howard Eiland and Kevin McLaughlin. Belknap Press, 1999.
Benjamin, Walter. *Illuminations*. Edited by Hannah Arendt, translated by Harry Zorn. Bodley Head, 2015.

Benjamin, Walter. *Selected Writings.* Vol. 4, *1938–1940,* edited by Howard Eiland and Michael W. Jennings. Belknap Press, 2003.

Bennett, Chad. "Being Private in Public: Claudia Rankine and John Lucas's 'Situation' Videos." *ASAP/Journal* 4, no. 2 (2019): 377–401.

Berkson, Bill. *A Frank O'Hara Notebook.* No Place Press, 2019.

Berlant, Lauren. *Cruel Optimism.* Duke University Press, 2011.

Berman, Marshall. *All That Is Solid Melts into Air: The Experience of Modernity.* Verso, 1983.

Bernes, Jasper. *The Work of Art in the Age of Deindustrialization.* Stanford University Press, 2017.

Best, Stephen, and Laura Marcus. "Surface Reading: An Introduction." *Representations* 108, no. 1 (2009): 1–21.

Bishop, Elizabeth. *Poems.* Farrar, Straus and Giroux, 2011.

Blasing, Mutlu Konuk. *Politics and Form in Postmodern Poetry: O'Hara, Bishop, Ashbery, and Merrill.* Cambridge University Press, 1995.

Bloch, Julia. "Alice Notley's Descent: Modernist Genealogies and Gendered Literary Inheritance." *Journal of Modern Literature* 35, no. 3 (2012): 1–24.

Bloch, Julia. *Lyric Trade: Reading the Subject in the Postwar Long Poem.* University of Iowa Press, 2024.

Bonneuil, Christophe, and Jean-Baptiste Fressoz. *The Shock of the Anthropocene: The Earth, History, and Us.* Translated by David Fernbach. 2013. Verso, 2017.

Boruch, Marianne. "Poets in Cars." *Massachusetts Review* 43, no. 4 (2002–2003): 521–40.

Bowman, Daniel. "Horsepower: Animals in Automotive Culture, 1895–1935." PhD diss., University of Sheffield, 2022.

Brigham, Ann. *American Road Narratives: Reimagining Mobility in Literature and Film.* University of Virginia Press, 2015.

Brossard, Olivier. "*The Last Clean Shirt:* A film by Alfred Leslie and Frank O'Hara." *Jacket2,* no. 23 (2003). http://jacketmagazine.com/23/bross-ohara.html.

Brown, Jericho. *The Tradition.* Picador, 2019.

Brown, Kurt, ed. *Drive, They Said: Poems About Americans and Their Cars.* Milkweed, 1994.

Brown, Stephen N. "Modernity and the Pleasures of Automobility in Middle-Class Poetry of the American West, 1910–1935." *Studies in Travel Writing* 17, no. 2 (2013): 160–73.

Buell, Frederick. "A Short History of Oil Cultures; or, The Marriage of Catastrophe and Exuberance." In *Oil Culture,* edited by Ross Barrett and Daniel Worden, 69–108. University of Minnesota Press, 2014.

Buell, Lawrence. *Writing for an Endangered World: Literature, Culture, and Environment in the U.S. and Beyond.* Belknap Press, 2001.

Burckhardt, Rudy, dir. *The Automotive Story.* Cittadura, 1954.

Burns, Ken, dir. *Unforgivable Blackness: The Rise and Fall of Jack Johnson.* PBS, 2004.

Bussey-Chamberlain, Prudence. *Queer Troublemakers: The Poetics of Flippancy.* Bloomsbury Academic, 2019.

Byers, Mark. *Charles Olson and American Modernism: The Practice of the Self.* Oxford University Press, 2018.

Calhoun, Ada. *Also a Poet: Frank O'Hara, My Father, and Me.* Grove Press, 2022.

Campbell, Rosa. "The So-Called New York School: A Feminist (Re)Vision in Six Poets." PhD diss., University of St Andrews, 2020.

Campbell, Rosa, Joel Duncan, and Jack Parlett. "Eileen Myles Now." *Women's Studies* 51, no. 8 (2022): 859-74.

Casey, Rogen N. *Textual Vehicles: The Automobile in American Literature.* Garland, 1997.

Cecire, Natalia. *Experimental: American Literature and the Aesthetics of Knowledge.* Johns Hopkins University Press, 2019.

Chatlos, Jon. "Automobility and Lyric Poetry: The Mobile Gaze in William Carlos Williams's 'The Right of Way.'" *Journal of Modern Literature* 30, no. 1 (2006): 140-54.

Chisholm, Dianne. *Queer Constellations: Subcultural Space in the Wake of the City.* University of Minnesota Press, 2005.

Clarke, Deborah. *Driving Women: Fiction and Automobile Culture in Twentieth-Century America.* Johns Hopkins University Press, 2007.

Clegg, John. "Black Representation After Ferguson." *Brooklyn Rail,* May 2016. https://brooklynrail.org/2016/05/field-notes/black-representation-after-ferguson.

Clegg, John, and Adaner Usmani. "The Economic Origins of Mass Incarceration." *Catalyst* 3, no. 3 (2019). catalyst-journal.com/vol3/no3/the-economic-origins-of-mass-incarceration.

Clune, Michael W. *American Literature and the Free Market, 1945-2000.* Cambridge University Press, 2010.

Coates, Ta-Nehisi. *Between the World and Me.* Spiegel and Grau, 2015.

Coates, Ta-Nehisi. *We Were Eight Years in Power.* Penguin, 2017.

Coleman, Wanda. *Wicked Enchantment: Selected Poems.* Penguin, 2020.

Comer, Krista. "Revising Western Criticism Through Wanda Coleman." *Western American Literature* 33, no. 4 (1999): 356-83.

Crawford, Margo Natalie. "The Twenty-First-Century Black Studies Turn to Melancholy." *American Literary History* 29, no. 4 (2017): 799-807.

Crawford, T. Hugh. *Modernism, Medicine, and William Carlos Williams.* University of Oklahoma Press, 1993.

Creeley, Robert. *The Collected Poems of Robert Creeley: 1945-1975.* University of California Press, 1982.

Culler, Jonathan. *Theory of the Lyric.* Harvard University Press, 2017.

Cummings, E. E. *Complete Poems: 1904–1962,* edited by George J. Firmage. Liveright, 1994.

Cvetkovich, Ann. *An Archive of Feelings: Trauma, Sexuality, and Lesbian Public Cultures.* Duke University Press, 2003.

Cvetkovich, Ann. *Depression: A Public Feeling.* Duke University Press, 2012.

Daggett, Cara. "Petro-Masculinity: Fossil Fuels and Authoritarian Desire." *Millenium: Journal of International Studies* 47, no. 1 (2018): 25–44.

Davidson, Ian C. "Mobilities of Form." *Mobilities* 12, no. 4 (2017): 548–58.

Davidson, Michael. *Guys Like Us: Citing Masculinity in Cold War Poetics.* University of Chicago Press, 2004.

Davidson, Michael. *The San Francisco Renaissance: Poetics and Community at Mid-Century.* Cambridge University Press, 1989.

Denning, Michael. *The Cultural Front: The Laboring of American Culture in the Twentieth Century.* 1997. Verso, 2010.

Dennison, Julia. "Williams and H. D. Figure It Out: Reconceiving the Childbirth Metaphor in 'His' *Paterson* and 'Her' *Trilogy.*" *Paideuma: Modern and Contemporary Poetry and Poetics* 33, nos. 2–3 (2004): 223–45.

Dettelbach, Cynthia Golomb. *In the Driver's Seat: The Automobile in American Literature and Popular Culture.* Greenwood Press, 1976.

Doctorow, E. L. *Ragtime.* 1975. Random House, 2007.

Dove, Rita. *On the Bus with Rosa Parks: Poems.* W. W. Norton & Company, 1999.

Duffy, Enda. *The Speed Handbook: Velocity, Pleasure, Modernism.* Duke University Press, 2009.

Duncan, Joel. "Frank O'Hara Drives Charles Olson's Car." *Arizona Quarterly: A Journal of American Literature, Culture, and Theory* 72, no. 4 (2016): 77–103.

Duncan, Joel. Review of *Whitman Noir: Black American and the Good Gray Poet.* Edited by Ivy G. Wilson. *Walt Whitman Quarterly Review* 32, no. 1 (2014): 83–86.

DuPlessis, Rachel Blau. *Genders, Races, and Religious Cultures in Modern American Poetry, 1908–1934.* Cambridge University Press, 2001.

DuPlessis, Rachel Blau. "Manifests." *Diacritics* 26, nos. 3–4 (1996): 31–53.

DuPlessis, Rachel Blau. *The Pink Guitar: Writing as Feminist Practice.* Routledge, 1990.

DuPlessis, Rachel Blau. *Purple Passages: Pound, Eliot, Zukofsky, Olson, Creeley and the Ends of Patriarchal Poetry.* University of Iowa Press, 2012.

Eisen-Martin, Tongo. *Heaven Is All Goodbyes.* City Lights Books, 2017.

Eliot, T. S. "Tradition and the Individual Talent." 1919. In *Selected Prose of T. S. Eliot,* edited by Frank Kermode. Harcourt Brace Jovanovich, 1975.

Ellison, Ralph. "Cadillac Flambé." *Callaloo* 24, no. 2 (2001): 442–53.

Ensor, Sarah. "The Ecopoetics of Contact: Touching, Cruising, Gleaning." *ISLE: Interdisciplinary Studies in Literature and Environment* 25, no. 1 (2018): 150–68.

Epstein, Andrew. *Beautiful Enemies: Friendship and Postwar American Poetry.* Oxford University Press, 2006.

Equal Justice Initiative. *Lynching in America: Confronting the Legacy of Racial Terror.* 3rd ed. 2017. https://lynchinginamerica.eji.org/report/.

Flink, James. *The Automobile Age.* MIT Press, 1988.

Fouirnaies, Christine. "'We Go': Gertrude Stein's Automobilism and WWI Writing." *Modernism/modernity* 31, no. 3 (2024): 447–68.

Franz, Kathleen. "'The Open Road': Automobility and Racial Uplift in the Interwar Years." In *Technology and the African-American Experience: Needs and Opportunities for Study,* edited by Bruce Sinclair. MIT Press, 2004.

Fraser, Kathleen. *Translating the Unspeakable: Poetry and the Innovative Necessity.* University of Alabama Press, 2000.

Fredman, Stephen. "The Contemporaries: A Reading of Charles Olson's 'The Lordly and Isolate Satyrs.'" In *Contemporary Olson,* edited by David Herd. Manchester University Press, 2015.

Freed-Thall, Hannah. *Modernism at the Beach: Queer Ecologies and the Coastal Commons.* Columbia University Press, 2023.

Freud, Sigmund. "Mourning and Melancholia." In *The Standard Edition of the Complete Psychological Works of Sigmund Freud.* Vol. 14, *1914–1916,* edited and translated by James Strachey, Anna Freud, Alix Strachey and Alan Tyson. Hogarth Press, 1957.

Friedlander, Benjamin. "Strange Fruit: O'Hara, Race and the Color Line." In *The Scene of My Selves: New Work on New York School Poets,* edited by Terence Diggory and Stephen Paul Miller. National Poetry Foundation, 2001.

Gallagher, Maureen. "The Didactic and Elegiac Modes of Claudia Rankine's *Citizen: An American Lyric.*" In *Revisiting the Elegy in the Black Lives Matter Era,* edited by Tiffany Austin, Sequoia Maner, Emily Ruth Rutter, and darlene anita scott. Routledge, 2020.

Ghosh, Amitav. "Petrofiction: The Oil Encounter and the Novel." *New Republic,* March 2, 1992, 29–34.

Gibson, Helen. "Joyriding Across the Color Line: Automotivity and Citizenship in the United States, 1895–1939." PhD diss., Freie Universität Berlin, 2021.

Gilroy, Paul. *Darker than Blue: On the Moral Economies of Black Atlantic Culture.* Belknap, 2010.

Gilroy, Paul. "Driving While Black." In Miller, *Car Cultures,* 81–104.

Giucci, Guillermo. *The Cultural Life of the Automobile: Roads to Modernity.* Translated by Anne Mayagoitia and Debra Nagao. University of Texas Press, 2012.

Glavey, Brian. "Having a Coke with You Is Even More Fun than Ideology Critique." *PMLA* 134, no. 5 (2019): 996–1011.

Goble, Mark. "'Our Country's Black and White Past': Film and the Figures of History in Frank O'Hara." *American Literature* 71, no. 1 (1999): 57–92.

Goldstein, Laurence. *Poetry Los Angeles: Reading the Essential Poems of the City.* University of Michigan Press, 2014.

Gooch, Brad. *City Poet: The Life and Times of Frank O'Hara.* Alfred A. Knopf, 1994.

Gray, Timothy. *Gary Snyder and the Pacific Rim: Creating Counter-Cultural Community.* University of Iowa Press, 2006.

Griffiths, Matthew. *The New Poetics of Climate Change: Modernist Aesthetics for a Warming World.* Bloomsbury Academic, 2017.

Halberstam, Jack. *Trans*: A Quick and Quirky Account of Gender Variability.* University of California Press, 2018.

Halter, Peter. "Williams and the Visual Arts." In *Cambridge Companion to William Carlos Williams,* edited by Christopher Macgowan. Cambridge University Press, 2016.

Harvey, David. *The Condition of Postmodernity: An Inquiry into the Origins of Cultural Change.* Blackwell, 1990.

Herd, David. "Stepping Out with Frank O'Hara." In *Frank O'Hara Now: New Essays on the New York Poet,* edited by Robert Hampson and Will Montgomery. Liverpool University Press, 2010.

Hickman, Ben. "Death in Life: The Past in 'As the Dead Prey Upon Us.'" In *Contemporary Olson,* edited by David Herd. Manchester University Press, 2015.

Holman, Matthew. "Class, Crisis, and the Commons in Eileen Myles's Late Work." *Women's Studies* 51, no. 8 (2022): 965–82.

The Honeyman. *Brother Bill (The Last Clean Shirt).* Red Bird, 1964.

Horkheimer, Max, and Theodor W. Adorno. *Dialectic of Enlightenment: Philosophical Fragments.* Edited by Gunzelin Schmid Noerr. Translated by Edmund Jephcott. Stanford University Press, 2002.

Horkley, Elizabeth. "The Double Bill as Dialogue: On Eileen Myles's 'The Trip' and Ivan Dixon's 'The Spook Who Sat by the Door.'" *Los Angeles Review of Books,* November 20, 2019. https://lareviewofbooks.org/article/the-double-bill-as-dialogue-on-eileen-myless-the-trip-and-ivan-dixons-the-spook-who-sat-by-the-door/.

Huber, Matthew T. *Lifeblood: Oil, Freedom, and the Forces of Capital.* University of Minnesota Press, 2013.

Hübinette, Tobias, and Catrin Lundström. "Three Phases of Hegemonic Whiteness: Understanding Racial Temporalities in Sweden." *Social Identities: Journal for the Study of Race, Nation and Culture* 20, no. 6 (2014): 423–37.

Hume, Angela. "Toward an Antiracist Ecopoetics: Waste and Wasting in the Poetry of Claudia Rankine." *Contemporary Literature* 57, no. 1 (2016): 79–110.

Hume, Angela, and Samia Rahimtoola. "Introduction: Queering Ecopoetics." *ISLE: Interdisciplinary Studies in Literature and Environment* 25, no. 1 (2018): 134–49.

Huttner, Tobias. "'The Possibility of Song': Paul Blackburn's Longue Durée Poetics of the Quotidian." Paper presented at Annual Meeting of the American Comparative Literature Association. Seattle, WA, March 28, 2015.

Irmscher, Christoph. "'Sharing with the Ants': American Ecopoetry from Lydia Sigourney to Ross Gay." In *A Companion to American Poetry*, edited by Mary McAleer Balkun, Jeffrey Gray, and Paul Jaussen. John Wiley & Sons, 2022.

Jackson, Virginia. "Lyric." In *The Princeton Encyclopedia of Poetry and Poetics*, edited by Ronald Greene, Stephen Cushman, Clare Cavanagh, Jahan Ramazani and Paul Rouzer, 826–34. Princeton University Press, 2012.

Jameson, Fredric. *The Political Unconscious: Narrative as a Socially Symbolic Act*. 1981. Routledge, 2002.

Jarmusch, Jim, dir. *Paterson*. Amazon Studios; Bleecker Street, 2016.

Javadizadeh, Kamran. "The Atlantic Ocean Breaking on Our Heads: Claudia Rankine, Robert Lowell, and the Whiteness of the Lyric Subject." *PMLA* 134, no. 3 (2019): 475–90.

Kane, Daniel. *Do You Have a Band? Poetry and Punk Rock in New York City*. New York: Columbia University Press, 2017.

Kane, Daniel. *We Saw the Light: Conversations Between the New American Cinema and Poetry*. University of Iowa Press, 2009.

Kane, Daniel. "Whimsy, the Avant-Garde and Rudy Burckhardt's and Kenneth Koch's *The Apple*." *World Picture*, no. 9, 2014.

Karpinski, Max, and Melanie Dennis Unrau, eds. "Poetics and Extraction." Special issue, *Canadian Literature*, no. 251 (2022).

Keller, Lynn. *Recomposing Ecopoetics: North American Poetry of the Self-Conscious Anthropocene*. University of Virginia Press, 2017.

Kennedy, David M. *Freedom from Fear: The American People in Depression and War, 1929–1945*. Oxford University Press, 1999.

Kerouac, Jack. *On the Road*. 1957. Penguin, 2016.

King, Martin Luther, Jr. *The Papers of Martin Luther King Jr.* Vol. 1, *Called to Serve: January 1929—June 1951*, edited by Clayborne Carson, Ralph Luker, and Penny A. Russell. University of California Press, 1992.

Kinnahan, Linda A. *Poetics of the Feminine: Authority and Literary Tradition in William Carlos Williams, Mina Loy, Denise Levertov, and Kathleen Fraser*. Cambridge University Press, 1994.

Knapp, James. *Literary Modernism and the Transformation of Work*. Northwestern University Press, 1988.

Knittle, Davy. "'Unruly Vernacular Riverfront': Eileen Myles's Queer Persistence in the Changing Climate of New York." *PMLA* 139, no. 3 (2024): 420–37.

Komunyakaa, Yusef. *Everyday Mojo Songs of Earth: New and Selected Poems, 2001–2021*. Farrar, Straus, and Giroux, 2021.

Kraus, Chris. *I Love Dick*. 1997. Serpent's Tale, 2016.

Lackey, Kris. *RoadFrames: The American Highway Narrative*. University of Nebraska Press, 1997.

Lacy, Suzanne. *Car Renovations.* 1972. http://suzannelacy.com/car-renovations/.
Ladd, Brian. *Autophobia: Love and Hate in the Automobile Age.* University of Chicago Press, 2008.
Latouche, John, dir. *Presenting Jane.* 1952.
Lawrence, D. H. *Studies in Classic American Literature.* Edited by Ezra Greenspan, Lindeth Vasey and John Worthen. Cambridge University Press, 2003.
Lawrence, N. R. "Frank O'Hara in New York Race Relations, Poetic Situations, Postcolonial Space." *Comparative American Studies: An International Journal* 4, no. 1 (2006): 85–103.
Lee, Benjamin. *Poetics of Emergence: Affect and History in Postwar Experimental Poetry.* University of Iowa Press, 2020.
Lehman, David. *The Last Avant-Garde: The Making of the New York School of Poets.* Doubleday, 1998.
LeMahieu, Michael. "Robert Lowell, Perpetual War, and the Legacy of Civil War Elegy." *College Literature* 43, no. 1 (2016): 91–120.
LeMenager, Stephanie. *Living Oil: Petroleum Culture in the American Century.* Oxford University Press, 2014.
Leslie, Alfred, dir. *The Last Clean Shirt.* 1964.
Levin, Sam. "US Police Have Killed Nearly 600 People in Traffic Stops Since 2017, Data Shows." *The Guardian,* April 21, 2022. https://www.theguardian.com/us-news/2022/apr/21/us-police-violence-traffic-stop-data.
Lewis, David L., and Laurence Goldstein, eds. *The Automobile and American Culture.* University of Michigan Press, 1983.
Lewis, Sinclair. *Free Air.* 1919. Dover Publications, 2018.
Link, Stefan J. *Forging Global Fordism: Nazi Germany, Soviet Russia, and the Contest over the Industrial Order.* Princeton University Press, 2020.
Livingston, Julie, and Andrew Ross. *Cars and Jails: Freedom Dreams, Debt and Carcerality.* OR Books, 2022.
Lowell, Robert. *Collected Poems.* Edited by Frank Bidart and David Gewanter. Farrar, Straus and Giroux, 2003.
Malm, Andreas, and Zetkin Collective. *White Skin, Black Fuel: On the Danger of Fossil Fascism.* Verso, 2021.
Mariani, Paul L. *William Carlos Williams: A New World Naked.* McGraw-Hill, 1981.
Marshall, Kate. *Novels by Aliens: Weird Tales and the Twenty-First Century.* University of Chicago Press, 2023.
Marx, Karl. *Capital: A Critique of Political Economy.* Vol. 1. Translated by Ben Fowkes. Penguin Books, 1976.
McCabe, Susan. *Cinematic Modernism: Modernist Poetry and Film.* Cambridge University Press, 2005.
McIvor, David W. *Mourning in America: Race and the Politics of Loss.* Cornell University Press, 2016.

McMullen, Chelsea, dir. "Rambling: Eileen Myles." *YouTube*, uploaded by NOWNESS, June 19, 2018. www.youtube.com/watch?v=u_no9pjee-M.

Meadowsong, Zena. "The Auto-Biography of Alice B. Toklas: Gertrude Stein and the Model T." Paper presented at Confluence and Division: The 16th Annual Conference of the Modernist Studies Association. Pittsburgh, PA, November 9, 2014.

Mendelson, Edward, ed. *W. H. Auden: Collected Poems*. Faber and Faber, 1976.

Michaels, Walter Benn. *Our America: Nativism, Modernism, and Pluralism*. Duke University Press, 1995.

Mickelson, Nate. *City Poems and American Urban Crisis: 1945 to the Present*. Bloomsbury Academic, 2019.

Miki, Roy. "Driving and Writing." In *William Carlos Williams: Man and Poet*, edited by Carroll F. Terrell. National Poetry Foundation, 1983.

Miller, Daniel, ed. *Car Cultures*. 2001. New York: Routledge, 2020.

Mills, Katie. *The Road Story and the Rebel: Moving Through Film, Fiction, and Television*. Southern Illinois University Press, 2006.

Mom, Gijs. *Atlantic Automobilism: Emergence and Persistence of the Car, 1895–1940*. Berghahn, 2015.

Mom, Gijs. *Globalizing Automobilism: Exuberance and Emergence of Layered Mobility, 1900–1980*. Berghahn, 2020.

Moore, Marianne. *A Marianne Moore Reader*. Viking Press, 1961.

Morin, Edgar. "The Case of James Dean." *Evergreen Review* 2, no. 5 (1958): 5–12.

Morton, Timothy. *Dark Ecology: For a Logic of Future Coexistence*. Columbia University Press, 2016.

Morton, Timothy. *Ecology Without Nature: Rethinking Environmental Aesthetics*. Harvard University Press, 2007.

Morton, Timothy. "Guest Column: Queer Ecology." *PMLA* 125, no. 2 (2010): 273–82.

Morton, Timothy. *Hyperobjects: Philosophy and Ecology After the End of the World*. University of Minnesota Press, 2013.

Myles, Eileen. *Afterglow (A Dog Memoir)*. Grove Press, 2017.

Myles, Eileen. "Already leaving." Instagram, March 2, 2021, https://www.instagram.com/p/CL5fmQ4lxkO/?hl=en.

Myles, Eileen. *Chelsea Girls: A Novel*. 1994. Ecco, 2015.

Myles, Eileen. *Cool for You: A Novel*. 2000. Soft Skull Press, 2017.

Myles, Eileen. "December 16." *Gulf Coast: A Journal of Literature and Fine Arts* 33, no. 1 (2021). https://gulfcoastmag.org/journal/33.1-winter/spring-2021/4-poems-myles/.

Myles, Eileen. "Eileen Myles: The Art of Poetry, No. 99." Interview by Ben Lerner. *Paris Review*, no. 214 (Fall 2015). https://www.theparisreview.org/interviews/6401/the-art-of-poetry-no-99-eileen-myles.

Myles, Eileen. Email to Joel Duncan. March 3, 2021.

Myles, Eileen. Email to Joel Duncan. May 2, 2021.

Myles, Eileen. *For Now.* Yale University Press, 2020.

Myles, Eileen. *The Importance of Being Iceland: Travel Essays in Art.* Semiotext(e), 2009.

Myles, Eileen. *I Must Be Living Twice: New and Selected Poems, 1975–2014.* Ecco, 2015.

Myles, Eileen. *Inferno: A Poet's Novel.* OR Books, 2010.

Myles, Eileen. "Interview with Eileen Myles." Interview by Morgan Parker. *The Literary Review* 57, no. 4 (Fall 2014): 178–93.

Myles, Eileen. *Maxfield Parrish: Early and New Poems.* Black Sparrow Press, 1995.

Myles, Eileen. "My Boy's Red Hat." In *Troubling the Line: Trans and Genderqueer Poetry and Poetics,* edited by TC Tolbert and Trace Peterson, 176–77. Nightboat Books, 2013.

Myles, Eileen. "Never Real, Always True: An Interview with Eileen Myles." Interview by Frances Richard. *Provincetown Arts,* no. 15 (2000–2001): 24–29.

Myles, Eileen. *Not Me.* Semiotext(e), 1991.

Myles, Eileen. "Oath." *Paris Review,* October 13, 2020. https://www.theparisreview.org/blog/2020/10/13/oath/.

Myles, Eileen. "Painted Clear, Painted Black." *Evening Will Come: A Monthly Journal of Poetics,* no. 29 (2013). https://www.thevolta-org.zulaufdesign.com/ewc29-emyles-p1.html.

Myles, Eileen, ed. *Pathetic Literature.* Grove Press, 2022.

Myles, Eileen. *School of Fish.* Black Sparrow Press, 1997.

Myles, Eileen. "'She was dying and I was there. I just started writing': Eileen Myles." Interview by Kaveh Akbar. *Divedapper,* January 20, 2015. https://www.divedapper.com/interview/eileen-myles/.

Myles, Eileen. *Skies.* Black Sparrow Press, 2001.

Myles, Eileen. *Snowflake / different streets.* Wave Books, 2012.

Myles, Eileen, dir. *The Trip.* Produced, shot, and edited by David Fenster. May 15, 2019. https://youtu.be/omcdaUy6JfE.

Myles, Eileen. *a "Working Life."* Grove Press, 2023.

Myles, Eileen, and Maggie Nelson. "Eileen Myles in Conversation with Maggie Nelson." *Women's Studies* 51, no. 8 (2022): 880–98.

Nealon, Christopher. *The Matter of Capital: Poetry and Crisis in the American Century.* Harvard University Press, 2011.

Nelson, Maggie. *Women, the New York School, and Other True Abstractions.* University of Iowa Press, 2007.

Ngai, Sianne. *Our Aesthetic Categories: Zany, Cute, Interesting.* Harvard University Press, 2012.

Nielsen, Aldon Lynn. *Reading Race: White American Poets and the Racial Discourse in the Twentieth Century.* University of Georgia Press, 1988.

Nielsen, Aldon Lynn. *Writing Between the Lines: Race and Intertextuality.* University of Georgia Press, 1994.

Notley, Alice. *Doctor Williams's Heiresses.* Tuumba Press, 1980.

Nyberg, Ferdinand. "Homing Change: Soul City as Re-Filiation." In *Un-Mapping the Global South,* edited by Gero Bauer, Nicole Hirschfelder, and Fernando Resende. Routledge, 2023.

O'Connor, Wanda. "Renovating the Open Field: Innovative Women Poets Reclaiming an Erasure History." In *The Cambridge Companion to American Poetry and Poetics Since 1990,* edited by Daniel Morris. Cambridge University Press, 2023.

O'Hara, Frank. *The Collected Poems of Frank O'Hara,* edited by Donald Allen. 1971. University of California Press, 1995.

O'Hara, Frank. "An Interview with Frank O'Hara." Interview by Edward Lucie-Smith. In *Standing Still and Walking in New York,* edited by Donald Allen. Grey Fox Press, 1975.

O'Hara, Frank. Letter to Joan Mitchell. August 28–29, 1963. Allen Collection of Frank O'Hara Letters, University of Connecticut Library.

O'Hara, Frank. Letter to Larry Rivers. July 21, 1963. Allen Collection of Frank O'Hara Letters, University of Connecticut Library.

O'Hara, Frank. *Lunch Poems.* City Lights Books, 1964.

O'Hara, Frank. *Poems Retrieved.* Edited by Donald Allen. Grey Fox Press, 1977.

Oldenburg, Claes. "I Am for an Art." In *100 Artists' Manifestos: From the Futurists to the Stuckists,* edited by Alex Danchev. Penguin, 2021.

Olson, Charles. *Collected Prose.* Edited by Donald Allen and Benjamin Friedlander. University of California Press, 1997.

Olson, Charles. *The Collected Poems of Charles Olson: Excluding the "Maximus" Poems.* Edited by George F. Butterick. University of California Press, 1987.

Olson, Charles. *The Maximus Poems.* Edited by George F. Butterick. University of California Press, 1983.

Packer, Jeremy. *Mobility Without Mayhem: Safety, Cars, and Citizenship.* Duke University Press, 2008.

Paes de Barros, Deborah. *Fast Cars and Bad Girls: Nomadic Women's Road Stories.* Peter Lang, 2004.

Parlett, Jack. *The Poetics of Cruising: Queer Visual Culture from Whitman to Grindr.* University of Minnesota Press, 2022.

Pearce, Lynne. *Drivetime: Literary Excursions in Automotive Consciousness.* Edinburgh University Press, 2016.

Perloff, Marjorie. *Frank O'Hara: Poet Among Painters.* University of Chicago Press, 1998.

Perloff, Marjorie. *The Poetics of Indeterminacy: Rimbaud to Cage.* Princeton University Press, 1981.

Perloff, Marjorie. *Radical Artifice: Writing Poetry in the Age of Media.* University of Chicago Press, 1994.

Perlow, Seth. *The Poem Electric: Technology and the American Lyric.* University of Minnesota Press, 2018.

Peterson, Tracy. "Trans Poetry and Poetics." In *A Companion to American Poetry,* edited by Mary McAleer Balkun, Jeffrey Gray, and Paul Jaussen. John Wiley & Sons, 2022.

Pizza, Joseph. *Dissonant Voices: Race, Jazz, and Innovative Poetics in Midcentury America.* University of Iowa Press, 2023.

Pound, Ezra. *Machine Art and Other Writings: The Lost Thought of the Italian Years.* Edited by Maria Luisa Ardizzone. Duke University Press, 1996.

Pound, Ezra. "Workshop Orchestration." *New Masses* 2, no. 5 (1927): 21.

Primeau, Ronald, ed. *Critical Insights: American Road Literature.* Salem Press, 2013.

Primeau, Ronald. *Romance of the Road: The Literature of the American Highway.* Bowling Green State University Popular Press, 1996.

Raine, Anne. "Modernism, Eco-Anxiety, and the Climate Crisis." *Modernism / Modernity Print Plus* 4, no. 3, November 21, 2019.

Rainey, Lawrence, Christina Poggi, and Laura Wittman, eds. *Futurism: An Anthology.* Yale University Press, 2009.

Ramazani, Jahan. *Poetry of Mourning: The Modern Elegy from Hardy to Heaney.* University of Chicago Press, 1994.

Rankine, Claudia. *Citizen: An American Lyric.* Graywolf Press, 2014.

Rankine, Claudia. "Claudia Rankine." Interview by Lauren Berlant. *Bomb,* October 1, 2014. bombmagazine.org/articles/claudia-rankine/.

Rankine, Claudia. "Claudia Rankine: How Can I Say This so We Can Stay in This Car Together." Interview by Krista Tippett. *On Being,* January 10, 2019. https://onbeing.org/programs/claudia-rankine-how-can-i-say-this-so-we-can-stay-in-this-car-together-jan2019/.

Rankine, Claudia. "Claudia Rankine on Blackness as the Second Person." Interview with Meara Sharma. *Guernica,* November 17, 2014. https://www.guernicamag.com/blackness-as-the-second-person/.

Rankine, Claudia. "The Condition of Black Life Is One of Mourning." In *Rebellious Mourning: The Collective Work of Grief,* edited by Cindy Milstein. AK Press, 2017.

Rankine, Claudia. *Don't Let Me Be Lonely: An American Lyric.* Graywolf Press, 2004.

Rankine, Claudia. *Just Us: An American Conversation.* Graywolf Press, 2020.

Rankine, Claudia. "The Making of *Citizen.*" Talk by Rankine. *YouTube,* uploaded by Harvard University, May 4, 2015. https://www.youtube.com/watch?v=8RyIFX9OG54&themeRefresh=1.

Rankine, Claudia. *Nothing in Nature Is Private.* Cleveland Poetry Center at Cleveland State University, 1994.

Rashid, Anne M. "Lucille Clifton's and Claudia Rankine's Elegiac Poetics of Nature." In *Revisiting the Elegy in the Black Lives Matter Era,* edited by Tiffany Austin, Sequoia Maner, Emily Ruth Rutter, and darlene anita scott. Routledge, 2020.

Rauscher, Judith. "Canadian Petro-Poetics: Masculinity, Labor, and Environment in Mathew Henderson's *The Lease.*" In *Energy in Literature: Essays on Energy and Its Social and Environmental Implications in Twentieth and Twenty-First Century Literary Texts,* edited by Paula Anca Farca. TrueHeart Academic Press, 2014.

Reed, Anthony. *Freedom Time: The Poetics and Politics of Black Experimental Writing.* Johns Hopkins University Press, 2014.

Rifkin, Libbie. *Career Moves: Olson, Creeley, Zukofsky, Berrigan, and the American Avant-Garde.* University of Wisconsin Press, 2000.

Riley, Peter. *Whitman, Melville, Crane, and the Labors of American Poetry.* Oxford: Oxford University Press, 2019.

Roffman, Karin. *The Songs We Know Best: John Ashbery's Early Life.* Farrar, Straus and Giroux, 2017.

Rogers, Richard P. *Voices and Visions: William Carlos Williams.* PBS, 1988. www.learner.org/series/voices-visions/william-carlos-williams/.

Ronda, Margaret. *Remainders: American Poetry at Nature's End.* Stanford University Press, 2018.

Ronda, Margaret, and Kristin George Bagdanov. "Energy Ecopoetics." In *The Routledge Companion to Ecopoetics,* edited by Julia Fiedorczuk, Mary Newell, Bernard Quetchenbach, and Orchid Tierney. Routledge, 2024.

Ronda, Margaret, and Lindsay Turner. "Introduction: Poetry's Social Forms," *Post45,* April 22, 2019. post45.org/2019/04/introduction-poetrys-social-forms/.

Rose, Jacqueline. "Stuart Hall: The Analyst." *New York Review of Books,* September 21, 2023, 49-51.

Ross, Kristin. *Fast Cars, Clean Bodies: Decolonization and the Reordering of French Culture.* MIT Press, 1995.

Rossetti, Dante Gabriel. *Poems.* Ellis & White, 1881.

Rubenstein, Michael, and Justin Neuman. *Modernism and Its Environments.* Bloomsbury Academic, 2020.

Ruscha, Edward, Mason Williams, and Patrick Blackwell. *Royal Road Test.* Published by the author, 1967.

Rymhs, Deena. *Roads, Mobility, and Violence in Indigenous Literature and Art from North America.* Routledge, 2019.

Sayre, Henry M. "American Vernacular: Objectivism, Precisionism, and the Aesthetics of the Machine." *Twentieth Century Literature* 35, no. 3 (1989): 328-42.

Scharff, Virginia. *Taking the Wheel: Women and the Coming of the Motor Age.* Free Press, 1991.

Schneiderman, Josh, ed. *'this pertains to me which means to me you': The Correspondence of Kenneth Kock and Frank O'Hara. Part 2, 1955-1956.* Lost and Found; The CUNY Poetics Document Initiative, 2009.

Schuster, Joshua. *The Ecology of Modernism: American Environments and Avant-Garde Poetics.* University of Alabama Press, 2015.

Sedgwick, Eve Kosofsky. *Touching Feeling: Affect, Pedagogy, Performativity.* Duke University Press, 2003.

Seiler, Cotten. *Republic of Drivers: A Cultural History of Automobility in America.* University of Chicago Press, 2008.

Seymour, Nicole. *Bad Environmentalism: Irony and Irreverence in the Ecological Age.* University of Minnesota Press, 2018.

Seymour, Nicole. *Strange Natures: Futurity, Empathy, and the Queer Ecological Imagination.* University of Illinois Press, 2013.

Seymour, Nicole. "Trans Ecology and the Transgender Road Narrative." In *Oxford Handbook Topics in Literature.* Oxford Academic, December 16, 2013. https://doi.org/10.1093/oxfordhb/9780199935338.013.152

Sharpe, Christina. *In the Wake: On Blackness and Being.* Duke University Press, 2016.

Sharpe, Christina. *Ordinary Notes.* Daunt Books Originals, 2023.

Shaw, Lytle. *Frank O'Hara: The Poetics of Coterie.* University of Iowa Press, 2006.

Sheller, Mimi. *Mobility Justice: The Politics of Movement in an Age of Extremes.* Verso, 2018.

Shukin, Nicole. *Animal Capital: Rendering Life in Biopolitical Times.* University of Minnesota Press, 2009.

Silliman, Ron. *The Age of Huts (Compleat).* University of California Press, 2007.

Silverberg, Mark. *The New York School Poets and the Neo-Avant-Garde: Between Radical Art and Radical Chic.* 2010. Routledge, 2016.

Siraganian, Lisa. *Modernism's Other Work: The Art Object's Political Life.* Oxford University Press, 2012.

Skillman, Nikki. "Lyric Reading Revisited: Passion, Address, and Form in *Citizen.*" *American Literary History* 31, no. 3 (2019): 419–57.

Slethaug, Gordon E., and Stacilee Ford, eds. *Hit the Road, Jack: Essays on the Culture of the American Road.* McGill-Queen's University Press, 2012.

Smith, Terry. *Making the Modern: Industry, Art, and Design in America.* Chicago University Press, 1993.

Snyder, Gary. *Danger on Peaks: Poems.* Shoemaker & Hoard, 2004.

Snyder, Gary. *Turtle Island.* New Directions, 1974.

Soloway, Joey, creator. *Transparent.* Amazon Studios, 2014–2019.

Soloway, Joey, and Sarah Gubbins, creators. *I Love Dick.* Amazon Studios, 2016–2017.

Song, Min Hyoung. *Climate Lyricism.* Duke University Press, 2022.

Sorin, Gretchen. *Driving While Black: African American Travel and the Road to Civil Rights.* W. Norton & Co., 2020.

Stein, Gertrude. *The Autobiography of Alice B. Toklas.* 1933. New York: Vintage Books, 1990.

Stein, Gertrude. *Bee Time Vine and Other Pieces, 1913–1927.* Vol. 3, *Yale Edition of the Unpublished Writings of Gertrude Stein,* edited by Carl Van Vechten. Books for Libraries Press, 1969.

Stein, Gertrude. *Geography and Plays.* 1922. Haskell House Publishers, 1967.

Stein, Gertrude. *Lectures in America,* 1935. Beacon Press, 1957.

Stein, Gertrude. *Useful Knowledge.* 1928. Station Hill Press, 1988.

Steinbock, Eliza. *Shimmering Images: Trans Cinema, Embodiment, and the Aesthetics of Change.* Duke University Press, 2019.

Steinman, Lisa M. *Made in America: Science, Technology, and American Modernist Poets.* Yale University Press, 1987.

Steven, Mark. *Red Modernism: American Poetry and the Spirit of Communism.* Johns Hopkins University Press, 2017.

Stevens, Wallace. *Letters of Wallace Stevens.* Edited by Holly Stevens. Faber and Faber, 1966.

Stodghill, Ron. "Black Behind the Wheel." *New York Times,* July 14, 2020. https://www.nytimes.com/2020/07/14/travel/Road-Trip-Detroit-Cars-racial-violence.html.

Stoneley, Peter. "O'Hara, Blackness, and the Primitive." *Twentieth Century Literature* 58, no. 3 (2012): 495–514.

Stryker, Susan. *Transgender History: The Roots of Today's Revolution.* Rev. ed. Seal Press, 2017.

Sugrue, Thomas J. "Driving While Black: The Car and Race Relations in Modern America." In *The Automobile in American Life and Society.* Henry Ford Museum and University of Michigan, 2005. www.autolife.umd.umich.edu/Race/R_Casestudy/R_Casestudy5.htm.

Szeman, Imre. "Literature and Energy Futures," *PMLA* 126, no. 2 (2011): 323–25.

Szeman, Imre. "Towards a Critical Theory of Energy." In *Energy Humanities: Current State and Future Directions,* edited by Matúš Mišík and Nada Kujundžić. Springer, 2021.

Terranova, Charissa N. *Automotive Prosthetic: Technological Mediation and the Car in Conceptual Art.* University of Texas Press, 2014.

Tichi, Cecelia. *Shifting Gears: Technology, Literature, Culture in Modernist America.* University of North Carolina Press, 1987.

Tucker-Abramson, Myka. *Cartographies of Empire: The Road Novel and American Hegemony.* Stanford University Press, 2025.

Tung, Charles. "Clocks: Modernist Heterochrony and the Contemporary Big Clock." In *The Edinburgh Companion to Modernism and Technology,* edited by Alex Goody and Ian Whittington, 36–50. Edinburgh University Press, 2022.

Unrau, Melanie Dennis. *The Rough Poets: Reading Oil-Worker Poetry.* McGill-Queen's University Press, 2024.

Unrau, Melanie Dennis. "'Tend the rusted steel like a shepherd': Petropoetics of Oil Work in Canada." PhD diss., University of Manitoba, 2019.

Urry, John. "The 'System' of Automobility." In *Automobilities,* edited by Mike Featherstone, Nigel Thrift, and John Urry. SAGE, 2005.

Vértiz, Vickie. *Auto/Body*. University of Notre Dame Press, 2023.
Vidal, Ricarda. *Death and Desire in Car Crash Culture*. Peter Lang, 2013.
Virilio, Paul. *Negative Horizon: As Essay in Dromoscopy*. 1984. Translated by Michael Degener. Continuum, 2005.
Vogel, Andrew. *Narrating a New Mobility Landscape in the Modern American Road Story, 1893–1921: Ambivalence and Aspiration*. Palgrave Macmillan, 2024.
von Hallberg, Robert. "The Politics of Description: W. C. Williams in the 'Thirties.'" *ELH* 45, no. 1 (1978): 131–51.
Warren, Kenneth W. "Rankine's Elite Status." *Los Angeles Review of Books,* January 7, 2016. v2.lareviewofbooks.org/article/reconsidering-claudia-rankines-citizen-an-american-lyric-a-symposium-part-ii/.
Watten, Barrett. *The Constructivist Moment: From Material Text to Cultural Poetics*. Wesleyan University Press, 2003.
Watts, Steven. *The People's Tycoon: Henry Ford and the American Century*. Vintage Books, 2006.
Wells, Christopher B. *Car Country: An Environmental History*. University of Washington Press, 2012.
Wenzel, Jennifer. "Foreword: Running to Stand Still." In "In Lieu of an Ending: Impasse," special issue, *Soapbox*, no. 3 (2022). https://www.soapboxjournal.net/print-editions/3-0-in-lieu-of-an-ending-impasse.
Whitman, Walt. *Poetry and Prose*. Library of America, 1996.
Williams, Eric. "Cars." *William Carlos Williams Newsletter* 3, no. 2 (1977): 1–5.
Williams, Candace. "Gutting the Sonnet: A Conversation with Jericho Brown." *The Rumpus,* April 1, 2019. https://therumpus.net/2019/04/01/the-rumpus-interview-with-jericho-brown/.
Williams, William Carlos. *The Autobiography of William Carlos Williams*. New Directions, 1967.
Williams, William Carlos. "Belly Music." 1919. "The Early Career of William Carlos Williams: A Critical Facsimile Edition of His Uncollected Prose and Manuscripts," edited by Eric White. *William Carlos Williams Review* 30, nos. 1–2 (2013): 62–69.
Williams, William Carlos. *The Collected Poems of William Carlos Williams*. Vol. 1, *1909–1939,* edited by Walton Litz and Christopher MacGowan. New Directions, 1991.
Williams, William Carlos. *The Collected Poems of William Carlos Williams*. Vol. 2, *1939–1962,* edited by Christopher MacGowan. New Directions, 1991.
Williams, William Carlos. *The Embodiment of Knowledge*. New Directions, 1974.
Williams, William Carlos. "The Five Dollar Guy." *New Masses* 1, no. 1 (1926): 19, 29.
Williams, William Carlos. *Imaginations*. New Directions, 1970.
Williams, William Carlos. *I Wanted to Write a Poem: The Autobiography of the Works of a Poet*. Edited by Edith Heal. New Directions, 1978.

Williams, William Carlos. *Paterson*. Edited by Christopher MacGowan. New Directions, 1992.

Windell, Maria A. "Citizenship in *Citizen*." *Los Angeles Review of Books,* January 6, 2016. v2.lareviewofbooks.org/article/reconsidering-claudia-rankines-citizen-an-american-lyric-a-symposium-part-i/.

Winters, Joseph R. *Hope Draped in Black: Race, Melancholy, and the Agony of Progress.* Duke University Press, 2016.

Wollen, Peter, and Joe Kerr, eds. *Autopia: Cars and Culture.* Reaktion, 2004.

Yaeger, Patricia. "Literature in the Ages of Wood, Tallow, Coal, Whale Oil, Gasoline, Atomic Power, and Other Energy Sources." *PMLA* 126, no. 2 (2011): 305–10.

Yau, John. "Wanda Coleman, the Great Poet of Los Angeles." *Hyperallergic,* May 23, 2020. https://hyperallergic.com/565242/wanda-coleman-the-great-poet-of-los-angeles/.

Yu, Timothy. "Modernist Poetry and Race." In *A History of Modernist Poetry,* edited by Alex Davis and Lee M. Jenkins. Cambridge University Press, 2015.

INDEX

Adorno, Theodor, 35, 63, 68, 78-79, 90; *Aesthetic Theory*, 68, 78-79
aesthetics: machine, 4, 35, 73; of mass automobility, 85; modernist, 55
AFFW Bulletin, 13, 173n46
African Americans: and automobility, 15-16, 133-34, 143-44; James Baldwin, 89, 90, 154, 156; Amiri Baraka, 60, 81, 88, 89, 95, 140, 182n86; Black Lives Matter, 128, 134, 137, 139-40, 143, 159; and cars, 16, 134, 155; Civil Rights Movement, 5, 7, 15, 60, 88-89, 136, 148, 157; and class, 150, 155; and deindustrialization, 138; dream of whiteness, 156, 157-58; driving while Black, 5, 7, 17, 18, 134-35, 137, 154, 159; and immobility, 146, 162; middle-class complicity, 154-55, 187n53; and mobility, 15, 137-38, 145; stopped cars, 5, 135, 136, 146-47, 158, 169; and violence, 17, 135, 138, 139, 150, 158. *See also* Coates, Ta-Nehisi; Coleman, Wanda; Dove, Rita; Rankine, Claudia
AIDS, 106, 113, 184n32
Aira, César, *Ghosts*, 128
Akbar, Kaveh, 120
Allen, Donald, 182n97; *The New American Poetry*, 60, 63, 78, 180n28
Altieri, Charles, 46

Alworth, David J., 58, 171n3
American Automobile Association (AAA), 15
American Dream, 92, 134, 154, 156, 158-59
Anderson, James Craig, 159-60, 161
Anderson, Stephanie, 98
Angel of History (Benjamin), 159
Anger, Kenneth, 179n23
Antheil, George, *Ballet Mécanique*, 11
Apple, The (1967), 85
Ashbery, John, 77, 128, 182n75; *A Nest of Ninnies*, 84-85
assembly line, 6, 8, 12-13, 60, 62, 67, 87, 178n60
Auden, W. H., 21
authenticity: and Myles, 122; and Olson, 59, 60-62, 67, 68, 83, 147; and white male poetics, 5, 58
Auto: On the Edge of Time (1993-94), 114
Automobile Tire Print (1953), 58
automobility: affordable, 8, 19, 28; and African Americans, 15-17, 133-34, 143-44, 157-58; and animals, 67, 86-87, 99, 105, 124; benefits of, 2, 18, 170; contradictions of, 3, 4, 7, 21, 26, 65, 99, 112, 133, 165-67; and economy, 1, 30, 78; and environment, 5, 6, 7, 21, 26, 97, 117-18, 132, 133, 156-57; and fascism, 9;

208 INDEX

automobility (*continued*)
and freedom, 5, 14, 15, 63, 105, 167; and gender, 14–15, 97, 98; and identity, 3, 5–6, 14–19, 122, 124, 159; "I Know a Man" (Creeley), 1–4, 19, 20, 59, 73, 114, 165; and Indigenous Canadian poetry, 172n14; inertia of, 148, 149, 158, 187n41; and masculinity, 2, 5, 8, 9, 14, 15, 18, 41, 63, 100; mass, 4, 5, 13, 14, 20, 23, 29–30, 40, 53–54, 63; and maternity, 31, 55, 178n60; and modernist literature, 4, 9, 10, 30, 49, 51; and music, 11, 67, 96, 117, 151–52; and patriarchy, 5, 128–29, 166; as petroculture, 20; pleasures and thrills, 1, 5, 83, 98; poets' critique of, 3–4, 13, 23, 30, 123, 175n100; privatized, 5, 18–19; and progress, 3, 17, 113, 133–34, 136, 158–59, 163, 167; and self-possession, 28, 38, 59, 65, 67, 72, 103, 117, 118, 120, 131, 132; and social connection, 19, 48, 49, 59, 79, 80, 82, 85, 88; stalled, 52, 53, 54; and status, 5, 28, 41; system of, 6, 144, 169; transfeminist reckoning with, 101, 114; and violence, 4, 15, 33, 34, 93, 105, 160, 162, 165, 166; as white male privilege, 5, 8, 18, 41; and whiteness, 14, 15, 17, 46, 67, 127, 144, 148, 156, 158; and white supremacy, 16, 88, 134–36, 144, 149, 162; and women, 5, 14, 31, 100, 105, 114. *See also* cars; drivers; driving; Fordism; gas stations; mass automobility; mass production; passengers; petropoetics; traffic
Automotive Story, The (1954), 59, 83, 85–88; Marge MacManus (character), 85–88
autopoetics, 171n5

avant-garde: multiracial, 93; O'Hara and, 78, 93; poetics, 104, 123; and Williams, 30, 31, 38, 40, 176n23; writing, 9, 60

Bagdanov, Kristin George, 22
Baker, R. C., 93
Baldwin, James, 89; *The Fire Next Time*, 154, 156; "The White Man's Guilt," 90
Ballard, J. G., 4, 76, 171n8
Baraka, Amiri (LeRoi Jones), 60, 81, 88, 89, 95, 140, 182n86
Baudelaire, Charles, 79
Becker, Jens Peter, 171n5
Benjamin, Walter, 103, 145, 149, 159, 186n5
Bennett, Harry, 49
Berkson, Bill, *A Frank O'Hara Notebook*, 71–72
Berlant, Lauren, 140, 144, 145; *Cruel Optimism*, 138
Berman, Marshall, 4, 59, 79
Bernes, Jasper, 78
Best, Stephen, 174n82
Bishop, Elizabeth, "The Filling Station," 23
Black Americans. *See* African Americans
Black Arts Movement, 179n20
Blackburn, Paul, "Shoeshine Boy," 180n36
Black Lives Matter, 128, 134, 137, 139–40, 143, 159
Black power, 139, 155–56
Blackwell, Patrick, 57
Bland, Sandra, 149
Blasing, Mutlu Konuk, 73
Bloch, Julia, 56, 178n63
Boruch, Marianne, "Poets in Cars," 172n14

Bowman, Daniel, 87
breath: and Creeley, 179n20; and Myles, 115; and O'Hara, 59, 72, 92, 95, 153; and Olson, 59, 61, 62, 64, 72, 95, 153, 166, 167, 179n20; poetics of, 59, 61, 72, 95, 179n20; and Rankine, 152, 162
Brigham, Ann, 3, 4, 15, 17
British Romantics, 21
Brossard, Olivier, 89
"Brother Bill (The Last Clean Shirt)" (song), 92
Brown, Jericho, 5, 167–68; "Duplex," 167; *The Tradition* (book), 167; "The Tradition" (poem), 168
Brown, Mike, 168
Brown, Stephen N., 172n14
Buell, Frederick, "A Short History of Oil Cultures; or, The Marriage of Catastrophe and Exuberance," 127
Buell, Lawrence, 178n54
Burckhardt, Rudy, *The Automotive Story*, 59, 83, 85-88
Bush, George W., 139–40
Bussey-Chamberlain, Prudence, 115
Byers, Mark, 62–63
Byrd, James, Jr., 139, 159

Cage, John, 58
Campbell, Rosa, 104, 120
cars: and American culture, 3, 6, 20, 30, 48, 50, 179n6; and animals, 66–67, 86–87, 105, 123–24; art, 58, 114; *The Automotive Story,* 59, 83, 85–88; breaking into, 161–62; crashes, 2, 6, 9, 33, 37, 38, 59, 60, 72, 73, 76–78, 82, 104, 116, 146, 166; and death, 58, 72, 76, 77, 78, 96; experimental films, 59–60; helped Black Americans escape ghetto, 133, 134, 158; "hot," 11, 40, 51; and killing, 104, 125; ownership, 14, 18, 19, 29, 58, 102, 166; parked, 6, 136, 143, 146–47, 169; poem titles of models, 168; and pollution, 24; production of, 7, 8, 9, 11, 22, 30, 50–51, 58; sitting in, 149, 153–59, 162, 169; as status symbols, 5, 16, 17, 134; stopped, 5, 135, 136, 146–47, 153–54, 158, 169; as symbols of freedom, 59, 134, 158, 160; and women, 15, 35, 45, 150–51; wrecked, 47, 52, 53, 59, 69, 101, 111. *See also* assembly line; automobility
Casper (character in *The Trip*), 127–29, 129, 130
Castile, Philando, 134
Cazalet, Ruth, 88
Cecire, Natalia, 10
Celan, Paul, 81, 140, 181n67
Chatlos, Jon, 43
Chauvin, Derek, 137, 153
Chavis, Benjamin, 149
Chelsea Girls (Myles), 18, 98, 100–105, 113, 114, 126, 183n2; "Madras," 103–4; "Popponesset," 98, 101–3, 111, 116, 131; "Violence Towards Women," 98, 103
Chicago, Judy, 114
Chisholm, Dianne, 103
Citizen: An American Lyric (Rankine), 135, 141–42, 143, 187n61; and mourning, 5, 21, 136–41, 144, 152, 153; and upward mobility, 150
citizenship, 141–42, 153, 158, 163; and street names, 145
Civil Rights Act of 1964, 60
Civil Rights Movement, 5, 7, 15, 60, 88–89, 136, 148, 157. *See also* Black Lives Matter; Black power

climate catastrophe, 18, 23; Ta-Nehisi Coates and, 157; Myles and, 5, 7, 118, 122, 124–25, 132, 184n43; and oil, 118, 121. *See also* petrocultures

Clune, Michael W., 79

Coates, Samori (son of Ta-Nehisi Coates), 154, 157, 158

Coates, Ta-Nehisi: and American Dream of whiteness, 156, 158; and automobility, 136, 153, 156–58, 159; *Between the World and Me*, 136, 153–59; biography, 154; "The Case for Reparations," 155; and climate catastrophe, 157; and Dreamers, 156–57; and ghettos, 157–58; letter to son, 154, 158; and middle-class African American complicity, 154–55; and mourning, 136, 153, 155, 158; own police stop, 154; poetic address, 158; sitting in car, 136, 153, 155–56

Coleman, Wanda, 7, 8, 21, 167, 173n73; *Bathwater Wine*, 19; "I Live for My Car," 18–19; *Imagoes*, 18; "Things No One Knows," 19

Comer, Krista, 19

crashing (car), 2, 6, 9, 19, 58–59, 72, 166; and Myles, 104; and O'Hara, 58–59, 73–74, 78, 79, 167; and Williams, 29, 36–37, 38

Crawford, John, 168

Crawford, Margo Natalie, 141

Creeley, Robert, 1–5, 8, 24, 62; "I Know a Man," 19, 20, 59, 73, 114, 165

Crisis, The (NAACP newsletter), 89

cruising: and Myles, 130; by O'Hara, 79–81, 181n70; by Williams, 34, 50, 109

Cummings, E. E., "XIX: she being Brand," 15

cuteness, 40, 123

Cvetkovich, Ann, 104

Dahlberg, Edward, 62

Davidson, Ian C., 119

Davidson, Michael, 2, 25, 62

Davis, Miles, 81, 181n69

Dean, James, 59, 179n23; O'Hara's elegies for, 73, 76–79, 82, 167, 179n23

death: of animals, 123–24; of Black drivers, 134, 137, 158, 167; of car, 112, 113; and car crashes, 2, 4, 36–37, 58, 72, 167; ecological, 7–8, 21, 125, 136; and the modern, 78–79

de Nagy, Tibor. *See* Tibor de Nagy Gallery

Denning, Michael, 9

Detroit Industry Murals (1932–33), 178n60

Diallo, Amadou, 139

Dickinson, Emily, 55, 72, 140; "After great pain a formal feeling comes," 72

Didion, Joan, *Play It as It Lays*, 184n23

DiPrima, Diane, 95; *Revolutionary Letters*, 25

Doctorow, E. L., *Ragtime*, 16

documentary poetry, 3, 143

dodgems (small magazine), 98, 185n62

Dove, Rita, 148; "Freedom Ride," 157; *On the Bus with Rosa Parks*, 148

Drive (magazine), 4

drivers: African American, 5, 15, 16, 17, 46, 88, 92, 134, 149, 150, 152, 163; becoming, 103, 105, 106, 109–10; guilty, 99; internal monologue, 146; police and Williams, 29, 34, 43; police stops of Black, 17, 134, 135, 137, 149–50, 154, 155; trans, 14, 125;

violence against Black, 5, 143–44, 146, 149, 153, 155, 163, 167, 168; white, 16–17, 161–62; women, 5, 14, 106, 108, 111, 114

driver's seat: Myles in, 105–6, 114, 116–17, 118, 166; of O'Hara, 73; of Olson, 132; of Williams, 28, 41, 42, 73, 132

driving: for African Americans in South, 15–16; and aliveness, 20–21, 63, 125; and contradictions of automobility, 4, 6, 26, 166; and death, 7, 21, 23, 73, 123; and environment, 5, 21, 100, 117, 121; interracial couple, 60, 83, 93, 150; for a queer Latina, 169–70; and typewriter, 57–58. *See also* open road; petropoetics

driving while Black, 5, 7, 17, 18, 134–35, 137, 154, 159; *The Negro Motorist Green Book*, 15, 135

DuBose, Samuel, 134

Duffy, Enda, 30, 176n21

DuPlessis, Rachel Blau, 33–34, 53, 62, 63, 64, 179n20, 180n24

Dylan, Bob, 118

ecological poetry. *See* ecopoetics

ecopoetics, 7, 21–22, 30, 100; queer, 98–99, 125. *See also* petropoetics

Edison, Thomas, 11

Edsel, 13–14

Eisen-Martin, Tongo, 167; "Heaven Is All Goodbyes," 134–35, 158

Eliot, T. S., 40, 42; *The Waste Land*, 177n39

Ellison, Ralph, *Cadillac Flambé*, 16

Elmslie, Kenward, 182n86

Emerson, Ralph Waldo, 12, 120

energy: ecopoetics, 22; and literature, 16, 19; in Olson, 62, 83; in petrocultures scholarship, 20, 174n83, 174n90; in Williams, 30, 38, 39, 40, 46, 49. *See also* petropoetics

Ensor, Sarah, 99, 125

environmental awareness, poets', 23, 25, 97, 100, 117, 121, 156–57

Epstein, Andrew, 59, 81

Evergreen Review (magazine), 77

feminist critique, 56, 114, 177n32

Fenster, David, 126

filling stations. *See* gas stations

Fisher, Eddie, 182n97

Fitzdale, Robert, 74

Fitzgerald, F. Scott, *The Great Gatsby*, 47

flaneur: O'Hara, 59, 71, 73, 166; Whitmanian ideal, 6. *See also* walking

Flink, James, 30, 58

Floating Bear (small magazine), 95

Floyd, George, 137, 153

Fondren, Hal, 74

Ford, Edsel, 13

Ford, Henry, 11, 12, 13, 28, 48, 49, 50–51, 54; *My Life and Work*, 8

Fordism: and aesthetics, 11; and alienation, 51, 58, 60, 63, 90, 94; and fascism, 9; gendered division of labor, 15, 34, 37–38; and mass automobility, 14–15, 86, 166; and modernism, 7, 8–14; postwar, 58, 83, 95, 138, 166; and regulated time, 67–68, 94, 95, 147; and social contract, 138; and society, 60, 79, 90, 138, 172n14. *See also* post-Fordism

Ford Motor Company, 13, 50–51

fossil fuels, 7, 20, 22, 24, 30, 100. *See also* oil; petrocultures

212 INDEX

Frank, Robert, 126
Franz, Kathleen, 133
Fraser, Kathleen, 179n20
Fredman, Stephen, 63
freedom: and African Americans driving, 80-81, 83, 93, 135, 136, 146, 167, 180n29, 181n73; automobile as symbol of, 59, 134, 158, 160; and automobility, 5, 9, 14, 15, 34, 63, 149, 165-66; and crashing, 73-79, 82, 96, 167; to drive, 4, 73-79, 82, 96, 167; fantasy of, 9, 108, 113; of movement, 34-35, 105, 108, 109, 134; of poetic expression, 152-53, 162. *See also* mobility
Freed-Thall, Hannah, 99
free verse, 10-11, 144, 151-53
Freilicher, Jane, 74, 84, 85
Freud, Sigmund, 63, 92, 138, 139
Friedlander, Benjamin, 88-89, 181n73
futurism, 35, 177n32. *See also* Marinetti, Filippo Tommaso

Gallagher, Maureen, 141, 152
Garner, Eric, 152, 168
Garvey, Marcus, 156, 157
gasoline. *See* oil
gas stations, 6, 29, 169; and Black drivers, 15; and Myles, 102-3, 104; and Williams, 25, 47, 48-49
General Motors Corporation, 49
Ghosh, Amitav, 20, 23
Gibson, Helen, 141
Gilroy, Paul, 17, 136; "Driving While Black," 134
Ginsberg, Allen, 82; *The Fall of America: Poems of These States, 1965-1971*, 118
Giucci, Guillermo, 15

Glavey, Brian, "Having a Coke with You Is Even More Fun than Ideology Critique," 78
Gold, Arthur, 74
Goldstein, Laurence, 6
Gooch, Brad, 70, 77
Grandma (2015), 185n62
Gray, Timothy, 175n106
Graywolf Press, 143
Guernica (magazine), 138, 153

Halberstam, Jack, 183n7
handshake: and Celan, 81, 181n67; of O'Hara and Baraka, 81, 140, 181n67
Harvey, David, 8
Heal, Edith, 53
Henry, John, 147, 169
Herd, David, 71
Heston, Charlton, 89
HIV, 167
Holiday, Billie, 83, 181n69; O'Hara elegy, 69, 70, 72, 73, 80, 95, 181n69
Holocaust, 90
Horkheimer, Max, 63
Howe, Susan, 179n20
Hübinette, Tobias, 139
Hume, Angela, 143, 183n12, 187n48

identity: and automobility, 3, 5-6, 14-19, 159; and futurists, 37; gender, 99, 183n7; and mobility, 3, 4; racial, 65-66, 141
Idusuyi, Johari Osayi, 148, 153
imagism, Williams and, 4, 6, 29, 32, 41, 51, 54, 166, 175n5
immobility: while pregnant, 31, 56; of prisoners and migrants, 129; sitting

in cars, 149, 153–59, 162, 169; stopped cars, 5, 135, 136, 146–47, 153–54, 158, 169; and violence, 99, 162
inequalities, 5, 105, 137, 150, 155, 165
infrastructure, 8, 18. *See also* automobility
Irmscher, Christoph, 23

Jackson, Lorri, 113
Jackson, Virginia, 142
Jameson, Fredric, *The Political Unconscious,* 174n79
Jarmusch, Jim, 28
Javadizadeh, Kamran, 142; "Atlantic Ocean," 175n100
Jim Crow, 15, 81, 133, 145, 155
Jim Crow Rd. (2008), 144–45, 145, 148
John Henryism, 147. *See also* Henry, John
Johnson, Jack, 16–17
Jones, Dr. Mabel, 155, 156, 157
Jones, LeRoi (Amiri Baraka), 60, 81, 88, 89, 95, 140, 182n86
Jones, Prince, 136, 154–55, 157, 158
Joyce, James, 39, 40
Jung, Carl, 63

Kahlo, Frida, 178n60
Kane, Daniel, 85, 93–94
Keats, John, 77
Keller, Lynn, 23, 99
Kerouac, Jack, 15, 59, 126; *On the Road,* 1, 3, 20, 58, 100, 104, 125, 184n23; Sal Paradise (*On the Road* character), 100, 104, 183n23
Killing Cycle, The (1967), 90
King, Martin Luther, Jr., 89, 145
Kinnahan, Linda, 34, 177n32
Knapp, James, 11

Koch, Kenneth, 69, 70, 71, 77, 85, 86–87, 182n86
Komunyakaa, Yusef, 82
Kraus, Chris, *I Love Dick,* 126

Lacy, Suzanne, 114
Ladd, Brian, 24
Lancaster, Burt, 89
Lang, V. R. (Bunny), 72, 77
Last Clean Shirt, The (1964), 82, 83, 88–96, 91, 108, 126, 127; interracial couple in, 60, 93, 150; time in, 93–94, 147
Latinx Americans, 142, 169. *See also* Vértiz, Vickie
Latouche, John, 72, 84
Lawrence, D. H., 10–11, 14; *Studies in Classic American Literature,* 10
Lawrence, N. R., 81, 181n67
Lee, Benjamin, 78
LeMenager, Stephanie, 20–21, 30, 118; *Living Oil: Petroleum Culture in the American Century,* 20
Leslie, Alfred, 59, 60, 88, 126. See also *Last Clean Shirt, The*
Lewis, Sinclair, *Free Air,* 3, 14
Lincoln, Abraham, 152
Litz, A. Walton, 35
Livingston, Julie, 137
Lowell, James Russell, "The Present Crisis," 89, 94
Lowell, Robert, "For the Union Dead," 23–24, 175n100; "Skunk Hour," 24
Loy, Mina, 177n32
Lucas, John, 136. See also *Situation*
Lucie-Smith, Edward, 72
Lundström, Catrin, 139
lynching, 80, 82, 83, 92, 134, 139, 152, 182n74

lyricization, 142–43
lyric poetry, 142–43, 158, 186n31

MacGowan, Christopher, 35
machinery: and O'Hara, 73, 93; and Olson, 60, 64, 65, 67, 118; and Williams, 33, 34–35, 38, 39, 40, 44, 50, 51, 175n5. See also *John Henryism*
Malcolm X, 145, 156
Malm, Andreas, 9
Marcus, Laura, 174n82
Mariani, Paul L., 175nn1–2, 178n54
Marinetti, Filippo Tommaso, 9–10, 11, 33, 37, 38; "Futurist Manifesto," 9, 37; "Technical Manifesto of Futurist Literature," 9
Martin, Trayvon, 137, 152, 158
Marx, Karl, 149; *Capital,* 180n26
masculinity, 9, 63, 99, 109; and automobility, 14, 15, 100; petromasculinity, 7, 97
mass automobility: early, 4, 5, 23, 29, 86, 166, 171n7; and Fordism, 8, 14–15, 166; in New York City, 49, 83, 85; and Olson, 63–64; pitfalls of, 7, 9, 20, 54, 118, 135; and Williams, 4, 13, 23, 29, 40, 49–50, 53–54, 58, 63, 166. See also automobility; *Automotive Story, The*
mass consumption, 8–9
mass production, 8–9, 12, 60. See also assembly line; Fordism; mass automobility; mass consumption
mass transportation, 17, 58
maternity: and automobility, 31, 55, 178n60; while pregnant, 31, 56; Williams and, 11, 27, 31, 38, 39–40, 50, 55, 64, 178n60, 178n62
Mayer, Bernadette, 27, 31–32, 55–56, 166

McCabe, Susan, 44
McIvor, David M., 158–59
McNair, Timothy, 153
Meadowsong, Zena, 12
mechanization, 9. See also machinery; Marinetti, Filippo Tommaso
melancholia, 139; mourning, 136–43
melancholic hope, 141
Memorial to Robert Gould Shaw and the Massachusetts Fifty-Fourth Regiment (1884), 24
Middle Passage, 156, 159
Miki, Roy, 41
Mitchell, Joan, 89
mobility: affordable, 19; African American, 133–35, 136, 137–38, 143–44, 158, 163; and class, 150–51; free, 4, 6, 15, 151–52; and freedom, 3, 13, 103, 134; hazards of, 4; and identity, 3, 17; justice, 17–18, 186n5; masculine, 103, 105; and Myles, 98, 99, 105, 106, 113, 129–30; and Olson, 60; politics of, 16, 88, 130, 169; racialized, 127; and social conflicts, 17; upward, 12, 16, 19, 37, 107, 150–51; white, 5, 100, 126–28, 151; and women, 15, 31, 56, 109, 113. See also automobility; cars; freedom
Model T, 8, 12, 16, 34, 134; of Williams, 27, 28, 29, 30, 31, 48
modernism, 28, 55, 68; aesthetics, 11, 27, 38, 55, 73; and Eliot, 42; European, 9–10, 39; and Fordism, 7, 8–14; literature and assembly-line production, 12; and violence, 37; of Williams, 4, 30, 31, 37, 38, 40. See also petromodernity
Mom, Gijs, 171n5
Montgomery Bus Boycott, 148
Moore, Marianne, 13–14, 86

Morin, Edward, "The Case of James Dean," 77–78
Morton, Timothy, 99, 122; *Ecology Without Nature: Rethinking Environmental Aesthetics*, 21–22
Moses, Robert, 74
mourning, 21, 72, 87, 132, 134, 153, 165; animals lost on road, 87; and Freud, 138, 139; ironic, 148; melancholic, 136–43; as political act, 135, 137, 139; sitting still in car as act of, 147, 158; and song, 147, 152, 162; violence against Blacks, 5, 134–35, 139, 141, 144, 146, 147; vulnerability of Black life, 139, 155, 158
Muhammad, Elijah, 156
Murphy, Michael David, 144
Myles, Eileen, 8, 53, 129, 169; *Afterglow*, 97, 118; "Already leaving," 185n53; and authenticity, 122; *auto*-fiction, 131; camera poems, 118–20, 184n49, 185n53; and car, 101, 106, 111, 112, 113, 116, 126; and climate catastrophe, 5, 7, 118, 122, 124–25, 132, 184n43; conception of transness, 98, 183n7; and crashing, 104; critique of masculinist poetics, 5, 104; "December 16," 127; "D. H.," 124–25; and driving, 21, 99, 100, 103, 105, 106–9, 112, 118, 120–21, 125, 130–31, 166; "En Garde," 110–12; and female body, 98, 115–16; female driver, 108, 109, 111, 114; and flow, 100, 119–20, 125, 127, 185n53; *For Now*, 117–18, 130–31; and gang rape, 18, 53, 101–2, 103, 104, 111, 166; "Heat," 116; "Iceland," 104; *Inferno*, 113; "LA/Driving poems," 99–100, 117–25; "The Lesbian Poet," 97–98, 113, 114–17, 166, 185n53; "Looking Out, A Sailor," 112–13; "Mal Maison," 106–9, 112, 113; *Maxfield Parrish*, 106, 109, 112; "More Oil," 123–24; "My Boy's Red Hat," 98; "My Light," 117; "1993," 100–101; *Not Me*, 106, 113; "#8 Car Camera," 118–19, 120, 184n50, 185n53; "#9 Destroying Us," 120–21, 123; "#10 Ball," 120, 121–22, 123, 129; and oil, 100, 118, 121–22, 123, 125, 127; as passenger, 100–101, 105, 132; *Pathetic Literature*, 97; petropoetry, 6, 100, 132; *The Real Drive*, 105–8; and self-possession, 5, 103, 117, 120, 131, 132; *Skies*, 116–17; *Snowflake / different streets*, 97, 99–100, 118, 123, 124, 128, 130; teaching, 117–18; and *they/them* pronouns, 97, 183n2; transfeminist petropoetics, 5, 97, 98–99, 116, 119, 129, 131, 166, 183n12; trans-species poem, 123–24; and trashed girls, 102, 103, 114, 115; *The Trip*, 100, 108, 126–30, 129, 130; truck, 118, 119, 130–31; "Weather," 117; and white supremacy, 128; and Whitman, 108, 109; a "Working Life," 127–28. See also *Chelsea Girls*

NAACP (National Association for the Advancement of Colored People), 89
Nabokov, Vladimir, *Lolita*, 20
National Association for the Advancement of Colored People (NAACP), 89
Nation of Islam, 156
Nauen, Elinor, 113
Nealon, Christopher, 140
Negro Motorist Green Book, The (AAA), 15, 135
Nelson, Maggie, 104, 184n49
Nest of Ninnies, A (Ashbery and Schuyler), 84–85

Neuman, Justin, 23
New American Poetry, 68, 72
New American Poetry, The (Allen), 60, 63, 180n28
New Criticism, 142
New Masses, 46, 49
New Republic, 20
New York School, 83, 104, 126
New York Times Magazine, 139
Ngai, Sianne, 40, 123
Nielsen, Aldon Lynn, 181n69
Nothing in Nature Is Private (Rankine), 159; untitled poem in, 161-63
Notley, Alice, 27, 31, 55-56, 178n63; "Doctor Williams's Heiresses," 55

Obama, Barack, 18, 137, 143, 158
Occupy movement, 137
O'Hara, Frank, 84; and African Americans, 80-81, 83, 93, 181n73; and avant-garde culture, 78, 93; "Bill's Body Shop," 74, 75-76; and Black men fetish, 46, 60, 81, 83, 92, 180n29; and crashing, 58-59, 73-74, 78, 79, 167; cut-up poetry, 89, 94, 95; "The Day Lady Died," 69, 70, 72, 73, 80, 95, 181n69; and deadly consequences of driving, 23, 73, 78; death of, 76, 90, 167; driving and Civil Rights Movement, 5, 88; elegies for James Dean, 73, 76-79, 82, 167, 179n23; film subtitles, 60, 88, 89-90, 94, 108; flaneur, 59, 71, 73, 166; and Fordism, 8, 60, 83, 90, 166-67; "For James Dean," 77; "Four Little Elegies," 76, 77; and fun automobility, 83, 86, 98; handshake with Baraka, 81, 140, 181n67; "Having a Coke with You," 182n83; homosexuality, 60, 79; and horses, 182n83; "I do this I do that," 59, 68, 71, 95; "In Memory of My Feelings," 182n83; *Lunch Poems,* 71; "Memorial Day 1950," 73; "Naptha," 182n83; "Ode: Salute to the French Negro Poets," 82, 83, 181n67; and Olson, 5, 6, 58, 58-59, 73-76, 79, 147-48, 167; and open field, 70; "Palisades," 74-75, 76; "Personal Poem," 81, 85, 88, 181n69; "Poem," 76; postwar prosperity, 73; and racist violence, 60, 79, 80-81, 83; "Rhapsody," 80-81, 82, 83, 92; "Second Avenue," 180n29; "Song (Did you see me walking by the Buick Repairs?)," 95; "Song (I am stuck in traffic in a taxicab)," 79; "A Step Away from Them," 46, 71, 72; "Steps," 79, 80; "3 Requiems for a Young Uncle," 73; and time signals, 6, 67-73, 93-96, 147-48; "To a Young Poet," 70; "To John Wieners," 70; and typewriters, 71; "Vincent and I Inaugurate a Movie Theatre," 82
oil: centrality to modern culture, 20-21, 22, 121, 156; criticism of, 5, 13, 30; as "hyperobject," 122. *See also* fossil fuels; petrocultures; petromodernity; petropoetics
Oldenburg, Claes, *I Am for an Art,* 57
Oldfield, Barney, 16-17
"Old Man River," 128
Olson, Charles: "Anubis will stare...," 71-72; anxiety about Indigenous and Black mobility, 60, 66-67; "As the Dead Prey upon Us," 63, 64-67, 68-69, 70, 76, 101, 180n24; and authenticity, 59, 60, 61, 67, 68, 83, 147; *Collected Poems,* 71; and commercial culture, 65, 70; and Fordism, 5, 8, 58, 59, 68; "Letter 22," 180n25; "The

Lordly and Isolate Satyrs," 46, 63-64, 67, 71, 179-80nn23-24; and masculine self-possession, 59, 60-62, 65, 67, 68, 72, 83, 118, 132; *Maximus Poems,* 65, 69-70, 180n25; and motorcyclists, 5, 46, 64, 67; and nonmetrical measure, 72; and O'Hara, 5, 6, 58, 58-59, 73-76, 79, 147-48, 167; phallicism, 62-64, 71; "The Post Office," 63; "Projective Verse," 5, 59, 60-65, 68, 70, 71, 179n20; time signals, 6, 62, 67-73, 79, 95, 147-48; and typewriters, 60-62; and white male privilege, 18, 67

On Being (podcast, Tippett), 133, 150-51, 158

open field, 61, 70

open road: genre, 3, 4; myth of, 4, 6, 9, 15-16, 59, 106, 136; poetry of, 10, 28, 171n7; thrills of, 1

optimism: American, 136-43, 156, 158-59; progressive, 148, 159, 163. See also *John Henryism*

Orlovsky, Peter, 82

Others (little magazine), 34

Packer, Jeremy, 17

Palisades Interstate Parkway, 74, 75

Parker, Morgan, 116

Parks, Rosa, 148

passengerhood, 100, 101, 105, 106

passengers: and drivers, 36, 53, 57, 99, 100, 104-5; female, 101-2, 105-6; traumatized, 99, 100, 104, 132

Paterson (2016), 28

pedestrianism. *See* flaneur; walking

Perloff, Marjorie, 30, 54, 175n5, 177n53; *The Poetics of Indeterminacy: Rimbaud to Cage,* 176n23

petrocultures: critique of, 123; scholars, 7, 20-22, 98-99. *See also* ecopoetics; energy; fossil fuels; oil; petropoetics

petromasculinity, 7, 97

petromodernity: addiction to, 22, 30, 55, 149; complicity of poetry, 99, 117, 121; ills of, 7, 23, 41, 99-100, 168; and Robert Lowell, 24

petropoetics, 7, 20-26, 174n90; Canadian, 174n92. *See also* ecopoetics

Pizza, Joseph, *Dissonant Voices,* 179n20

poetic drive: of Jericho Brown, 167-68; of Ta-Nehisi Coates, 136; of Wanda Coleman, 19; defined, 3, 7; of Tongo Eisen-Martin, 135; in "I Know a Man" (Creeley), 4; of Myles, 98, 132; of O'Hara, 58, 60, 79, 95; of Olson, 58, 60; of queer poets of color, 167; of Rankine, 136, 159, 162, 166; of Gertrude Stein, 13; of Vickie Vértiz, 167; of Williams, 35, 38, 41, 53, 54

Poetry (magazine), 77

poetry: documentary, 3, 143; reparative, 21, 125, 132

Poetry Foundation, 2

Poetry New York (magazine), 60

Poets Theatre, 69

policing, racialized, 133, 134, 137, 139, 150-55, 167. *See also* Black Lives Matter; driving while Black

Pollock, Jackson, 72

pollution, 24

post-Fordism, 8, 78, 127, 138, 166. *See also* Fordism

Pound, Ezra, 7, 10-12, 13; *Cantos,* 172n34; ideogram, 38-39; *Kulchur,* 88; "Machine Art," 11, 13; poetics, 11, 69-70, 72; Pound-Olson tradition, 94

Presenting Jane (1952), 83-85, 84, 182n75

progress: and automobility, 3, 17, 133-34, 136; narratives of, 7, 140, 141, 144, 148; and O'Hara, 73; and protest, 149; symbols of, 17, 40; technological, 3, 17, 146; and Williams, 38-40. See also progressive optimism
progressive optimism, 148, 159, 163
Provincetown Arts (magazine), 126
Pull My Daisy (1959), 126

Queen and Slim (2019), 3
queer: driver, 106, 169; ecology, 122; ecopoetics, 98-99, 125
queer poets. See Brown, Jericho; Myles, Eileen; O'Hara, Frank; Stein, Gertrude; Vértiz, Vickie

racial profiling, 143. See also driving while Black; policing, racialized
racism: environmental, 149; and homophobia, 167; and technological progress, 10, 146-47. See also Black Lives Matter; Civil Rights Movement; driving while Black; white supremacy
Rahimtoola, Samia, 183n12
Raine, Anne, 55
Rambling (2018), 98, 119
Rankine, Claudia, 8, 18; and anti-Black racism, 138, 142, 143, 163; being driven, 150-51; and Black drivers, 5, 17, 18, 143, 146, 147, 149, 150, 152, 153, 169; and Black Lives Matter, 137, 139-40; blossoms, 152, 187n48; and citizenship, 141-42, 153, 158, 163; and class, 150-51, 155, 163; "The Condition of Black Life Is One of Mourning," 139; and despair, 139-40; *Don't Let Me Be Lonely: An American Lyric,* 135, 140, 143, 159; and *Jim Crow Rd.,* 144-46; *Just Us: An American Conversation,* 135, 138, 141, 142, 148, 150, 151, 186n5; and Latinx and Asian people, 142; and loafing, 151-52; and lyric tradition, 142-43; melancholic mourning, 136-43; poetic address, 153, 158, 160, 161; and progress, 140, 141, 159; prose poems and film scripts, 6, 135; sitting still, 133, 143-53; teaching, 146; and time, 147-48, 159, 162-63, 167; and white supremacy, 138, 143, 150, 151, 154, 155, 159, 160, 162. See also *Citizen: An American Lyric; Nothing in Nature Is Private; Situation*
rape: Myles and gang rape, 18, 53, 101-2, 103, 104, 111, 166; Williams and rape fantasies, 53, 166
Rauschenberg, Robert, 58
Reed, Anthony, 142
Reilly, Evelyn, 23
reparative poetry, 21, 125, 132
"republic of drivers," 5
Rifkin, Libbie, 62, 67
Riley, Peter J., 78
Rivera, Diego, 178n60
River Rouge Complex, 49, 50. See also Ford Motor Company
Rivers, Larry, 88
road: movie, 3, 20, 100, 108; novel, 1, 3, 4, 15, 20, 38, 171n7; trip, 3, 9, 16, 107, 118, 129
Roberson, Ed, 23
Roffman, Karin, 84-85, 182n75
Ronda, Margaret, 7, 21, 22, 25; *Remainders,* 99
Rose, Jacqueline, 129
Ross, Andrew, 137
Ross, Kristin, 22
Route 126 (1972), 114

Royal Road Test (1967), 57, 59
Rubenstein, Michael, 23
Ruscha, Edward, 57, 58, 59

Sayre, Henry M., 176n5
Scharff, Virgina, 14
Schuster, Joshua, 22, 30
Schuyler, James (Jimmy), 77, 114; *A Nest of Ninnies*, 84-85
Scorpio Rising (1964), 179n23
Sedgwick, Eve Kosofsky, 21, 174n83
Seiler, Cotten, 3, 5, 14, 15, 28, 63
self-possession: and automobility, 28, 38, 59, 65, 67, 72, 103, 117, 118, 120, 131, 132; masculine, 28, 59, 60, 65, 67
Seymour, Nicole, 21, 99
Sharpe, Christina, *In the Wake: On Blackness and Being*, 140-41; *Ordinary Notes*, 141
Shaw, Lytle, 182n86
Sheeler, Charles, 50-51
Sheller, Mimi, 14-15, 17-18, 105
Shelley, Percy Bysshe, 77
Shukin, Nicole, 87
Silliman, Ron, *Ketjak*, 57
Sinclair, Upton, *Oil!*, 20
Siraganian, Lisa, 39-40
sit-ins, 148-49. *See also* Civil Rights Movement
Situation (videos, Lucas and Rankine), 135-36; *In Memory of James Craig Anderson*, 159-60; *In Memory of Trayvon Martin*, 152-53; *Situation 8*, 149; *Stop-and-Frisk*, 149, 151
Skillman, Nikki, 160
Snyder, Gary, 7, 175n106; *Danger on Peaks*, 25; "Mimulus on the Road to Town," 25-26, 168; "Plain Talk," 24; "Tomorrow's Song," 25; *Turtle Island*, 24-26; "Why Log Truck Drivers Rise Earlier than Students of Zen," 26
Soloway, Joey, 126
Song, Min Hyoung, *Climate Lyricism*, 165
Sorin, Gretchen, 15
space: in cars, 135, 163; male-dominated, 105, 108-9, 111, 112; queer taking up, 112; road, 132; and white privilege, 17, 151
Spahr, Juliana, 23
speed: of assembly line, 62; of automobility, 158; and driving, 17, 28, 59; of economic progress, 149; and poetic "I," 119; and pop culture, 30; and violence, 4
Spook Who Sat by the Door, The (1973), 128
stalled: hopes of the Civil Rights Movement, 157, 159; junk and Williams, 30, 46, 52-53; poetic drive of Rankine, 136, 153, 162
Stein, Gertrude, 7, 9, 10, 22, 55, 94, 115, 171n5, 173n46, 176n23; *The Autobiography of Alice B. Toklas*, 12, 113; "The Ford," 12; "Portraits and Repetition," 12; *Useful Knowledge*, 12; "The Work," 13; "Work Again," 13
Steinbeck, John, *The Grapes of Wrath*, 178n60
Steinbock, Eliza, 129
Steven, Mark, 54
St. Mark's Poetry Project, 114
Stodghill, Ron, 134
Stoneley, Peter, 92-93
strikes, 49, 149
Stryker, Susan, 98
subtitles: by O'Hara, 60, 88, 89-90, 94, 108; of Rankine's trilogy, 141-43, 151
Sugrue, Thomas J., 138

Szeman, Imre, 20, 23; "Towards a Critical Theory of Energy," 174n83

Taylor, Frederick Winslow, 67
technology: and American poets, 5–6, 73; and Henry, 147; and Myles, 118–19, 128; and O'Hara, 73, 94; and Williams, 33, 175n5, 176n21
Thelma and Louise (1991), 3
There Will Be Blood (2007), 20
Tibor de Nagy Gallery, 84
Tichi, Cecelia, 175n5
time: clocked, 68, 71; progressive, 148, 159
Tippett, Krista, 133, 150–51, 158
Tomlin, Lily, 185n62
Totem Press, 60
touring narratives, 14
traffic: and *Automotive Story*, 85, 88; and Myles, 100; and O'Hara, 59, 60, 71, 79–82, 83, 90, 95, 166; stops, 134, 137, 149, 154; and Williams, 29, 47, 51–52
Transcendentalists, American, 21
trans cinema, 129–30
transfeminist: petropoetics, 5, 97, 98–99, 116, 119, 129, 131, 166, 183n12; reckoning with automobility, 101, 114; stakes and technology, 118–19
trans identity, 97, 98, 99–100, 104, 124, 126, 129–30
Transparent (2014–19), 126
trashed: cars, 16, 113, 114; girls, 103, 104, 114; Myles, 102, 114–15
Trump, Donald, 127, 137, 148
Tucker-Abramson, Myka, 3; *Cartographies of Empire*, 171n7
Turner, Lindsay, 7

Tuumba Press, 55
typewriters, 57–58, 60, 61, 65, 67, 71

United Auto Workers, 9, 49
Unphotographable (ongoing), 144
Unrau, Melanie Dennis, 22; *Rough Poets*, 174n90
Urry, John, 6
US Steel, 49

Vértiz, Vickie, 4, 5, 167, 168–70; *Auto/Body*, 4, 168, 169; "Dictation," 169; "'69 Chevy Impala," 168–69
Vietnam War, 89, 93, 94
Villon, François, "The Ballad of the Dead Ladies," 76
violence: against animals, 87; and automobility, 4, 33, 34, 37, 93, 162, 165–66; and class, 155; and driving, 33, 34, 38, 99, 119, 166; environmental, 99, 156; and immobility, 162; male, 18, 53, 79, 98, 99, 101–5, 106, 109, 110–11; police, 149, 150, 153, 155, 167; racist, 5, 60, 73, 79, 80–81, 136, 138, 146, 149, 150, 152, 158, 159–60; white, 5, 80, 93, 153
Virilio, Paul: "The Metempsychosis of the Passenger," 105; *Negative Horizon*, 105
vision: double, of automobility, 3; of Olson, 61; poetic, of Myles, 120; of Pound, 11; of Rankine, 159; and Williams, 15, 27–29, 31, 34, 35, 37, 40–44, 45–46, 47, 52, 53, 54, 166, 177n53
Vogel, Andrew, 3; *Narrating a New Mobility Landscape*, 171n7
Voices and Visions (documentary), 28

von Hallberg, Robert, "Politics of Description," 178n55

walking, 24-25, 30, 54, 59, 75, 95, 96, 179n10. *See also* flaneur
Wallace, Darrell, Jr., 17
Warren, Kenneth, 150
Warsh, Lewis, 55
Watten, Barrett, 9, 12, 13, 172n34
Wenzel, Jennifer, 179n10, 187n41
West, Cornel, 140, 148
Whalen, Philip, 55
White, Ian, 94
White, Richard, 88
white melancholia, 139
whiteness: and automobility, 14, 15, 17, 46, 67, 127, 144, 148, 156, 158; dream of, 156, 157-58; privileges of, 17, 29, 46, 151
white supremacy, 90, 128, 134, 135, 159; and African Americans, 16-17, 134-35, 136, 137, 142, 143, 144, 148, 150, 154, 155, 163; and automobility, 16, 88, 134-36, 144, 149; and class, 150; protesting, 135, 141, 149; and violence, 80-81, 134. *See also* Black Lives Matter; Civil Rights Movement; racial profiling; racism
Whitman, Walt, 55, 61, 79, 108, 109; and automobility, 10-11, 14; *Leaves of Grass,* 34, 51, 151-52; loafing, 151-52; sounds in throat, 152-53; "When Lilacs Last in the Dooryard Bloom'd," 152
Wieners, John, 69, 70, 114
Williams, Eric (William Eric; Bill) (son of William Carlos Williams), 28, 31, 32, 175n1
Williams, Florence (Floss; Flossie) (wife of William Carlos Williams), 29, 31, 32

Williams, William Carlos: and aesthetics, 4, 29, 35, 55, 176n5, 176n21; and African Americans, 41, 46, 152; *The Autobiography of William Carlos Williams,* 28-29, 34, 43, 175n1, 177n39; and automobility, 13, 18, 23, 30-31, 41, 49, 54-55, 58, 166; and avant-garde, 30, 31, 38, 40, 176n23; "Belly Music," 34-35; and crashing, 29, 36-37, 38; and dangerous automobiles, 29, 31, 32, 33, 34, 37, 48; *The Descent of Winter,* 49-51, 54, 178n55; *An Early Martyr and Other Poems,* 51, 53, 54; early poems, 15, 28, 32-38; and Eliot, 40, 42, 177n39; *The Embodiment of Knowledge,* 13; and futurists, 33, 37, 177n32; *The Great American Novel,* 11, 31, 38-40, 46, 47, 51; imagism, 4, 6, 29, 32, 41, 51, 54, 166, 175n5; later poems, 49-56; and leaves, 34-35; libel suit, 47, 49; line breaks, 29, 34, 37, 43-44; literary heiresses, 31-32, 55-56, 169; and machines, 13, 33, 34-35, 39, 40, 44, 46, 50, 51, 175n5; and maternity, 11, 27, 31, 38, 39-40, 50, 55, 64, 178n60, 178n62; and modernism, 4, 30, 31, 37-38, 40, 176n21; objectifying women, 15, 31, 166; and oil, 30, 38-39, 49-50; *Paterson,* 28, 53, 54, 55, 176n23, 178n54, 178n62; *Pictures from Brueghel and Other Poems,* 28, 54; and rape fantasies, 53, 166; "The Raper from Passenack," 49, 53, 166; and reckless driving, 28-29, 32, 34, 43; "The Right of Way," 42-43, 44, 45, 50, 53, 54; "Romance Moderne," 33, 35-37, 38, 41, 177n32; and self-possession, 28, 31, 33, 38, 54; "Sketch for a Portrait of Henry Ford,"

Williams, William Carlos (*continued*) 30, 49, 53–54; *Spring and All,* 31, 32, 37, 40–46, 47, 54; "To Elsie," 44–46; "View of a Lake," 49, 51–53, 54, 74, 177n54; and vision, 15, 27–29, 31, 34, 35, 37, 40–44, 45–46, 47, 52, 53, 54, 166, 177n53; and words, 30, 35, 38–39, 47, 48, 175n5; and working class, 28, 41, 45, 46; "XIX," 45; "The Young Housewife," 15, 30, 31, 32–34, 37–38, 47, 50, 53, 109

Windell, Maria, 141–42

Winters, Joseph R., 141; *Hope Draped in Black: Race, Melancholy, and the Agony of Progress,* 140

women: violence against, 99, 103; workers, 41, 44–45

Yaeger, Patricia, 20, 174n79

Yau, John, 19

Yu, Timothy, 10

Zetkin Collective, 9

CULTURAL FRAMES, FRAMING CULTURE

No Exit: Contemporary American Literature and the State
SETH MCKELVEY

Spectacle Earth: Media for Planetary Change
ANDREW KALAIDJIAN

*Changed Men: Veterans in American
Popular Culture after World War II*
ERIN LEE MOCK

*We, Us, and Them: Affect and American
Nonfiction from Vietnam to Trump*
DOUGLAS DOWLAND

Criminal Cities: The Postcolonial Novel and Cathartic Crime
MOLLY SLAVIN

Skimpy Coverage: Sports Illustrated *and
the Shaping of the Female Athlete*
BONNIE M. HAGERMAN

*Story Revolutions: Collective Narratives from
the Enlightenment to the Digital Age*
HELGA LENART-CHENG

*Institutional Character: Collectivity,
Agency, and the Modernist Novel*
ROBERT HIGNEY

*Walk the Barrio: The Streets of Twenty-First-
Century Transnational Latinx Literature*
CRISTINA RODRIGUEZ

*Fashioning Character: Style, Performance, and
Identity in Contemporary American Literature*
LAUREN S. CARDON

*Neoliberal Nonfictions: The Documentary
Aesthetic from Joan Didion to Jay-Z*
DANIEL WORDEN

Dandyism: Forming Fiction from Modernism to the Present
LEN GUTKIN

*Terrible Beauty: The Violent Aesthetic and
Twentieth-Century Literature*
MARIAN EIDE

Women Writers of the Beat Era: Autobiography and Intertextuality
MARY PANICCIA CARDEN

Stranger America: A Narrative Ethics of Exclusion
JOSH TOTH

*Fashion and Fiction: Self-Transformation in
Twentieth-Century American Literature*
LAUREN S. CARDON

*American Road Narratives: Reimagining
Mobility in Literature and Film*
ANN BRIGHAM

The Arresting Eye: Race and the Anxiety of Detection
JINNY HUH

*Failed Frontiersmen: White Men and Myth in the
Post-Sixties American Historical Romance*
JAMES J. DONAHUE

www.ingramcontent.com/pod-product-compliance
Lightning Source LLC
Chambersburg PA
CBHW050340241125
35865CB00036B/765